George Bernard Shaw
and the
Socialist Theatre

GEORGE BERNARD SHAW
AND THE
SOCIALIST THEATRE

TRACY C. DAVIS

PRAEGER

Westport, Connecticut
London

The Library of Congress has cataloged the hardcover edition as follows:

Davis, Tracy C.
    George Bernard Shaw and the socialist theatre / Tracy C. Davis.
      p. cm.—(Contributions in drama and theatre studies, ISSN
0163–3821 ; no. 56) (Lives of the theatre)
    Includes bibliographical references and index.
    ISBN 0–313–27611–0 (alk. paper)
    1. Shaw, Bernard, 1856–1950—Political and social views.
2. Socialism and literature—Great Britain. 3. Socialism and
theater—Great Britain. I. Title. II. Series.
PR5368.S6D38   1994
822'.912—dc20   93–49613

British Library Cataloguing in Publication Data is available.

A hardcover edition of *George Bernard Shaw and the Socialist Theatre* is available from
the Greenwood Press imprint of Greenwood Publishing Group, Inc. (Contributions in
Drama and Theatre Studies, Number 56; ISBN: 0–313–27611–0).

Library of Congress Catalog Card Number: 93–49613
ISBN: 0–275–93764–X (pbk.)

First published in 1994

Praeger Publishers, 88 Post Road West, Westport, CT 06881
An imprint of Greenwood Publishing Group, Inc.

Printed in the United States of America

To C.Y.S.
for the first twenty years
and Annie
whom I only knew for five

Contents

Photographs follow page 56.

Foreword

This book stems from the Greenwood Press series *Lives of the Theatre*.
To facilitate use in college and university courses, some volumes have
been selected to appear in paperback. This is such a volume. *Lives of the
Theatre* is designed to provide scholarly introductions to important periods
and movements in the history of world theatre from the earliest instances
of recorded performance through to the twentieth century, viewing the
theatre consistently through the lives of representative theatrical practitioners. Although many of the volumes will be centred upon playwrights,
other important theatre people, such as actors and directors, will also be
prominent in the series. The subjects have been chosen not simply for their
individual importance, but because their lives in the theatre can well serve
to provide a major perspective on the theatrical trends of their eras. They
are therefore either representative of their time, figures whom their contemporaries recognised as vital presences in the theatre, or they are people
whose work was to have a fundamental influence on the development of
theatre, not only in their lifetimes but after their deaths as well. While the
discussion of verbal and written scripts will inevitably be a central concern
in any volume that is about an artist who wrote for the theatre, these scripts
will always be considered in their function as a basis for performance.

The rubric "Lives of the Theatre" is therefore intended to suggest both
biographies of people who created theatre as an institution and as a medium
of performance and of the life of the theatre itself. This dual focus will be
illustrated through the titles of the individual volumes, such as *Christopher
Marlowe and the Renaissance of Tragedy*, *George Bernard Shaw and the*

Socialist Theatre, and *Richard Wagner and Festival Theatre*, to name just a few. At the same time, although the focus of each volume will be different, depending on the particular subject, appropriate emphasis will be given to the cultural and political context within which the theatre of any given time is set. Theatre itself can be seen to have a palpable effect upon the social world around it, as it both reflects the life of its time and helps to form that life by feeding it images, epitomes, and alternative versions of itself. Hence, we hope that this series will also contribute to an understanding of the broader social life of the period of which the theatre that is the subject of each volume was a part.

Lives of the Theatre grew out of an idea Josh Beer put to Christopher Innes and Peter Arnott. Sadly, Peter Arnott did not live to see the inauguration of the series. Simon Williams kindly agreed to replace him as one of the series editors and has played a full part in its preparation. In commemoration, the editors which to acknowledge Peter's own rich contribution to the life of the theatre.

Josh Beer
Christopher Innes
Simon Williams

Preface

Numerous archives have generously offered assistance, advice, and access to unique collections while this book was in preparation. My sincere thanks goes to the archivists and reading room staff at the British Library Department of Manuscripts, John Hay Library at Brown University, Archival and Special Collections at the University of Guelph, British Library of Political and Economic Science (London School of Economics), Harvard College Library, Special Collections at Northwestern University, University of Calgary Library, and Harry Ransom Humanities Research Center at the University of Texas, Austin. Jennifer Lee, Russell Maylone, and Melissa Miller-Quinlan warrant singling out for personal thanks, along with Sidney P. Albert and Dan H. Laurence, whose collections of Shaviana deposited respectively at Brown University and the University of Guelph made my task much easier. I wish to thank Susan Bennett, Peter A. Davis, and William Worthen for invaluable colleagial assistance and advice, and Miriam Stanford, Kathi Duncan, and Fred Graber for their hospitality in the name of friendship and scholarship. This book exists because of John Roberts's initiative; I also appreciate Josh Beer's patience, encouragement, and advice throughout the period of writing as well as Christopher Innes's and Simon Williams's eagle eyes and close readings. At a crucial juncture, Catherine Cole took time from her own endeavors to assist with verifications and manuscript preparation, though any remaining errors or omissions are my own.

Abbreviations

BS   Michael Holroyd. *Bernard Shaw.* 5 vols. London: Chatto and Windus, 1988–93.

CL   Dan H. Laurence. *Bernard Shaw, Collected Letters.* 4 vols. London: Max Reinhardt, 1965–88.

CPP   *Complete Plays with Prefaces.* 6 vols. New York: Dodd, Mead and Co., 1963.

Introduction

There is a belief somewhat prevalent in the late twentieth century that GBS is an excruciating bore: his diatribes are interminable, his self-advertisements intolerable, and whatever currency he held in his own time (usually thought to extend only between 1892 and 1914), he has no relevance now. Surely anything worth noting about Shaw has already been written, reviewed, and copiously quoted.

I would be the last to assert that, following so soon after the publication of Michael Holroyd's authorized biography, this book dares to challenge that multivolume set for space on the library shelf. Nor does it necessarily jockey with anything that poses as a definitive reading of Shaw, whether geared to the esoteric or more general reader. As my title suggests, I am interested in Shaw, socialism, and the theatre, which leaves a great deal out. I offer a chronological orientation to Shaw's life with emphasis on certain polemical traits, yet this is not the Marxist life that has been foreseen;[1] more biographical detail should certainly be sought from Holroyd and other sources, and the bibliographic essay that concludes the book is addressed particularly to student readers who can benefit from a manageably sized orientation to the mountain of Shavian scholarship. Critical analysis of selected works bearing particularly on Shaw's socialist convictions and experimentation with various genres of writing and public performance may be expected, though readers should respect economy in each selection. I highlight what I think is most interesting, give the crucial background, weave a linking narrative, and let the bibliographic essay lead readers to discussions it would be fruitless to duplicate. This is more of a history of ideas and cultural representations with Shaw at the centre than a conventional biography.

As Shaw's activities and exploration of different kinds of writing and social performance multiplied, the course of his life became more complex. Consequently, the first chapters of this book are able to follow a chronological line while the latter chapters cannot. Instead, a selection of themes, activities, and critical strategies determine the narrative of the second half of Shaw's life.

Like many of Shaw's friends, acquaintances, and mortal enemies, I find myself simultaneously intrigued and exasperated by GBS. The qualities I admire in him are qualified with at least as many grave concerns. Nevertheless, the energy with which he pursued his work—and the many fronts on which he was able to maintain a presence—cannot fail to inspire wonder. He finished five novels, nearly thirty full-length plays, and over twenty short plays of farce, comedy, and philosophy; his reprinted art, music, theatre, and literary criticism for the popular press amounts to nine very substantial volumes; he probably wrote more letters than anyone else of his time (at least a quarter of a million by Dan Laurence's count), responding at length to a multitude of correspondents almost as soon as a note was received; and he wrote dozens of tracts and blue book commentaries, hundreds of articles, prefaces for his own and others' work, and numerous books of social commentary. In short, he had an opinion on everything from Arthur Balfour to Gabrielle Wietrowetz, and expressed it in an impressive variety of genres ranging from amatory notes penned for the most glamorous actresses of two centuries to the fall-guys and lackeys of *Major Barbara* and *Pygmalion*, and most everything in between.

Though only a handful of his five dozen mature contributions to the stage are frequently read, Shaw's stature in the late twentieth century is based virtually entirely on his prodigious dramatic output. Perhaps there is good reason for this: plays have the virtue of splitting up GBS's writing persona so one is not constantly bombarded with the full force of the facets of him one personally finds most odious or overbearing. Under these circumstances his genuine wit and talent for inventing situations can best survive the onslaught of words. It is as a playwright that Shaw is now chiefly remembered, and it is on that basis that he is included in this series of books; however there is more to his legacy than drama. He aspired, above all, to have an impact on his society, and though his career in elected politics was brief, he exhibited a political zeal in all his writings and actions. Drama was just one form of stating his message and the theatre just one format for performing it.

How could one human being have been so prolific? From the beginning of his writing career he embraced each new communicative method—shorthand, typewriter, telephone—and as soon as he could afford it, he hired others to do the ancillary tasks and saved for himself the imaginative act of composition. Just as when he was a young man he tried a succession of platforms for social outreach (the Shelley Society, Zetetical Society, Land Reform Union, and Fabians), he practised a range of writing genres (poetry, novels, pamphlets, articles, and plays) until he found niches where he could both excel authorially and exert his influence politically. The results show that he never really abandoned any of these genres. The dialogues in his plays bounce and reverberate with speech that is as nearly poetic as anything without regular meter might be. The prefaces to plays, a category in which Shaw was as prolific as he was unorthodox, ring with the rhetoric of stump speeches, the pressing argument of political tracts, and the long, complex interworking of thought and incident that might be found in an epistolary novel. Never one to waste or hide away an accomplishment, he exploited his rhetorical prowess in pedantic monographs such as *The Intelligent Woman's Guide to Socialism and Capitalism* and the novella *The Adventures of the Black Girl in Her Search for God*.

Since his death in 1950, Shaw has inspired thousands of articles, hundreds of learned books, and at least half a dozen journals devoted solely to his life and work. Holroyd's four-volume biography runs to nearly two thousand pages. Would this prodigious half-century of scholarship have pleased GBS? Most assuredly. To be the subject of inquiry, debate, and serious attention was his lifetime goal. The vast quantities of material would flatter and console him while affirming his own not inconsiderable self-opinion that he was a notable man. Perhaps second only to Shakespeare, he commands acreage on library shelves and a place in English curricula reflecting not only the vastness of his oeuvre but also its perpetual ripeness for critical plunder. For the first few decades, scholarship concentrated on putting Shaw in the context of other nineteenth- and twentieth-century literati. Play festivals sprang up to assert his place among playwrights of both centuries. Most recently, he has become a sounding board for feminist, postmodernist, and postcolonial critics who use him anew to understand the ideological formations he shaped and was shaped by. Once again, he is being read in the context of his contemporaries, only this time the guest list has changed to include discourses—such as feminism—that operated in tandem with Shaw but which he never managed to capture.

An iconoclast in dress, diet, and politics, Shaw held his opinions with conviction and never hesitated to proselytize. He loathed certain conventions of English writing. In defence of his first volume of plays, he fired a counter salvo to a Scottish reviewer who chastised his punctuation: "I have used the apostrophe in every case where its omission could even momentarily mislead the reader; for example, I have written she'd and I'll to distinguish them from shed and ill. But I have made no provision for the people who cannot understand dont unless it is printed don't. If a man is as stupid as that, he should give up reading altogether."[2] He was not quite as belligerent about spelling reform and the "alfabet," though he would have liked to be. These are some of the battles he did not win.

A lot of his battles were unwinnable. Some of the most intensely argued positions were meant simply to provoke, without the remotest hope of convincing anyone. When, for example, in *Androcles and the Lion* he provides a diatribe on the "true" communist doctrines of the New Testament and Christianity, he might sweep his readers along with the sheer bravado of the argument, but casting Jesus as Economist in the preface pulled the genre of the toga play a little too far. Casting Jesus as communist in his writings on postrevolutionary Russia is perhaps more in keeping with the genre of political commentary:

> The famous execution on Calvary . . . has never been challenged in respect of the two thieves who suffered on that occasion along with the Communist. The principle of the execution is fully admitted. All the controversies have arisen on the point whether the execution of the Communist was not a mistake—whether he was not rather the sort of person who should be encouraged rather than liquidated.[3]

Some ideas are remarkably prescient of the postmodern political climate. In the preface to *Misalliance* he offers a treatise on children's rights. Proclaiming in 1910 that "in any decent community, children should find in every part of their native country, food, clothing, lodging, instruction, and parental kindness for the asking" sets out an agenda far beyond the scope of Dr. Barnardo's and presages the aims of UNESCO and a remarkable new direction in legal thought we are only just beginning to explore. But in his characteristically perverse style, Shaw imbeds these views in the midst of a diatribe against formal schooling, which suggests as much autobiographical anguish as a serious suggestion for social policy.

Misalliance and *Getting Married* are both single, long incidents that bear at least as much resemblance to the television genre of the situation comedy or the cinematic auto-analysis of Woody Allen as their contemporaneous category, the discussion play. In form and content alike, Shaw was always prepared to do whatever he thought necessary to shake up his fellow beings. This is summed up aptly in a statement that suffices as his philosophy of playwriting:

> I am not an ordinary playwright in general practice. I am a specialist in immoral and heretical plays. My reputation has been gained by my persistent struggle to force the public to reconsider its morals. In particular, I regard much current morality as to economic and sexual relations as disastrously wrong; and I regard certain doctrines of the Christian religion as understood in England today with abhorrence. I write plays with the deliberate object of converting the nation to my opinions in these matters. . . . I mention these facts to shew that I have a special interest in the achievement by my profession of those rights of liberty of speech and conscience which are matters of course in other professions.[4]

But, as many have found to their peril, taking Shaw at his word is always dicey. Consider the following passage:

> I believe in preserving the unities as the Greeks did. Exactly to the extent that a dramatist sacrifices the unities he sacrifices the effect of his play. So it has always been my aim to preserve the unities, even though I may be obliged to represent as happening in one day events that might have taken twelve months to occur.[5]

The fallacies should be apparent to any adept theatre history student: first, that the Greeks observed "unities," for the concept is a seventeenth-century French invention, and second that Shaw religiously observed unities of time, place, or action. *Man and Superman, Pygmalion,* and *St. Joan* play havoc with the concepts, as much as *The Devil's Disciple, Getting Married,* and *Heartbreak House* are masterful examples of compression and restraint. Shaw is not necessarily the best authority on Shaw. In the preface to *The Apple Cart* he exhorts us not to take his plays at face value—a good maxim.

Is this a fault or merely an idiosyncracy? His life, work, and utterances are full of contradictions but also paradoxes. This is one thing that makes him perennially interesting. In me, it spawns a hitherto unfamiliar writing posture—abiding aggravation—with (I grudgingly admit) admiration for the breadth and sheer feats of human endurance, ingenuity, and conviction that Shaw the "writing machine" represents.

NOTES

1. Margot Peters, "The State and Future of Shaw Research: The MLA Conference Transcript. Biography," *Shaw* 2 (1982): 183.

2. Letter to *Glasgow Herald*, 26 April 1898; reprinted in Shaw, *Agitations: Letters to the Press 1875–1950*, ed. Dan H. Laurence and James Rambeau (New York: Frederick Ungar, 1985), 42.

3. Harry M. Geduld, ed., *The Rationalization of Russia* (Bloomington: University of Indiana Press, 1964), 122–23.

4. "Preface to *The Shewing-Up of Blanco Posnet*," based on the statement Shaw submitted to the Select Committee on Stage Plays (Censorship) 1909; reprinted in *Complete Plays with Prefaces*, 6 vols. (New York: Dodd, Mead and Co., 1963), 5: 190–91. All subsequent references to Shaw's plays and prefaces are from this edition and abbreviated in the text as CPP.

5. "Less Scenery Would Mean Better Drama," 1909; reprinted in *Shaw* 3 (1983): 27.

George Bernard Shaw
and the
Socialist Theatre

Chapter 1

Shaw before Playwriting

Do not talk of the middle class: the expression is meaningless except when it is used by an economist to denote the man of business who stands in the middle between land and capital on the one hand, and labor on the other, and organizes business for both. I sing my own class: the Shabby Genteel, the Poor Relations, the Gentlemen who are No Gentlemen.[1]

During his lifetime of ninety-four years, Shaw took pains to leave a paper trail heavily strewn with autobiographical information, including largely ghostwritten biographies of himself. These sources are no more definitive than the ersatz memoirs he embedded in a variety of kinds of writings: prefaces, criticism, introductions and afterwords to colleagues' books, essays, lectures, journalism, and thousands of letters. There is no shortage of material, though anything written by Shaw about himself is always subject to doubt on the grounds of exaggeration, misinformation, or outright fabrication. Skepticism—an approach Shaw encouraged in others—is a prudent attitude. Though Shaw is the principal source for information on his own early life, the outline is relatively straightforward and trustworthy.

As a young man, his father, George Carr Shaw, was a clerk in an Irish ironworks. When in his mid-thirties, his family name landed him a post in the Four Courts (Public Record Office), where he could languish in complete idleness. When this position was eliminated through legal reforms, he was compensated with a government pension of £44 a year.[2] Then, at the age of thirty-eight, he became engaged to the twenty-year-old Bessie Gurly, whose fortune he counted on to help him buy into a wholesale business. Appalled by her choice in mates, Gurly's family disinherited her, dashing George Carr Shaw's hopes of prosperity. He sold his pension for £500 and eventually went into an unprofitable grain-milling partnership.

George Bernard, born on 26 July 1856, was the last of three children and the only boy resulting from the marriage. His parents were severely disappointed with each other but were, on the whole, civil when they could not avoid one another's company. They were not strict with their children; Shaw describes their childrearing method as "anarchy." Consequently, Shaw was obliged to find his own way in the world, his predeliction to shyness fighting with precocity. The family abandoned religious services by the time Shaw was ten, and he was henceforth encouraged to take an unorthodox skeptical view of everything concerned with religion, even though Protestant allegiances were ingrained. He grew up in a household without illusions or love but seemed to suffer less from these deficiencies than the excesses of his father's drinking and the restraints that put on their welcome into society. Social relations revolved around the family, not so much because of the strict genteel snobbery that the Shaws maintained despite obvious poverty, but because George Carr Shaw gained a thoroughly deserved reputation for drunkenness and belligerent humour. Beyond the family and Vandeleur Lee (Bessie Shaw's music tutor) few would associate with them.

Everyone in Shaw's extended family played musical instruments, some more bizarre than others. Congenial musicales were a feature of their mutual entertainment. Shaw's mother took the avocation seriously and aspired to a singing career under the guidance of Lee, a man with highly eccentric methods which seemed nonetheless to work. In 1866, the Shaws moved in with Lee. Much speculation has occurred about the adults' ménage à trois, particularly since Shaw's plays are saturated with romantic yet largely sexless triangles. The arrangement seems to have been harmonious musically, economically, and socially. With Lee in the household, Shaw became familiar with an extensive repertoire of vocal music and later taught himself to be an adequate accompanist on the piano, a skill that gave him access to many drawing rooms and possibly boudoirs. He was taken to the opera and countless amateur recitals. This exposure, in conjunction with frequent visits to Ireland's public art collection, was formative in Shaw's intellectual development. His knowledge of sculpture and painting came from the books of Louis Duchesne and Giorgio Vasari and free access to the National Gallery in Dublin, which he exploited much more enthusiastically than his other educational opportunities. A friend who often accompanied him recalled: "It is odd to look back at the long hours we spent there and to see us again, two schoolboys of twelve or thirteen years old, one short and dark, the other tall and fair, going from one picture to another, not as chance visitors, but earnest critics. The attendants must have wondered at us and been secretly amused."[3]

The National Gallery of Ireland opened in 1864 with acquisitions based on the collection of Cardinal Joseph Fesch, an uncle to Napoleon Bonaparte. During Shaw's years of study, the gallery featured a respectable assortment of old masters, eighteenth- and nineteenth-century canvases collected by the Irish aristocracy on their European grand tours, and a comprehensive collection of Irish work. This self-education was so formative in Shaw's life that he granted the institution one third of his residual estate for a period of fifty years following his death. The bequest significantly improves what was already a substantial treasure.

By Shaw's own admission he benefitted minimally from years of formal secondary education. He refers to his various schools as prisons and claims to have learned nothing in them except that the mathematical sciences are foolish. Performing well in an English essay contest meant a great deal to him but nothing to his teachers, for only proficiency in Latin impressed them. It may have been the instructors or possibly what Shaw calls his utter inability to comprehend other languages that prevented him from picking up Latin or any other tongues. Only music made foreign languages accessible to him, which meant that his vocabulary was somewhat esoteric. He later remarked: "My command of operatic Italian is almost copious, as might be expected from my experience as a musical critic. I can make love in Italian; I could challenge a foe to a duel in Italian if I were not afraid of him; and if I swallowed some agonizing mineral poison, I could describe my sensations very eloquently."[4] He could manage at least as much in French.

When Shaw was sixteen, his mother followed Lee to London to pursue a singing career for her daughter Lucy (she performed with the Carl Rosa Opera Company and later with D'Oyly Carte). Back in Dublin, it was imperative that Shaw turn his attention to earning a living. He was launched on the world without knowing anything by conventional standards of preparatory school and university education while knowing a very great deal by virtue of keeping his eyes and ears open to what was around him at home. His grasp of history came from novels and plays, which may explain why he felt no compunction about liberally infusing his autobiographical narratives and historical plays with fiction. His grasp of philosophy and political science came from reading eclectically in the uncanonized European masters, which accounts for why he was an iconoclast among most of the educated middle class in Britain, with views occasionally brilliant and invariably unconventional. His allegiance to Ireland, its scenery, literature, and sensibilities, also kept him apart from intellectuals in the English and European mainstream.

In Victorian Dublin politics, religion, and moral hypocrisy were as indelibly imprinted on the city as human geography. The Shaws were determined to assert status absurdly out of proportion with their means. The snobbery of the family—adamant that their surname carried aristocratic prestige—greatly affected what Shaw could and could not do in his early years, which schools he would attend, what he would do for a living, and how he attempted to present a prosperous face to the world. All of Dublin society played into the protocol of deference based on family, trade, and religion. Middle-class professions lost financial ground to the skilled working class, yet the prejudices of the old order still prevailed. Shaw could not afford to go to university, even though a fine one existed in the city, and so he was forced to turn to the world of commerce as his father had done. For Protestants such as the Shaws, putting their teenage son into a trade or retail merchandising was anathema, though the most menial position in a wholesale firm was acceptable if commercial pursuits became the only option. Shaw saw and felt the absurdity of the situation of being placed as a clerk even though he was doomed to earn less than a mechanic, yet the middle class still could not abide to see sons in "blue-collar" occupations.

His uncle secured him a position in Uniacke Townshend's land agency. The job promised him professional status without compromising the family's dignity as Shaws. He was not an apprentice like the university-educated men around him, for such a position required cash investments from young men's families. He was merely an office boy. Shaw cultivated the company of the abundant gentlemen apprentices, whom he described as having "paid large fees for the privilege of singing operatic selections with me when the principals were out." This, presumably, was the Victorian equivalent of *karaoke*, and the anecdote was related by Shaw to characterize his unsuitability for office life as well as his unquenchable enthusiasm for art. His literary compositions ruthlessly condemn the drudgery of office work, yet when referring explicitly to his personal experience he recalled "there was nothing to complain of socially, even for a Shaw; and the atmosphere was as uncommercial as that of an office can be. Thus I learnt business habits without being infected with the business spirit."[5]

There were repercussions of this work later in Shaw's life. His promotion to cashier brought him in closer connection with the machinery of business and firsthand experience with capitalist accumulation at the expense of the poor, though he could not rationalize his distaste for the system until he became acquainted with the theories of Henry George nearly a decade later. Like school, he refers to the office as a prison, and fled it in 1876 when his mother invited him to join her entourage in London. As he later wrote, he had traded the status of being a Dublin Shaw to being a nobody amongst the vast middle class of a London suburb, and even that status grew hard to maintain as his clothes wore out.[6]

During his first years in London, he spent a short time working in the nascent telephone industry, gratefully abandoning it at the first opportunity. Unlike the character Edward Connolly, self-reflectively invented by Shaw for a novel composed in 1880, neither Shaw's inventive nor musical genuis was fortuitously discovered while installing or promoting a telephone. No doubt this was a severe disappointment. In 1880 the family moved from Brompton to an address near Regent's Park, which put the British Museum within easy reach. Shaw used the famous Reading Room as his base: the seats were comfortable, an incomparable library was at his disposal, and light, ink, and blotting paper were free. He aspired to earn his living as an author, submitting a few unsolicited articles and, for a year, ghostwriting music criticism for the *Hornet* on behalf of Vandeleur Lee. He gives his total income for literary efforts as £6 over a period of nine years, a sum that could be accumulated by a manual labourer in almost as many weeks. The principal claim to his time was novel writing, which he pursued with dogged regularity at the rate of 250 shorthand words every fifteen minutes, adding up to precisely five quarto pages a day. Reaching the bottom of the fifth page he would stop regardless of his place in the sentence to resume work the following day. With this degree of application he finished five novels in as many years.

The first, *Immaturity*, ran to 200,000 words (the length of *Great Expectations*) and was not published for fifty years. Two others, *The Irrational Knot* (1880) and *Love among the Artists* (1881), were serialized in Annie Besant's socialist periodical *Our Corner* in 1885–87 and 1887–88. The last of Shaw's novels, *An Unsocial Socialist* (1883), was the first to be published (the next year in J. L. Joyne's periodical *To-Day*) and the most directly relevant to his lifetime preoccupations with socialist reform. He received no payment but at least he was read. *Cashel Byron's Profession* (1882) appeared in the same periodical, and in addition the editor published the novel in book form, from which Shaw was promised one twelfth of the shilling sale price. The edition was far from successful, as Shaw commented, "I have never seen an advertisement, never met a human being who had ever seen one, never expect to meet one."[7]

Socialist rhetoric in *Cashel Byron's Profession* is evident, though not too strident. Cashel Byron shows how all life is a struggle for someone, if not oneself personally. Every silver spoon gets earned by someone somehow. Cashel is the son of a famous actress; he runs away from the private school he abhors, joins the crew of a ship, lands in Australia, and apprentices with a boxer. His fame as a devastating pugilist takes him back to England, where his gentlemanly breeding wins the attention of an aristocratic and learned woman, Lydia, who meanwhile remains ignorant of his victories in the ring. Despite themselves, other characters are forced by circumstances to learn to recognize the system (science) and wisdom (art) in Cashel's life view, which he developed through pugilistic study.

One of the oddest chapters in the novel depicts Lydia and her "advanced thinking" companion Alice in attendance at an entertainment staged in honour of a visting African king. Various kinds of English combats are demonstrated, including cavalry charges, medieval tilts at arms, sword-play, and boxing. Unbeknownst to Lydia, the defending boxing champion is Cashel Byron. The match begins with proper displays of prowess and concludes in a melée very foreign to the Marquis of Queensbury's rules. Cashel, the apparent victor, is presented to the African guest:

> The king informed him, through an interpreter, that he had been unspeakably gratified by what he had just witnessed; expressed great surprise that Cashel, notwithstanding his prowess, was neither in the army nor in Parliament; and finally offered to provide him with three handsome wives if he would come out to Africa in his suite. Cashel was much embarrassed; but he came off with credit, thanks to the interpreter, who was accustomed to invent appropriate speeches for the king on public occasions, and was kind enough to invent equally appropriate ones for Cashel on this.[8]

Shaw's meaning is ambiguous almost to the point of obscurity. This emphasizes the worth of the man who blends physical skill with tactical finesse to gain an advantage over an opponent, while also equating the value of such individuals with a system of feudal patronage. Presenting such forms of historical combat as general entertainment glorifies the arts of war, yet they are far more engaging than the archaeologically "accurate" stage production of *King John* Cashel's mother prepares for earlier in the chapter. Because of Lydia's prejudices, a marriage is possible between her and Cashel only if he will renounce fighting, and only then after his fortune is made by inheriting from his long-lost aristocratic father. She settles down to write learned treatises and oppose conventional education while he is pursued by the Radicals (a party interested in working-class causes) to run for Parliament, where his unorthodox views of science, art, and society can be expounded. Together they breed a new generation of children, hybrids of their best characteristics.

The composition of the later novels coincides with Shaw's integration into London's political and social milieux. First attempts were awkward and unsuccessful, though Shaw persisted in trying out clubs and attending lectures until he found both congenial companionship and his own intellectual identity. The early 1880s are characterized by his exploration of individualism, especially the quest for the individuality that blossomed as "GBS." He frequented the New Shakespeare, Browning, and Shelley Societies seeking literary fellowship. Such migratory allegiance is typical of his peers. During the same period, Shaw read papers and developed debating skills in the Zetetical Society, a branch of the Dialectical Society following the school of neoclassical economics based on John Stuart Mill and Thomas Malthus, subsequently also trying the Land Reform Union after he came in contact with Henry George, the American author of *Progress and Poverty.*

George explained the link between rising production and increasing poverty: "Wealth in all its forms being the product of labor applied to land or the products of land, any increase in the power of labor, the demand for wealth being unsatisfied, will be utilized in procuring more wealth, and thus increase the demand for land."[9] The economic cycle is arrested, according to George, by assessing a single tax on the value of land rather than its products; this would equalize the tax burden, encourage investment, and maintain levels of production. There would be even less incentive to crowd the poor into tenements, establish monopolies, or waste resources if land was nationalized. The theory is not concerned with redistributing wealth profoundly or reconsidering the economic goals of society at large. It is thoroughly capitalist in intent, yet ironically it was George who led Shaw to the ideas of socialism through his 1882 London lecture. After an infatuation with George, Shaw rapidly turned from *Progress and Poverty* to *Capital* (*Das Kapital*), switching allegiance from the Land Reform Union to the Social Democratic Federation, a Marxist group led by H. M. Hyndman.

The nineteenth century is notable for entrenching principles of economic theory into common parlance. There was no economics profession per se, and so even the greatest theorists wrote for a general readership.

Most of this discourse revolved around the idea of "progress" founded in Social Darwinism and a belief in historical evolution: free markets and free trade were championed with as little regulatory interference as possible and were believed to evolve and operate for the mutual benefit of investors, employers, and the employed. John Stuart Mill, the leading laissez-faire economist, sympathized with the plight of factory workers and advocated government regulation of the length of a working day and inspections to guard against inhumane practices. Hand in hand with such liberal politics, Mill and his neoclassical revisers had unquenchable faith in the forces of the marketplace and the benefit of retaining incentives for profit making. Karl Marx's economic concepts represented a radical new position in the British milieu, though the ideas of communal living and de-alienating workers from the means of production expounded by Robert Owen achieved a following earlier in the century. According to Marx, the value of a capitalist economy was based on the total amount of labour input, with the difference between labourers' wages and the total output representing profit accruing exclusively to a separate class of masters (the theory of surplus value). Disseminating awareness of the inequitable operations of this system, including the capitalist class's interest in maintaining the workers' wages at a bare subsistence level, would lead inevitably to class friction and inexorably to mass action, revolutionizing the social and economic order. More than any of his contemporaries, Marx described economics historically, accounting for the origins of the contemporaneous agricultural and manufacturing bases and their effects on the working classes, with projections for future conflict. For him, economics was dynamic and evolutionary.

The first volume of *Capital* was written in 1867, translated from German to French five years later, and made available in English in 1886. *The Communist Manifesto* (1848) was equally slow to appear in English. In 1880, when Hyndman discovered *Capital* in the French edition, he was probably the first Briton to read Marx systematically or sympathetically. In the years that followed, *Capital* took hold of a generation of young socialists to the extent that the 1880s represent a crucible for radical thought. After decades of incipient organization, labour unions took hold, culminating in the 13 November 1887 march on Trafalgar Square famous for the altercations memoralized as "Bloody Sunday," which most agree was a fiasco demonstrating the pitfalls of confrontational tactics. Shaw proceeded to the square but was not personally involved in the confrontations between soldiers and police (some 4,600 strong) and John Burns's contingent of protectors. He arrived too late to be gaoled.[10] In contrast, the peaceable Matchgirls' Strike of 1888 organized by Annie Besant and strikes of dockers and gasworkers in 1889 demonstrated the power of collective action when supported by public sympathy. By 1893 unions were strong enough to precipitate formation of the Labour Party under Keir Hardie, a Scottish miner whose 1892 election to Parliament was a milestone in working-class politics. When, in 1883, Shaw struggled through the French text of *Capital* (seventeen years before Lenin, as Shaw fondly pointed out), it was at the commencement of socialist challenges to the English state that registered for a century. It also coincided with Marx's death.

For Shaw, reading *Capital* brought about nothing short of an epiphany. It gave him both a creed and a direction. "I immediately became a Socialist," he professed, "and from that hour I was a man with some business in the world," taking every opportunity to proselytize on economic topics for as long as an audience would tolerate him. Shortly after his conversion, he was invited to speak for an hour before a working men's club:

> I thought at first of writing a lecture & even of committing it to memory; for it seemed hardly possible to speak for an hour without text when I had thitherto [*sic*] only spoken for ten minutes in a debate. But I saw that if I were to speak often on Socialism—as I fully meant to do—writing and learning by rote would be impossible for mere want of time. . . . The lecture was called Thieves, and was a demonstration that the proprietor of an unearned income inflicted on the community exactly the same injury as a burglar does. (CL 2:487)

At the outset of this new phase of his life, Shaw worked on his last novel, *The Unsocial Socialist*, which bears the flavour of such speeches. The pseudo-Shavian character Trefusis abandons his wife after six months of marriage, preferring to live as a rural labourer and promote socialism among the proletariat. (Opting for the "simple life" was popular among socialists such as Charlotte Wilson and Kate and Henry Salt, later acquaintances of Shaw's.) During an accidental encounter, Trefusis explains to his estranged wife in a lengthy monologue how his father's wealth was created from the surplus value of exploited labourers' efforts. Men were desperate for employment in the tight labour market of mid-Victorian Manchester and willing to take whatever conditions the capitalist imposed:

> My father offered them the use of his factory, his machines, and his raw cotton on the following conditions: They were to work long

and hard, early and late, to add fresh value to his raw cotton by manufacturing it. Out of the value thus created by them, they were to recoup him for what he supplied them with: rent, shelter, gas, water, machinery, raw cotton—everything, and to pay him for his own services as superintendent, manager, and salesman.

He paid the workers just enough to keep them from starving and kept the rest "to reward me for my virtue in saving money."[11]

> The workmen abstained from meat, drink, fresh air, good clothes, decent lodging, holidays, money, the society of their families, and pretty nearly everything that makes life worth living. . . . Yet no one rewarded them for their abstinence. The reward came to my father, who abstained from none of these things, but indulged in them all to his heart's content.[12]

The more the workers abstained, the richer Trefusis' father became, justifying his wealth "as the reward of his risks, his calculations, his anxieties, and the journeys he had to make at all seasons and at all hours." With the profits of others' waged labour, he expanded his operations, became richer, retooled his factories, fired the men and hired docile women and children who would work for less, and contrived to get a seat in Parliament, where he preserved the laws that made all this possible. He lived the life of a landed gentleman, married the daughter of another landed gentleman, and produced a son who would inherit a fortune without exerting himself in the slightest way.

Trefusis accepted this formula until it occurred to him that there was merely a distinction of nomenclature between the industrialist and the criminal. Here, Shaw the novelist cribbed from Shaw the lecturer:

> If he had lived a century earlier, invested his money in a horse and a pair of pistols, taken to the road, his object—that of wresting from others the fruits of their labor without rendering them an equivalent— would have been exactly the same, and his risk far greater, for it would have included risk of the gallows. Constant travelling with the constable at his heels, and calculations of the chances of robbing the Dover mail, would have given him his fill of activity and anxiety.[13]

While explaining the distaff side of his family—particularly his maternal grandfather's culpability in throwing the peasants off his land and creating the labour pool for factory owners like his father—Trefusis fleshes out the second side of the capitalist triangle. The third consists of his own generation (including his wife) which lives luxuriously on rent from land and interest from investments, genteely removed from all taints of commerce and manufacturing.

Shaw's conversion of Marx's turgid prose on the dialectics of historical materialism to a dramatis personae and plot was a commendable achievement in the early 1880s. In his youth, Marx sketched the plots of novels but destroyed all evidence of them when he launched a more sedate career in economics, going from country to country in search of a culture tolerant enough for him to publish without censorship. Ultimately, which version is more likely to win converts, Shaw's or Marx's? This passage from *Capital* explains the same set of phenomena as Trefusis' confession in *An Unsocial Socialist*:

> In themselves, money and commodities are no more capital than the means of production and subsistence are. They need to be transformed into capital. But this transformation can itself only take place under particular circumstances, which meet together at this point: the confrontation of, and the contact between, two very different kinds of commodity owners; on the one hand, the owners of money, means of production, means of subsistence, who are eager to valorize the sum of values they have appropriated by buying the labour-power of others; on the other hand, free workers, the sellers of their own labour-power, and therefore the sellers of labour. . . . The free workers are therefore free from, unencumbered by, any means of production of their own. With the polarization of the commodity-market into these two classes, the fundamental conditions of capitalist production are present. The capital-relation presupposes a complete separation between the workers and the ownership of the conditions for the realization of their labour. As soon as capitalist production stands on its own feet, it not only maintains this separation, but reproduces it on a constantly extending scale.[14]

The key question for both novelist and philosopher was: what can be done to break the cycle? This is what Trefusis grapples with: if he gives up his wealth it will be subsumed into the fortunes of other capitalists who will perpetuate its destructive use. Instead, he retreats from society to the company of precisely the class of workers that had been exploited by his ancestors, and attempts to convince them to join the international movement of workers. His wealth is used for printing and distributing pamphlets, hiring lecturers, and publishing a journal addressed to the working classes. This had to be done covertly or capitalists would suppress it, and it had to be done incognito or the proletariat would distrust his motives.

After his wife's illness and death (brought about after a wintry journey sparked by jealousy—a subplot providing the book's conventional "love interest"), Trefusis abandons the policy of rural infiltration and life among the working classes who had given him so much abuse. The incidents surrounding the commissioning and construction of his wife's grave marker demonstrate the effects of workers' competition with each other, profoundly effecting Trefusis' outlook. Against his father-in-law's wishes, a famous artist is not selected, and instead a skilled stonemason (who would have executed the famed artist's design anyway) is hired. But the stonemason subcontracts the work, skimming a profit that ultimately allows him to set himself up as a capitalist employer. This closely parallels a set of transactions Shaw unwittingly instigated during this period:

> I remember once, at a time when I made daily use of the reading-room at the British Museum . . . I gave a £2 copying job to a man whose respectable poverty would have moved a heart of stone: an ex-school-master, whose qualifications were out of date, and who, through no particular fault of his own, had drifted at last into the reading-room as less literate men drift into Salvation Army Shelters. . . . His first step in the matter was to obtain from me an advance of five shillings; his next, to sublet the commission to another person in similar circumstances for one pound fifteen, and so get it entirely off his mind and return to his favorite books. This second, or rather, third party, required an advance of one-and-sixpence to buy paper, having obtained which, he handed over the contract to a fourth party, who was willing to do it for one pound thirteen and sixpence. Speculation raged for a day or two as the job was passed on; and it reached bottom at last in the hands of the least competent and least sober copyist in the room, who actually did the work for five shillings.[15]

Trefusis abandons his two-room cottage in favour of a decaying country estate and gives up proselytizing among the poor in order to make direct appeals to the ruling classes to provide the leadership necessary for massive social change. He confronts the enemy in its own territory, trapping it with its preferred luxuries.

Trefusis lures Chester Erskine, a maudlin poet of irresolute republican sentiments, and Sir Charles Brandon, a leisured aristocrat and artistic dabbler, to his ramshackle country retreat to view his collection of photographs. In contrast to etchings, photography is propounded as the purer art, unencumbered by dishonesty in subject or technique. The collection consists of albums systematically documenting the lives and working conditions of industrial labourers in developed and colonized nations, along with the machines that created riches for their owners and poverty for their operators. It juxtaposes photographs of ladies and pit lasses, peers and barge operators, communists and kings, to demonstrate that the classes have no natural basis for segregation. The tactic was not new: in 1795 William Pitt, the Prime Minister, was taken by a Halstead host to visit the poorest townspeople's homes. Pitt was dumbstruck, not realizing that anyone in England lived in such misery. Trefusis adds a socialist homily for his guests, convincing them that the current system of private property cannot be sustained much longer, with efficient foreign competition for raw and finished goods growing at an exponentially greater rate than England can match, especially as unions demand a more equitable share of surplus value. Capital will migrate abroad where profits are greater; labour will follow. The British industrial and agricultural bases will collapse, and the ruling class will starve in a reductio ad absurdum of free trade. The workers will turn on their former masters and show no mercy.

Shaw presents this scenario dystopially: the Marxist vision of the future is not the beginning of a new and better order but the collapse of all order. Trefusis offers an alternative. They can forestall the dystopia if they join the socialist cause and lend their names to the ranks calling for reform. The principle is still evolutionary, but it is not Marx's revolution. Trefusis is able to appeal to the self-interest of his class: they will give a greater share to the disenfranchised while retaining wealth more proportionately to their real needs. This strategy of infiltrating and influencing the upper classes also promised Shaw—a "shabby genteel" whose Dublin family clung to aristocratic prestige—a legitimate place in the socialist firmament.[16] Like Shaw and his fictional creation Trefusis, the bulk of this generation of British socialists were from the middle classes or above, advocating reform *for* the working classes but not *among* them. Shaw soon found his political niche in a new organization of similarly disposed radical thinkers.

The autobiographical component of Shaw's novels shows most markedly in the leading male protagonists: eloquent, brainy, freethinking individualists who know society's rules but refuse to perform the inane and hypocritical choreography demanded by politeness. In *Love among the Artists*, the Wagneresque composer Owen Jack and the Polish pianist Mlle Szczympliça share the honours as inspired social misfits. An early manifestation of the mechanical genius Conolly (hero of *The Irrational Knot* which chronologically precedes this book, though it was written next) who "would make an excellent God, but a most unpleasant man, and an unbearable husband" rounds out the complement of characters.[17] Conolly, Cashel, and Trefusis do not mince words or perpetuate empty salutations or ceremonies, but given a chance to lecture on population control, religious shams, class and occupational prejudice, and teetotalism, or to liken the cruelties of vivisection and combat, they never decline. They argue with a full arsenal of personal testimony, historical example, and metaphor. Their convictions are strongly held, and the evidence of such integrity is always irresistible for women of equally promising stature. This new breed of worthy men attracts females who are unequivocally gentlewomen who mate and defy the prejudices of the social order within its most prestigious bastions. Convictions run higher than romantic passions, which can probably be accounted for by the failure of the scrawny, ill-dressed Shaw—who showed no prospects of earning a living—to warrant women's attention. He had no sexual experience whatsoever.

In the novels, fighting from within the ruling class and presenting an alternative through personal example is a situation contrived by plot and character. In 1884, when Shaw abandoned the novel form, it became possible to adopt this as a political strategy within the newly founded Fabian Society, which he embraced. Raymond Williams's theory about the relationship between a writer's choice of medium and the social practices of politics has direct relevance to this coincidence in Shaw's career.

> Significantly, since the late nineteenth century, crises of technique—which can be isolated as problems of the "medium" or of the "form"—have been directly linked with a sense of crisis in the relationship of art to society, or in the very purposes of art which had previously been agreed or even taken for granted. A new technique has often been seen, realistically, as a new relationship, or as depending on a new relationship. Thus what had been isolated as a medium [such as novel writing], in many ways rightly as a way of emphasizing the material production which any art must be, came to be seen, inevitably, as social practice; or, in the crisis of modern cultural production, as a crisis of social practice. This is the crucial common factor, in otherwise diverse tendencies, which links the radical aesthetics of modernism and the revolutionary theory and practice of Marxism.[18]

As usual, Williams does not specify whom he was thinking of but presents the idea as an open-ended observation, leaving others to test its applicability. There is no evidence that Shaw suffered a "crisis of technique" in the sense that his plot-making ability was blocked, his daily flow of words came to a stop, or the novel form lost credibility either in society at large or among his new circle of associates. Yet as a novelist he undeniably failed to make an impact on society: up to the time of his Marxist epiphany his novels were unpublished, unremunerated, and unappreciated. Clearly, they were displaying no political utility. There is evidence that Shaw grew embarrassed by them as expressions of youth; his new experiences rapidly helped him improve on what had been the distant and unphysical love making as well as naive accounts of political economy. The interest in theatre and particularly actresses, whose milieu is more artistically and morally permissive—demonstrated in *Love among the Artists*, *The Irrational Knot*, *Cashel Byron's Profession*, and *An Unsocial Socialist*— abided and culminated in Shaw's first serious attempt at playwriting in 1884. The project was also his first literary collaboration (with the Liberal theatre critic William Archer), pursued intermittently for several years and then laid aside until 1892. Significantly, this project intertwined with Shaw's other reading (such as royal commissions on housing), writing (particularly pamphlets and political journalism), and lecturing (see Illustration 1). In 1887 he attempted a new novel but it went nowhere. By 1890 he could state with conviction: "No thank you: no more novels for me. Five failures are enough to satisfy my appetite for enterprise in fiction." (BS 1:277)

He had tried a medium that had brought prestige to George Eliot, Mrs. Gaskell, Charles Dickens, and a host of other reform-minded writers. The novel was a prestigious medium in English letters, but it brought Shaw no prestige, so he abandoned it. The drama was a maligned medium that promised no prestige but held out two intriguing possibilities: livelihoods were comfortably sustained by prolific writers such as H. J. Byron and Charles Reade, and being shy of political content the stage was ripe for a maverick infusion of ideological polemics. The fight against the Lord Chamberlain, whose office censored or banned plays at will, and entrenched conventions of dramatic composition would be strenuous, but Shaw was evidently either undaunted or unaware of the extent of the struggle ahead. It certainly was not the art form to which he was most drawn or in which he was most experienced, for his artistic inclinations had up until that time taken him into galleries and concert halls far more regularly than theatres.

The transition years between Shaw's wholehearted pursuit of novel writing and concerted push at playwriting extended from 1884 to 1892, by which time the techniques of the stage had come under a new relation to politics through productions of Henrik Ibsen's social dramas. Shaw probably saw the potential but lacked a context for his plans. To publish a novel, an author needed to convince only one reader; to produce a play, a legion of backers, actors, and unofficial critics needed to be convinced of the text's and the author's worth. In the meantime, Shaw laboured to create a new political landscape through the Fabians and to profoundly challenge aesthetic tastes through his newspaper columns.

The Fabian Society struggled into existence late in 1883. The first meetings were attended by a variety of people who had very little in common except a willingness to attend meetings and a desire to change their lives in some way. Preferences for social, spiritual, and political focuses conflicted. Not exactly an auspicious beginning. What emerged under the leadership of Edward Pease, Frank Podmore, and Hubert Bland was a small band devoted to high moral principles, interested in social reform on the lines of the Social Democratic Federation (minus hard-line Marxism), but completely devoid of political experience or working-class connections. They professed that "if Capital be socialised, Labor will benefit by it fully; but while Capital is left in the hands of the few, Poverty must be the lot of the many."[19] Nevertheless, when Edward Pease quit his job as a stockbroker and went to work as a carpenter in a Newcastle cooperative, whatever illusions he had of working-class prospects were shattered: "I never met a shop-mate . . . who took the remotest interest in politics or socialism, or trade unionism or co-operation. They *were* interested in racing . . . they were simply breadwinners."[20]

The Fabians believed that different tactics had to be devised for transforming society on socialist lines. They were determined not to be another group of "street-corner agitators" who

marshal columns of hollow-cheeked men with red flags and banners inscribed with Scriptural texts to fashionable churches on Sunday, and . . . lead desperate deputations . . . to the Local Government Board office and back again, using stronger language at each official rebuff from pillar to post. These were the days when . . . Mr. Hyndman was expelled from his club for declaring on the Thames Embankment that there would be some attention paid to cases of starvation [only] if a rich man were immolated on every pauper's tomb.[21]

The club was named after Fabius Cunctator, a Roman general whose tactics in the campaign against Hannibal were believed to be cautious yet forthright. He patiently waited, suffered censure, chose his moment, and then struck with determination and success. This strategy (though of dubious historical authenticity) would be the Fabians' modus operandi.

Shaw rapidly attained influence in the Social Democratic Federation but was disenchanted with Hyndman's leadership and decided that the group had a disadvantageous proportion of zealots to intellectuals. He attended his first Fabian meeting on 10 May 1884. The middle-class, tolerant, educated clique that sought to reform society by argument, brain power, and superior organization rather than working-class revolt was consonant with Shaw's own philosophies. They would proceed at first with research and writing, develop their credentials, let a platform evolve, and then launch the full force of their influence to make an egalitarian state managed by people just like themselves. The next week Shaw delivered a speech the Fabians embraced as their manifesto. From that point he was an indispensable part of the society.

The ease with which Shaw traded one form of writing for another shows in the propagandistic nonfiction he composed for the Fabians. In 1889 he was entrusted with the task of editing *Essays in Fabian Socialism*, a volume that sold surprisingly well. It consists of detailed essays by leading members on the history of laissez-faire capitalism and the basic planks in the Fabian platform for "municipal socialism," a program it meant to expound in London's new County Council, the first unified government the metropolitan area had ever had. One of Shaw's contributions, "Economic," works out precisely the same narrative as Trefusis delivered to Henrietta in *An Unsocial Socialist*, only this time it was overt political philosophy. Either way, capitalism was to end in a tremendous "smash-up."[22]

The Fabian Society was growing slowly but very advantageously. Annie Besant was the most famous recruit, but the civil servants Sidney Webb and Sydney Olivier, along with the classics teacher Graham Wallas and sociologist Beatrice Webb, were among the society's most dedicated members, providing much needed leadership. They became fast friends with Shaw. Along with a circle of sympathizers in Hampstead, they traded papers on the Poor Laws, trades unions, feminism, and the history of socialism.

They avoided rigid doctrine, preferring permissive consensus on procedural matters. This kept them free of the divisive factional fighting that plagued other socialist groups. Common planks emerged over the next decade, but for the most part the group was so diverse in background, temperament, and sophistication that they needed a long period in which they could openly debate, rally information, and test ideas. Most significantly, they argued themselves away from some of the mainstays of Marx. They agreed with his historical account of how capitalism evolved but disagreed about what should happen in the future. They advocated common ownership of the means of production, but did not see this coming about through overthrow of the parliamentary system: democracy should be extended gradually, not abandoned suddenly. They also differed in their ascription of how value came about. Marx saw labour as the ultimate denominator of value; the Fabians replaced this idea with the "law of rent." In a throwback to David Ricardo (on whose ideas Marx extensively relied) and Henry George, Fabians saw land as the ultimate denominator of value and the foundation of capitalist production, giving differential advantages to the classes. Significantly, they argued that these differential advantages were perpetuated at the expense of the entire nation, not just one class, hence their advocacy of government takeovers of the means of production (e.g., socialization of utilities and factories).

While preparing to change Britain, Shaw needed a livelihood. He never charged for lecturing, saw no potential as a novelist, abhorred the commercial world, and lacked the education for a civil service career. His potential is symbolized by the seeming disorder of Trefusis' study, which contains the remnants of plaster statuary (used for target practice), athletic equipment, art materials, a camera, library, desk, and lounging sofas. At this juncture, biographies and commentaries invariably relate the story that Shaw was discovered in the British Library simultaneously reading the score of Richard Wagner's opera *Tristan and Isolde* alongside *Capital*. The implicit suggestion is that two contemporary works more different in subject or ideology could hardly be found, and that their coincidence on Shaw's desk accounts for intense individualism and intellectual iconoclasm. This may be true; however it is more important to ask what was behind his verve to absorb Wagner and Marx simultaneously. What kind of a synthesis could this possibly produce in a young man eager for authorhood and desperate for a livelihood?

Recently, Wagner has been somewhat rehabilitated after having fallen out of fashion as an anti-Semite embraced by German Nazis. In Britain of the 1880s, he was obscure on every count. Shaw recognized in Wagner a musical talent unequalled by any of his contemporaries. He probably first heard part of *Tristan and Isolde* in 1877; he noted the concert performance of an excerpt in a *Hornet* review, but had not yet had the opportunity to form an opinion of Wagner's theatrical qualities. In 1882 the opera was performed in its entirety at the Theatre Royal, Drury Lane.

Soon after meeting Shaw, William Archer recognized his predeliction for discerning good musical performance and sensibilities in sympathy with his own agenda for artistic reform. Under Archer's influence, Shaw became music critic for the *Dramatic Review* and book reviewer for the *Pall Mall Gazette*. He graduated to the *Star*, where his musical persona "Corno di Bassetto" was invented. By 1889 he could command £3 3s. a month, still not a labourer's living wage. Corno di Bassetto had difficulty constraining his columns to musical criticism, which in part accounts for their unprecedented popularity. The next year he transferred to Archer's paper, the *World*, where he stayed for four years.

From 1884 until 1898, Shaw lived by his pen, critiquing other people's artistic endeavors. Much of this was dogsbody work, done purely for money. He grew impatient with reviewing bad novels and poetry, writing, "there ought to be legislation against this sort of thing—on the lines of the Factory Acts."[23] Stanley Weintraub's assessment is apt:

> For Shaw the art of criticism, especially when it came to music and theater, was easy; but his purely literary criticism, once he no longer had to produce it, was irregular in appearance and often uninspired. At its best it was intellectually agile, complementary to the philosophical biases of his play, and a joy to read. Pillaged from the prefaces, looted from the lectures, or extricated from his journalism, his major statements on writers and writing demonstrate that however strong was his commitment to literary art, it was that extra dimension of a criticism of society that, to him, gave life to literature. Having declared that for art's sake alone he would not have produced a single sentence, he remained impatient with writers who were mere virtuosos with words, literary fiddlers playing stylistic cadenzas. One needed something worth saying.[24]

His financial resources were more plentiful, but he still had difficulty looking better than the "shabby genteel." He lived frugally, on vegetables and water, in his mother's household. He attended more concerts and read more books than he cared for free of charge. His earnings went further than they should.

When his father died in 1885, Shaw inherited the proceeds from a life insurance policy. With part of the £100, he bought his first new set of clothes in many years: the infamous Jaeger suit. Dr. Gustave Jaeger, whose name graces what has grown to be one of the most prestigious clothing stores in Britain, was in the 1880s on the radical fringe of the rational dress movement. He advocated natural animal fibers and nonrestricting cuts, testifying that their superior capability to release the body's fumes cured a variety of ills ranging from obesity to haemorrhoids. Shaw chose an undyed wool knitted into a stretchy fabric called stockinette, cut in an eccentric pattern of jacket and knee breeches. "With his red hair and beige suiting, an acquaintance remarked, Shaw looked like 'a forked radish in a worsted bifurcated stocking.'"[25] It was quite a fashion statement, and Shaw adopted it permanently in shades of red and brown, eventually bowing to the custom of trousers. In 1892 Keir Hardie made a bold class statement by striding into the Houses of Parliament wearing a cloth cap. Shaw's public construction of himself was more individualistic and eccentric, but also less class-marked.

Stanley wore a Jaeger when in search of Dr. Livingstone, Scott wore a Jaeger on expedition to the North Pole, but Shaw wore his on a different kind of quest. One of his first acts in this new persona was to seduce his mother's friend Jenny Patterson. It was his twenty-ninth birthday. Perhaps wool does have beneficial effects on the body's exhalations, just as Jaeger claimed. His next lasting liaison was with Annie Besant, editor, prolific author of books and pamphlets, notorious birth control advocate, and recent recruit to the Fabian Society. His repertoire of piano duets was also practised in other quarters.

Victorians drew a wavy line between "popular culture" and "art." For some members of each class art was the popular choice, yet for most people class-based tastes in entertainment veered away from what only radical iconoclasts and history has judged to be truly artistic and toward populist preferences for conservatism in painting, spectacularism in theatre, and the more bombastic expressions of music. Fabians were interested in reforming popular culture and propagandizing through new aesthetics. This is nowhere more apparent than in Besant's judgment of the entertainments available in London in 1886. She praises the concerts at St. James's Hall, where for one shilling anyone can enjoy "an evening of music as good as any crowned head could buy,"[26] and notes expressions of republican sentiments along with the audience's behaviour, the cheapness of admission, and proportion of working-class clientele in music halls and theatres throughout the city. "Middle-class art," she concludes, "is as low as middle-class morals, a whited sepulchre, filled with all uncleanness."[27]

Entertainments were available in all districts, and Besant is eager to praise what gives pleasure to labourers, yet laments that the provision for exclusively working-class patrons did little more than please:

> If we sum up East End amusements, and the amusements open to the
> poor all over London, we must sorrowfully confess that the gates of

art are closed and barred against them. Amusements there are, but art there is not, and from the nobler and higher enjoyments they are shut out. The music-hall is better, far better than nothing; but where are the music, the painting, the drama, that delight, that elevate, that refine? "The poor would not understand, would not care for these," say the well-to-do. And that is the condemnation of our society. We put out the eyes of the poor, and then make their blindness an excuse for our selfish neglect, and argue that they do not miss beauty and light and color. Throw open all treasures of art to the workers. . . . Let art, the great humaniser, bring them under its gracious sway, softening manners, purifying thought, and gladdening life.[28]

This does not mean proletarianizing the most exclusive theatres, for she condemns Henry Irving because he "chooses great plays which appeal to the intellect, and smothers them under upholstery that gratifies only love of display," while Herbert Beerbohm Tree and Madge Kendal produce trivial texts and Wilson Barrett wallows in sensational melodramas.[29] Ian Britain argues that Fabians believed the labouring classes would be rescued from inequitable social organization by reorganizing both economics and culture (i.e., the arts).

While the roots and aims of Fabian socialism were strongly aesthetic in nature, its adherents were aware—and none more so than the Society's most famous artist, Shaw—that the arts could work no magic on their own in humanizing and refining the mass of mankind. This was especially the case when, as at present, art itself was liable to be corrupted by ignorant idolatry, or by its association with the luxury and opulence of the prosperous few. Generally, Fabians recognized that for art to be fully effective as a humanizing force, a radical reordering of society as a whole was required, and one which would entail considerable changes in the present conditions and organization of artistic production, if not in the nature of art itself.[30]

What Besant suggests is a levelling of opportunities for workers to choose self-improvement: high art at the discretion of all, achieved by reforming politics and taste simultaneously.

Ultimately, Fabians proposed that leisure be a branch of municipal government. It was a necessity and should be provided with reliable quality at the lowest possible cost, rather like water and sanitation. It was not necessary to bludgeon the working classes with entertainment that portrayed the Fabians' political utopia: a "useful" mission for art such as the

Socialist Realism propounded in Stalin's Soviet Union. Instead, they called for removing art from the exigencies of a commercial system while retaining heterogeneity.[31]

The Fabian Society as a whole has been portrayed as lacking concern for art. Sometimes this is a way of singling out Shaw as an extraordinary talent rising above the political mire of his philistine colleagues: a lone specimen of socialist *and* Wagnerite. Sometimes this is in blatant defiance of the private lives and public pursuits of the most prominent society members, including lesser dramatists, performers, and poets. It is true that William Morris and his followers had a much more abiding confidence in the responsibility and potential of art to reform society and put much more energy into designing the products of artisans' crafts, the system of producing those crafts, and the communities that could replace the ubiquitous factories. Shaw, an early convert to vegetarianism and teetotalism, added rational dress to his fads; this choice is related to Morris's reforms, yet Shaw actually took a more intellectual route to connect his passion for the arts with a growing economic critique. His five novels chart this growing sophistication.

Later in his life, Shaw explained how he came to hear the two strains in his nature urging him harmoniously to seek social change: "Ruskin, beginning as an artist with an interest in art—exactly as I did myself, by the way—was inevitably driven back to economics, and to the conviction that your art would never come right whilst your economics were wrong. . . . You may aim at making a man cultured and religious; but you must feed him first."[32] By reading *Capital* and *Tristan and Isolde* in tandem Shaw fed both parts of himself.

In 1876, the centennial of the American Revolution, Shaw arrived in London. It is easy—and quite common—to argue that at that moment Europe was on the eve of another kind of revolution, for on the Continent the theatre was undergoing profound challenges to literary, presentational, and organizational conventions. Ibsen's *Peer Gynt* was performed in Christiania (Oslo), marking a transition from the romantic verse drama of the earlier part of the century to a raunchier depiction of life rounded out by greed and moral vapidity in the age of commerce and colonialism. In this case, an old form (epic verse drama) showed adaptability to new philosophical perspectives. In the same year, Wagner's Festival Theatre opened in Bayreuth for presentations of his four-opera cycle *The Ring of the Nibelungs*. This event marks profound changes in operatic composition, performance, and theatre design in an attempt to unite the musical, dramatic, and visual arts. Meanwhile, the duke of Saxe-Meiningen's troupe toured Europe with carefully researched historically accurate costumes and sets, impressing a generation of future directors with meticulous staging, choreographed crowd scenes, and evenness of acting throughout the cast.

In 1873 Emile Zola adapted his novel *Thérèse Raquin* for the stage. Five years later, in his article "Naturalism in the Theatre," he expressed the hope that a great playwright would emerge to take up the movement toward scientific enquiry and analysis and lead theatrical art into a new era. He urged that exaggerated melodramatic acting, laboured rhetoric, and action at the expense of character analysis should be abandoned. The literary and presentational aspects of the "well-made play" epitomized by Victorien Sardou were to be replaced. Instead, artists should delve into life of the here and now, replicate how people talk and think, make reality function with all its power to convey the raw human condition, and depict people in the environments that make them who they are and that cannot be regarded separately from them. In some respects, Zola's vision sounds remarkably like what had been a curiosity of English repertoire for the previous couple of decades.

James Greenwood's series of personal exposé *Pall Mall Gazette* articles, "A Night in a Workhouse," fascinated readers in 1866. They were quickly adapted for presentation at the Marylebone, Pavilion, and Britannia Theatres. For the middle-class Greenwood, his voluntary stay in the Lambeth workhouse was regarded as an act of bravery; for the working and impoverished classes the workhouse was a spectre of doom that prodded them to endure miseries independently until the last possible moment when charity could be avoided no longer. The attraction of adapting Greenwood's series for the theatre lay in documenting the casual ward of the workhouse, a repository of the destitute in the precursor of the welfare state, where the poorest citizens of the parish resorted in shame that made poverty itself seem criminal. Pictorial realizations of familiar settings and heightened emotions were the mainstays of Victorian melodrama theatres' profits. In one adaptation, the warder "Old Daddy" who figures sentimentally in Greenwood's articles was exhibited in his own character, adding to the realism of the workhouse's rows of beds and cranks for grinding the daily measure of flour.[33]

Henry Mayhew, who wrote a few plays when he was younger, collected interviews with the least prosperous citizens of the capital and published them as *London Labour and the London Poor* (1861–62). Concern over migration, crowding, disease, and depravity amongst the urban poor prompted several such studies, varying from the sensational journalism of Andrew Mearns and George R. Sims to the social surveys of Charles Booth. These forays into Darker England were the impetus for many dramas that capitalized on precisely the kinds of scenes that Zola called for: "inside a factory, the interior of a mine, the gingerbread market, a railway station, flower stalls, a racetrack. . . . All the activities of modern life."[34] Zola does not discount this genre, but bemoans his contemporaries' failure to complete the illusion:

> What we need is detailed reproduction: costumes supplied by tradespeople, not sumptuous but adequate for the purposes of truth and for the interest of the scenes. . . . At one stroke they could satisfy the public hunger for spectacle and the need for exact studies which grows more pressing every day. Let us hope, though, that the playwrights will show us real people and not those whining members of the working class who play such strange roles in boulevard melodrama.[35]

Zola's preferred degree of naturalism was eventually provided by André Antoine at the Théâtre Libre in Paris and by David Belasco in the U.S.A.

In contrast to this development toward stage naturalism, the art theatre cultivated in London during the 1870s and 1880s is epitomized by Henry Irving, who took over management of the Lyceum Theatre in 1878. The Lyceum equalled the Meininger company in attention to visual detail but exceeded it in romantic lavishness of production and was its antithesis in its promotion of star players. Like the Bayreuth Festival Theatre, the Lyceum employed prominent visual artists and composers (Laurence Alma-Tadema and Arthur Sullivan are among those still famous over a century later) and was a mecca for playgoers with sophisticated tastes. Irving and his leading lady, Ellen Terry, excelled in Shakespeare, in which they specialized, along with a repertoire of historical and romantic melo-dramas that has not lasted beyond their lifetimes. Aesthetically, the reforms Zola propounded were anathema to Irving, who preferred grandeur, majes-ty, and rip-roaring acting effects, deploring the introduction of the squalid and tawdry misery of everyday matters on the stage.

The actor-manager system (in which the same personage ruled onstage, presided over artistic decisions, and chose and produced the repertoire) was supreme in London's West End theatres in the last third of the nineteenth century. J. L. Toole, Squire Bancroft, John Hare, and George Alexander all flourished under this system. In the East End, family-based managements were the norm, whether or not the proprietor was also the leading actor: Morris Abrahams at the Pavilion, George Conquest at the Surrey, and Sara Lane at the Britannia are among the longest lived. Melodrama was the most popular dramatic genre, though some theatres in the West End were able to specialize in burlesque, opera, and extravaganza, while others across the river presented circuses year-round. Pantomime, produced exclusively in the winter, was the financial salvation of many enterprises in London and the provinces. Other managements made up the difference between production expenses (ever increasing with the demand for spectacle, the sophistication of new technology, and increases in stars' wages) and West End receipts with summer tours of the provinces or extensive foreign journeys most often through North America, Australia, and southern Africa. Continental European actor-managers operated under the same commercial constraints yet were not necessarily so oblivious to developments in what was called the "New Drama." Eleonora Duse, an Italian actress of great renown, performed in *Thérèse Raquin* in 1879 and later championed several of Ibsen's social plays. Why could an Italian embrace the modernist repertoire but not an English actor-manager?

Music halls were resolutely populist. They offered a varied fare of comic singers, acrobats, dancers, and balladists in venues all over the nation, catering to clientele from every social class. Music hall per se had only existed since the 1850s, when it metamorphosed from male-only singing rooms, supper clubs, and judge and jury clubs into a highly lucrative new medium for artists and audiences of both sexes. By the early 1890s, London's thirty-five principal halls accommodated fourteen million visitors annually.

Theatrical entertainment was available for virtually every taste and pocketbook. Illegal theatres attracted ragged customers in poor neighbour-hoods for a penny a head (the price of a cooked meal), while a serious middle-class theatregoer attending the West End houses could easily spend the equivalent of a labourer's annual income by attending every other week in the year. The irony was lost on most Victorians. "It was no sign of national prosperity," as the historian Ian Britian cites the Fabian Sidney Webb, "that 'a thousand pound prima donna' should be 'faintly amusing a languid audience' at the moment when 'forty thousand children may be without bread, and several persons dying of starvation.' "[36] Theatre was a big business, and where a profit could be anticipated the investment was made. A few reformers questioned the social utility of theatre, bought out going concerns, and offered a more "uplifting" repertoire without the coincident sale of liquor in an effort to educate, proselytize, or augment the opportunities for threadbare patrons. Generally, however, the theatre went unchecked and unimproved by anything but the marketplace. Ian Britain sums it up succinctly:

In considering the question of whether the supply of this commodity
should be increased or not, no attempts would be made by those
responsible for the decision to assess either general social need or
the "intensity of desire" exhibited by particular groups within
society. This question . . . would be resolved merely by the momentary whim of a few hundred families with the money to invest in
such ventures, the direction of their whim being determined by
whether or not they thought the venture in question would add to
their personal fortune.[37]

Some Victorians—particularly in the dissenting Protestant sects—stayed
away from the drama on religious grounds. Among such believers,
Shakespeare was read in Bowdler's purified edition, and stage dancing
was believed to be a certain path to perdition for dancer and spectator
alike. Nevertheless, among this sector of the population attendance at
musical concerts was permissible, Sunday services held in opulent music
halls were commonplace, and blackface minstrel shows at the St. James's
Hall were a staple diversion. The paradox is evident to those with a
modern sensibility, but not to Victorians.

A range of other entertainments were targeted as improving influences
for the working classes. Seaside resorts served factory workers in industrialized Lancashire, while institutions like the Alexandra Palace were accessible
to Londoners on the new long holiday weekends. Special places and dates
for working-class leisure were instituted in the Victorian period to eliminate
rowdy traditions often destructive of property and to break down ancient
work habits derived from agricultural and religious calendars. Victorians
explored ways in which to unite leisure pursuits with technological dis-
coveries; the crowning achievement in this vein was the Great Exhibition
of 1851 installed in the Crystal Palace. In order to encourage the working
classes to attend, admission rates were relatively low, yet to placate the
middle-class obsession for regulated space, there were higher rates on
designated days, ensuring an exclusively genteel crowd. Other institutions,
such as the London Zoo, melding educational with recreative functions,
also scaled entry fees for different times in the week.

At the same time that organized leisure became so splendid, spon-
taneous community-based leisure declined. Sports were professional-
ized, regulated, and changed from largely participatory games to a
spectatorial activity. Music hall likewise was commercialized and pro-
fessionalized at the expense of the communal pub sing-along. Amateur
theatricals flourished among the middle classes, while their less comfortably off counterparts were herded into the galleries to enjoy professional

fare. Though enjoyed by all classes, the leisure industries were ideologically responsible for regulating working-class behaviour and presenting
material that entertained while asserting the value of the status quo. To
some critics, this meant the fare was moribund. Others regarded it as
wholesome affirmation of Christian ethics.

For many freethinkers, socialists, and radicals, Ibsen's plays contained
the promise of breaking up this log jam. Before translations and literary
criticism were widely available, social contacts were important in spread-
ing the message about Ibsen. One important Ibsenite clique, consisting of
Eleanor Marx Aveling (Karl Marx's daughter), Edward Aveling, and Olive
Schreiner, inspired a later member, Havelock Ellis, to edit a volume of
plays that proved to be Ibsen's first conquest of the English reading public.
As evangelical socialists, the Avelings felt affinity with what they believed
to be Ibsen's political outlook. Eleanor Marx Aveling closely identified on
a personal level with characters like Nora (*A Doll's House*), Ellida (*The
Lady from the Sea*), and possibly Stockman (*An Enemy of the People*) and
harboured an unfulfilled dream to perform professionally.[38] As an actress,
however, her only experiences of the roles were in private readings she
organized between 1884 and 1886. In the summer of 1884 she and Aveling
read part of Henrietta Lord's translation of *A Doll's House* (known as *Nora*)
to Schreiner. Later they read the play again before a larger group of friends.
In May 1885 Marx Aveling tried to organize another reading with various
friends taking part, and consulted Shaw about the casting.[39] The event
finally came off in January the next year in the Avelings' Bloomsbury flat.
May Morris read Mrs. Linde, Edward Aveling read Torvald, Eleanor Marx
Aveling read Nora, and Shaw "impersonated Krogstad at her request with
a very vague notion of what it was all about."[40]

Ibsen was, as William Archer commented, "the god of a few fanatics."[41]
The reasons are clear. As writers who entertained advanced ideas about
marriage and women's rights, Schreiner felt kinship with Ibsen's avant-
garde literary sensibility while Ellis found inspiration in Ibsen's rendering
of sexual psychology. As evangelical socialists, the Marx Avelings felt
affinity with what they believed to be Ibsen's political outlook.

As Ibsen makes Helmer say to Nora, "Home life ceases to be free and
beautiful directly its foundations are borrowing and debts." But
borrowing and debts, when one is a member of community, and not
an isolated man fighting for his own hand, can never come. Intellectual likeness. The same education for men and women; the bringing
up of these twain side by side, until they join hands at last, will ensure
a greater degree of this.[42]

Ibsen's most infamous play, *Ghosts*, was serialized in the socialist magazine *To-Day*, a rival to *Our Corner*, both of which published Shaw's novels. Yet the circulation of these periodicals was minuscule compared to Ellis's edition of Ibsen's *An Enemy of the People*, *The Pillars of Society*, and *Ghosts*, which was published in Walter Scott's shilling Camelot series in 1888. It was released simultaneously in New York, Toronto, and London, selling over fourteen thousand copies within five years. Unlike Shaw, Webb, Fabian pamphleteers, and Ellis, Ibsen was no longer an "exotic of the library" found only in the collections of malcontents and eccentrics.[43]

Shaw was not an active Ibsenite until 1888, long after Marx Aveling's reading of *A Doll's House*. As Archer's and Ellis's friend, he had access to each new Ibsen play and translation, yet there is no indication that he took more than a passing interest until his enthusiasm was sparked by reading Ellis's Camelot texts. In September 1888 Archer and H. L. Braekstad concocted a plan to read *Peer Gynt* aloud to Shaw, render it in literal translation, then turn Shaw loose to "put it into shape."[44] For a time, Shaw took language lessons so he could better understand the Dano-Norwegian original. The project disintegrated, yet Shaw remained a prime enthusiast.

Ibsen had sufficient British supporters to get his plays read; what was needed was a forum in which they could be sensitively performed (i.e., without "Bowdlerization") and attract a wide audience. Under such circumstances both a dramatic revolution and a political renaissance could be bred.

NOTES

1. *Shaw: An Autobiography 1856–1898*, ed. Stanley Weintraub (New York: Weybright and Talley, 1969), 12.

2. In the old system of British currency, a pound (£) equalled twenty shillings (s.), each of which contained twelve pence (d.).

3. Edward McNulty, "Memoirs of G.B.S.," *Shaw* 12 (1992): 11.

4. Quoted in Weintraub, *Shaw: An Autobiography*, 50.

5. Ibid., 68.

6. Letter, 3 December 1942, in *Bernard Shaw: Collected Letters*, 4 vols., ed. Dan H. Laurence (London: Max Reinhardt, 1965–88), 4: 653. Subsequently abbreviated in the text as CL.

7. Quoted in Michael Holroyd, *Bernard Shaw*, 4 vols. (London: Chatto and Windus, 1988–92), 1: 120. Subsequently abbreviated in the text as BS.

8. *Cashel Byron's Profession*, in *Selected Novels of G. Bernard Shaw* (New York: Caxton House, 1946), 459.

9. Henry George, *Progress and Poverty: An Inquiry into the Cause of Industrial Depressions, and of Increase of Want with Increase of Wealth. The Remedy* (New York: D. Appleton, 1881), 224.

10. Thomas Lloyd Humberstone, *Battle of Trafalgar Square* (London: Ridgill Trout, 1948), 14.

11. *An Unsocial Socialist*, in *Selected Novels*, 571.

12. Ibid., 573.

13. Ibid., 573–74.

14. Karl Marx, *Capital: A Critique of Political Economy*, vol. 1, trans. Ben Fowkes (New York: Vintage, 1977), 874.

15. Shaw, "Socialism for Millionaires," *Contemporary Review*, February 1898; reprinted in *Fabian Tract* 107 (1901): 7–8.

16. Later in life, Shaw developed a third alternative for heirs in Trefusis's predicament. In 1944 he inherited Irish property from his great-grandfather. Paul A. Hummert writes:

To wipe the slate clean, he offered the property to the [local] Council on Trust in Carlow with the stipulation that it be used "for purposes which exclude its sale to private owners, the use of its revenue to relieve the rates directly, or for alms giving of any kind confining it to improvements, home modernization, and experimental innovations." He also insisted that "it shall not be a closed trust but the nucleus of a civic improvement fund well advertised and open to all citizens who desire to follow my example."

Based on British Museum Add. Ms. 50699, fol. 14, reproduced in Paul A. Hummert, *Bernard Shaw's Marxian Romance* (Lincoln: University of Nebraska Press, 1973), 61.

17. *Love among the Artists* (1880; reprint, New York: Brentano's, 1913), 320.

18. Raymond Williams, *Marxism and Literature* (Oxford: Oxford University Press, 1977), 163–64.

19. "Why Are the Many Poor?" *Fabian Tract* 1 (1884): 3.

20. Quoted in Norman and Jeanne MacKenzie, *The Fabians* (New York: Simon and Schuster, 1977), 67.

21. Shaw, "The Fabian Society: Its Early History. A Paper Read at a Conference of the London and Provincial Fabian Societies at Essex Hall on the 6th February, 1892," *Fabian Tract* 41 (1899): 7.

22. The famous phrase "Socialism or Smash" is introduced in *An Unsocial Socialist*, *Selected Novels*, 683, and recurs as "the object of our campaign with its watchwords, 'EDUCATE, AGITATE, ORGANIZE' was to bring about a tremendous smash-up of existing society, to be succeeded by complete Socialism"; *Fabian Tract* 41 (1892): 4.

23. Quoted in Dan H. Laurence, gen. intro., *Widowers' Houses: Facsimilies of the Shorthand and Holograph Manuscripts and the 1893 Published Text* (New York and London: Garland, 1981), vii.

24. Stanley Weintraub. *The Unexpected Shaw: Biographical Approaches to G.B.S. and His Work* (New York: Frederick Ungar, 1982), 137.

25. Quoted in MacKenzie, *The Fabians*, 50.

26. Annie Besant, "How London Amuses Itself: West End and East," *Our Corner* 8 (1886): 14.

27. Ibid., 13.

28. Ibid., 116.

29. Ibid., 14–15.

30. Ian Britain, *Fabianism and Culture: A Study in British Socialism and the Arts c. 1884–1918* (Cambridge: Cambridge University Press, 1982), 4.

31. Chris Waters, *British Socialists and the Politics of Popular Culture, 1884–1914* (Manchester: Manchester University Press, 1990), 1–2.

32. Shaw, *Ruskin's Politics* (London: Christophers, 1921), 19–21.

33. See Jim Davis, "A Night in the Workhouse, or the Poor Laws as Sensation Drama," *Essays in Theatre* 7.2 (May 1989): 111–26.

34. Emile Zola, "Naturalism in the Theatre," in *The Theory of the Modern Stage: An Introduction to Modern Theatre and Drama*, ed. Eric Bentley (Harmondsworth and New York: Penguin, 1968), 368–69.

35. Ibid., 369.

36. Britain, *Fabianism and Culture*, 118. Also see Webb, "The Difficulties of Individualism," *Fabian Tract* 69 (1896).

37. *Britain, Fabianism and Culture*, 118.

38. See Chushichi Tsuzuki, *The Life of Eleanor Marx 1855–1898: A Socialist Tragedy* (Oxford: Clarendon Press, 1967), 165–66.

39. See Olive Schreiner's letter to Havelock Ellis, 16 November 1885, in *The Letters of Olive Schreiner, 1876–1920*, ed. S. C. Cronwright-Schreiner (London: T. Fisher Unwin, 1924), 87.

40. Shaw Diaries, 4 May 1885 (Blanche Patch's transcriptions in the Library of Political and Economic Science, London School of Economics). See also J. L. Wisenthal, ed., *Shaw and Ibsen: Bernard Shaw's "The Quintessence of Ibsenism" and Related Writings* (Toronto: University of Toronto Press, 1979), 5–6.

41. William Archer, *About the Theatre: Essays and Studies* (London: T. Fisher Unwin, 1886), 2.

42. Edward and Eleanor Marx Aveling, *The Woman Question* (London: Swan Sonnenchein, Lowrey, 1887), 15–16.

43. J. B. Halvorsen. *Bibliografiske Oplysninger til Henrik Ibsens Samlade Vaerker* (Copenhagen: Glydendalske, 1901); from a comment in Malcolm Salaman's introduction to Arthur Wing Pinero, *The Profligate* (London: Heinemann, 1891), v.

44. Shaw Diaries, 28 August and 14 September 1888 (Library of Political and Economic Science, London School of Economics).

Chapter 2

Apprenticeship as a Playwright

For one thing, at least, we have to thank Henrik Ibsen in England
to-day as in Norway a dozen years ago. He has set people talking and
thinking about the drama as they have not talked or thought about it
for years . . . all this is well; and if the brief passing of Ibsen is to make
our intellectual public turn once more to the theatre—even though they
only turn to it to abuse it—his exceeding bitter medicine will not have
been tasted in vain.

Era[1]

In the interval between the controversial *A Doll's House* production of
1889 (produced by the Fabian actor Charles Charrington) and the renewal
of the Ibsen debate in 1891, the public's and press's attitudes toward the
drama changed enough to alter the climate into which Ibsen's acolytes
could tender projects. In the haunts of literary and cultured people as well
as at formal and informal meetings of playgoing enthusiasts of all back-
grounds, the latest West End successes were discussed and there seems to
have been a widespread revival of interest in theatrical matters.[2] In
reaction, many periodicals increased the space allotted to theatrical reviews and news. Since 1880, but especially since William Archer's
repeated accusations of British backwardness and dramatic philistinism in
1889, London's progressive playgoers became interested in the Continental theatres of André Antoine and Otto Brahm, in the new playwrights and
their realism and naturalism, and in up-to-date alternatives to the Adelphi-

style melodrama and the French well-made play that had monopolized English playbills up until that time.

In the autumn of 1890 Herbert Beerbohm Tree (Henry Irving's heir apparent as premier West End actor-manager of serious drama) set aside Monday nights "for the production of plays 'calculated to delight and charm the few' but ill suited to the grosser tastes of vast audiences." As Thomas H. Dickinson remarked in 1917, "this was the first sign of a disposition to adapt the professional stage for the new movements in playwriting and pointed the way to a more flexible organization of the stage."[3] This could have led to a more adventurous repertoire, challenges for actors, and the reeducation of mainstream playgoers. Unfortunately, Tree was impervious to the idea of ensemble acting and used his Monday night laboratory to augment his star status; playgoers attended with the ideals of Sardou's well-made plays firmly in tow and saw little to challenge them. The experiment was soon abandoned. Ibsen's audience, instead, was reclaimed from the ranks of ex-playgoers who were wearied and dissatisfied by traditional and native drama, and from all sorts of playgoers curious about the assertions that great dramatic literature was being created in their own time.

Despite Ibsen's predominantly bad press—or perhaps because of it—Victorians, for the first time, bought printed plays by a contemporary foreign writer. During this period lengthy articles on the theatre's progress, development, and popularity appeared frequently in prestigious review periodicals. At the time Shaw was still writing music criticism, but he took every opportunity to include Ibsen's name in his reviews and write about drama instead of music. In 1891 playgoers were shown a serious, literary alternative in productions of Ibsen's *Rosmersholm* (for which Robert Buchanan somewhat facetiously proposed Shaw—"A Socialist Clown"—as Rosmer),[4] *Ghosts*, *The Lady from the Sea* (which Shaw unsuccessfully pressed on both Alma Murray and Florence Farr),[5] and *Hedda Gabler*. For the first time, playgoers flocked to see unfamiliar plays in matinees and scratch conditions, and even in one case under conditions of questionable legality in a back-street third-rate playhouse. The "Ibsen craze" that briefly stung London in 1889 was renewed, with a vengeance, and while detractors frequently pronounced its demise, they were repeatedly thwarted by announcements of yet more forthcoming productions. Awareness of Ibsen crossed class boundaries to a remarkable degree, and he was indubitably the sensation of 1891. Interest was not only fanned by the unprecedented persistent commentary that Ibsen was accorded by the press and by word of mouth in pubs, clubs, and drawing rooms, but also by the mystique of Ibsen himself, an exiled Norwegian bourgeois who dared to write con-

troversial plays in an obscure "unreadable" language, and whose forty
years of labour seemed to burst upon London without warning. The
Quarterly Review declared Ibsen "a phenomenon worthy of study" in
the serious, academic manner that scholars grant all Great Authors.[6]

Accordingly, the Playgoers' Club invited the notorious freethinker
Edward Aveling to read from *Ghosts* early in February 1891 (a month
before the production). The subsequent discussion was lively, and Eleanor
Marx Aveling and Shaw found themselves "much in the position of a pair
of terriers dropped into a pit of rats." The debate was so popular, with what
Shaw called "an assemblage of barloafing front-row-of-the-pit-on-a-first-
night-dilettanti" swelling the crowd, in addition to socialists, that it was
resumed five times before year's end (CL 1: 288). On the last occasion
Tree addressed the club on the subject of "Some Interesting Fallacies of
the Modern Stage."[7] Among the fallacies that he discussed was the idea
that independent theatres would free the stage from the tyranny of actor-
managers. He regarded Ibsenism as a passing fad without importance
except, perhaps, for its effect on native drama:

> What I maintain is, that the work of such writers as Ibsen will not
> hold a permanent place upon our stage, for, interesting as it undoubt-
> edly is, it can only be a transient phase, bearing the same relation to
> home-grown art as a crinoline does to the human form, as the tail of
> the tadpole does to the frog. It cannot be expected to take its place as
> a permanent and native growth. It serves, however, as an admirable
> manure for the future, a dung-hill from which many a fair flower of
> the drama may bloom.[8]

This is reminiscent of the language William Archer culled from reviews
of *Ghosts* which Shaw reprinted as "*Ghosts* and Gibberings" in *The
Quintessence of Ibsenism*, compiled in the summer of 1891. Shaw saw
market potential in a book on the controversial dramatist: privy to the small
group of zealous supporters who wrote weekly in the best journals, Shaw
knew how to rankle the large group of detractors who read the best journals
but wrote for the popular dailies and weeklies, gaining publicity for
himself and his work.

Until *The Quintessence* was published in October 1891, Shaw was not
distinguished as an exponent of Ibsenism to a significantly greater extent
than Graham Wallas, Annie Besant, or other Fabians. Ibsen's plays were
redolent with scandal, and his ideas were sufficiently remote from the
person of average education that authoritative explanations were desired.
This was the perfect outlet for Shaw's didactic flare, comfortably fitting

the Fabian credo of "practical socialism" by engaging the middle class in intellectual dialogue. Originally planned as an extension of his "Ibsen as a Socialist" lecture delivered to the Fabians in July 1890, *The Quintessence* evolved into an explanation of how and why some English people recognized in Ibsen a genius of the highest order while others denounced him as revolting and described him in obscene terms. The result—a jumble of philosophy, political theory, literary criticism, personal testimony, theatre history, and social commentary—was published by the same press that issued his novel *Cashel Byron's Profession* and the *Fabian Essays in Socialism*. By 1897 only two thousand copies had been sold. The book's fame and wide readership are twentieth-century developments, created by enlarged editions published after Shaw had attained world renown; neglect of this fact has substantively determined how the history of Ibsen's reception in England has been told. *The Quintessence*'s significance lay in honing Shaw's philosophy to a dramatic sensibility, not in proselytizing Ibsen during the height of controversy over his plays.

In *The Quintessence* Shaw argues that the logical outcome of rationalism in the modern world is denial of God (atheism, or as clerics would say, impiety). When individuals are motivated by will, an internal force, rather than by obligations to external entities, they progress toward greater freedom, eventually throwing off all the shackles of duty.[9] This is the stance of the visionary realist (in the sense of mental conviction, not aesthetics) which is attacked by idealists and philistines alike. The attack is most apparent when the realist is a woman who repudiates duty and compliance to men and the hearthside, refusing to conform in favour of achieving her own emancipation. "A typical Ibsen play," therefore, "is one in which the leading lady is an unwomanly woman, and the villain an idealist . . . by virtue of his determination to do nothing wrong."[10]

This is precisely the situation in *Rosmersholm*, which Shaw was instrumental in having produced early in 1891. Because the Ibsenites were a disparate group, only loosely linked by their mutual admiration of the playwright, they were sometimes completely unaware of each other's plans and there was confusion over who intended to produce which play. Shaw's meddling eliminated duplication. In the autumn of 1890 an American actress named Marion Lea contemplated a production of *The Lady from the Sea*, but so did Florence Farr. When Farr requested that Shaw oblige her by playing the part of the Stranger ("She said that as I had a red beard she thought I would look the part in a pea jacket," wrote Shaw, but "I pleaded ineptitude and declined"), he advised her to tackle *Rosmersholm* instead. Shaw "delivered to her so powerful a discourse on *Rosmersholm* that she was resolved to create Rebecca or die."[11] His flirtation with Farr blossomed while he coached her in minute detail over pronunciation and character interpretation of the reviled heroine whose unrequited lust and incestuous origins are discovered by political hypocrites. The non-Ibsenite press did not like *Rosmersholm*, they did not enjoy watching it, and they were not "converted" to Ibsenism by it, but most critics (by their own estimation) gave it a fair hearing and criticized it on dramatic principles. It was spared the insulting epithets showered on *Ghosts*, which presented a more profound threat both in its subject matter and quasi-illegal presentation.

Shaw was confident that the new drama would find an honoured place in the repertoire, radically reforming taste until the old drama was extinguished. The "old drama" in this sense particularly connotes the repertoire of melodramas and heroic dramas devoid of social criticism, rather than Shakespeare or other enduring contributors to the English canon. Ibsen was seen as a transitional figure who would instill the spirit of change then gradually slip from sight. As Shaw admitted, " 'A Doll's House' will be as flat as ditchwater when 'A Midsummer Night's Dream' is still fresh as paint; but it will have done more work in the world; and that is enough for the highest genius, which is always intensely utilitarian."[12] This change was to affect writing, staging, producing, and spectating, but at first Ibsen was odious to mainstream managers, so beyond their own select circle reformers faced considerable resistance. In 1913 Shaw could optimistically reflect on the progress achieved; however the writing he championed was still a small minority of the dramatic output:

> In vain does the experienced acting manager declare that people want to be amused and not preached at in the theatre; that they will not stand long speeches; that a play must not contain more than 18,000 words; that it must not begin before nine nor last beyond eleven; that there must be no politics and no religion in it; that breach of these golden rules will drive people to the variety houses; that there must be a woman of bad character, played by a very attractive actress, in the piece; and so on and so forth. All these counsels are valid for plays in which there is nothing to discuss. They may be disregarded by the playwright who is a moralist and a debater as well as a dramatist.[13]

Lacking a theatre dedicated to the new drama of debate, English actors became their own producers by borrowing against future profits as Charles Charrington and Janet Achurch had done to mount *A Doll's House* in 1889, or presenting through more modest means an ad hoc matinee or two, as Elizabeth Robins initially did for *Hedda Gabler* and John Todhunter did for Florence Farr's two performances of *Rosmersholm*. A third alternative—private producing societies on the Continental model—proved the most enduring solution. The Parisian Théâtre Libre, founded by a gas company clerk named André Antoine in 1887, was the first independent theatre in Europe to champion the work of the realist and naturalist schools. Beginning with an adaptation from Zola, the club gained wide notoriety with productions of Ibsen and lesser French writers. In 1889 a German critic named Otto Brahm founded a similar enterprise in Berlin, the Freie Buhne, opening with *Ghosts*. The "independent" theatres' common repertoire solidified around Ibsen, Gerhart Hauptmann, Bjornstjerne Bjornson, Leo Tolstoy, Emile Zola, August Strindberg, and Ludwig Anzengruber. They were also known for challenging the rehearsal process and performance conventions in line with a more intimate acting style, realistic environments, and psychological accuracy.

These examples encouraged Britons to create a comparable (though not necessarily similar) organization for the production of plays that would not otherwise be seen in London. Various schemes for an uncommercial independent theatre were proposed, with repertoire companies, subscription seasons, company management, unification of amateur clubs, and entrepreneurial funding figuring in the plans. Jacob Grein, London manager of the Dutch East India Company, who shared his time between his commercial job and theatre reviewing, germinated plans for a purely artistic theatre as early as 1889. For unknown reasons his first plans did not come to fruition. In 1891 he allied with George Moore, Henry James, Thomas Hardy, George Meredith, William Archer, and others to propose a subscription season of five performances (at £2 10s. per membership) that would include great European plays and English drama inspired by foreign examples. With £50 earned promoting the plays of Arthur Wing Pinero and Henry Arthur Jones (whose fame as yet rested in farce, melodrama, and romance) in Holland and £30 in translator's fees, Grein formed the Independent Theatre Society of London (ITS). When the ITS's plans to produce *Ghosts* were announced at a Playgoers' Club meeting, resistance to the idea of a "free" theatre, to a foreign repertoire, and to the specific characteristics of *Ghosts* (which bases a family history on adultery, incest, venereal disease, clerical hypocrisy, and prostitution) were immediately expressed. *Ghosts* was unlicensable. It was useless to ask the Lord Chamberlain—who authorized all plays for performance and was shortly to block Shaw from putting a play before an audience—to affix his stamp of approval. Consequently, it could only be presented to a "private" audience who paid no fees at the door. Unlike Tree, Grein believed that star actors and expensive scenery, costumes, and props were not necessary to convey a great play, especially *Ghosts*, "a work of art overpowering in its extreme simplicity, and therefore useful as a lesson in the craft of playwriting."[14] The original investment was recovered, leaving the principal intact for subsequent projects.

This production was the centre of the maelstrom over the theatre of ideas, and a challenge went out to English writers—particularly novelists—to take up playwriting and demonstrate that modernity was not the exclusive prerogative of foreigners. None of the founders of the ITS took up the challenge, while Elizabeth Robins, Mrs. Hugh Bell, John Todhunter, "Michael Field" (Katherine Harris Bradley and her niece Edith Emma Cooper), and Dorothy Leighton were among the indigenous dramatists who came forward and had plays produced in the next few years. Percy Bysshe Shelley's *Cenci* was revived, along with plays by Zola, Willem Van Nouhuys, and more Ibsen.

Like it or not, they were encouraged to extract the essence of Ibsen's appeal (with or without also adopting his "indiscretions," depending on the advocate's critical stance) and to use his innovations to inspire the second English dramatic renaissance. Pundits were disappointed. A surprise submission in 1892 was from a writer who turned out to be the society's most productive and long-lasting prodigy: George Bernard Shaw. Shaw's critique of slum landlords and capitalist complicity was in keeping with the didactic tone of Ibsen's so-called "social" plays, particularly *The Pillars of Society* and *An Enemy of the People*, and not unlike Shaw's agitational writings on housing from the mid-1880s.

Shaw had early dramatic ambitions, but they were for the most part subsumed into novels and didactic writing in the 1880s. Moved by Andrew Mearns's 1883 penny pamphlet "The Bitter Cry of Outcast London," Shaw launched two responses, the Fabian Tract number three "To Provident Landlords and Capitalists" (1885) and sections of *An Unsocial Socialist*. Land ownership was the topic that turned him into a socialist writer. In 1888 he began a play based on Archer's outline of Emile Augier's *Ceinture Dorée* which they renamed *Rheingold*. Their efforts took precisely the form of adaptation from the kind of French original they complained was the force behind conservatism and the guarantee of triviality on the English stage, though this irony seemed to elude them. When Archer objected to how Shaw had worked out the structure, the project was shelved. Shaw rediscovered the manuscript in July 1892 and resumed work. Grein accepted it at once and went into rehearsal 14 November, opening 9 December. Shaw puffed it up in every newspaper that would give him a hearing: the *Era*, *Speaker*, and *Star*. Critics were less than enthusiastic—including Ibsenites and Shaw's closest socialist firends—yet in Shaw's ambitious mind the production was his catapult to international fame.

Various details of "The Bitter Cry of Outcast London" resonate in *Widowers' Houses*. Mearns begins his exposé with a reference to Christian ministers' useful work in publicizing the appalling conditions in which the poorest classes live. Just such a minister exposes Shaw's villain Sartorius to the Royal Commission on the Housing of the Working Classes as the worst slum landlord in London, immune to prosecution because he is a vestryman in the local government. Mearns reveals details of the "pestilential human rookeries" where people are crowded in unimaginable conditions:

> To get into them you have to penetrate courts reeking with poisonous and malodorous gases arising from accumulations of sewage and refuse scattered in all directions and often flowing beneath your feet. . . . You have to ascend rotten staircases, which threaten to give way beneath every step. . . . Walls and ceiling are black with the accretions of filth which have gathered upon them through long years of neglect. It is exuding through cracks in the boards overhead; it is running down the walls; it is everywhere.[15]

While Mearns is concerned about the effects of such conditions on inhabitants' spiritual, physical, moral, and material well-being, Shaw concentrates on the class that necessitates and perpetuates their misery. At the same time, he extends existing Fabian arguments about the theory of rent (usually grounded in agricultural examples) to the realities of subletting halves or quarters of rooms in urban tenements.[16]

Drawing on his early experience as a clerk in a Dublin land agency, where he kept account of other peoples' fortunes, Shaw depicts the accumulation of wealth in the "upper ten thousand" that marries and recreates only with itself. A younger son obliged to find his own living in a profession meets and is hastily engaged to a "vital and energetic" heiress. The prospective groom, Dr. Trench, has a £700-a-year income derived from investments he believes to be ethical. His fiancée's father, Sartorius, insists that Trench get his aristocratic relatives' written congratulations to news of his engagement, explicitly indicating that they will treat Blanche Sartorius as their equal despite the fact that her father's wealth is self-made. Trench believes himself to be without prejudice and agrees to the condition. In the second act, Trench is appalled to discover that Sartorius derived his self-made wealth from slum tenements and forbids Blanche to accept any money from the ill-gotten proceeds after they are married. Not

knowing the full basis of Trench's objection, she refuses and breaks off
the engagement. Trench's high moral stance is exploded when Sartorius
points out to him that the source of his own income—interest from a
mortgage on Sartorius's slums—is a higher order of the same reprehensible phenomenon whereby a rent collector named Lickcheese extracts
money from tenants living in the most appalling conditions.

SARTORIUS (forcibly). Yes: a mortgage on my property. When I, to use
    your own words, screw, and bully, and drive these people to pay what
    they have freely undertaken to pay me, I cannot touch one penny of
    the money they give me until I have first paid you your seven hundred
    a year out of it. What Lickcheese did for me, I do for you. He and I
    are alike intermediaries: you are the principal. It is because of the
    risks I run through the poverty of my tenants that you exact interest
    from me at the monstrous and exorbitant rate of seven per cent,
    forcing me to exact the uttermost farthing in my turn from the tenants.
    (CPP 4: 534).

One of Shaw's responsibilities in the Dublin clerkship was to make a
weekly round by tram to collect rents from slum dwellers, so he had
performed Lickcheese's work for an employer in Sartorious's position.
The play bitterly portrays the greed that begets complacency when many
suffer for the benefit of the few, to the extent that Sartorius's impoverished
tenants become prostitutes so that his daughter Blanche (granddaughter of
a laundress) can become a real lady.

As Michael Holroyd observes, *Widowers' Houses* is a socialist play
without a socialist in it (BS 1: 284). Even the morally indignant Trench is
ultimately co-opted into the scramble after greater wealth: the slums will
be improved but only in order to exploit a development project seeking to
tear the properties down for street improvements. The mortgagor Trench,
ground landlord Lady Roxdale (Trench's aunt), mortagee Sartorius, and
Sartorius's former rent collector Lickcheese (newly self-made through
investing in just such a scheme in East London) easily conspire to take the
slight risk:

TRENCH. As I understand it, Robbins's Row is to be pulled down to
    make way for the new street into the Strand; and the straight tip now
    is to go for compensation. . . . Well, it appears that the dirtier a place
    is the more rent you get; and the decenter it is, the more compensa-
    tion you get. So we're to give up dirt and go in for decency. (CPP
    4: 51–52).

The play originally aimed at instructing voters for an upcoming municipal election, reflecting both the Fabians' platform and gradualist reform tactics.[17] The brand new London County Council had power over negligent landlords, but Shaw calls voters' attention to a new magnitude of swindling which municipal regulation actually facilitated:

LICKCHEESE. Theres no doubt that the Vestries has legal powers to play old Harry [i.e., to play the devil] with slum properties, and spoil the houseknacking game if they please. That didnt matter in the good old times, because the Vestries used to be us ourselves. Nobody ever knew a word about the election; and we used to get ten of us into a room and elect one another, and do what we liked. Well, that cock wont fight any longer; and, to put it short, the game is up for men in the position of you and Mr. Sartorius. My advice to you is, take the present chance of getting out of it. Spend a little money on the block at the Cribbs Market end: enough to make it look like a model dwelling, you know; and let the other block to me on fair terms for a depot of the North Thames Iced Mutton Company. Theyll be knocked down inside of two year to make room for the new north and south main thoroughfare; and youll be compensated to the tune of double the present valuation, with the cost of the improvements thrown in. Leave things as they are; and you stand a good chance of being fined, or condemned, or pulled down before long. (CPP 4: 552)

Shaw sought to teach by negative example, but some of the plotting is weak and it lacks the explicit raisonneur who made some of his later dramas as tedious as their message was unmistakable. The purpose in *Widowers' Houses* is more oblique, residing in a twist on a biblical passage: "Beware of the scribes, which love to go in long clothing, and love salutations in the market places, and the chief seats in the synagogues, and the uppermost rooms at feasts: Which devour widows' houses, and for a pretence make long prayers; these shall receive greater damnation" (Mark 12:38–40).

Perhaps the most original aspect of the play is the debunking of the "motherless" ingenue Blanche Sartorius. She aggressively woos her way into a relationship with Trench, jumps at the prospect of an engagement, easily dismisses both the plight of the poor and her complicity in making them impoverished, and restores her engagement with the wiles of a chief executive officer in heat. As Martin Meisel points out, Blanche takes the role of an ingenue but all her actions are those of a heavy heroine (also known as the villainess in melodrama).[18] This accounts for much of the critics' opposition to the play. The most extraordinary display of her personality—and one that for many commentators is utterly incongruous—occurs between Blanche and her maid just after Blanche breaks up with Trench. The maid enters while stifling sobs, apparently subject offstage to a verbal and/or physical beating by her rejected mistress. When Blanche enters, "the maid looks at her with abject wounded affection and bodily terror." She tries to bundle up Trench's gifts and letters, pleading her devotion, while Blanche dumps all the verbal vituperation on her that is really felt for her ex-suitor. The brief scene culminates with Blanche's hands around the maid's throat, the victim imploring "Let me go, Miss Blanche: you know youll be sorry: you always are. Remember how dreadfully my head was cut last time" (CCP 4: 538).

This scene—so inexplicable to some—is a feminized domesticated version of the commercial brutalization that the men carry out. What Blanche imposes on the working class in cold fury, Sartorius, Lickcheese, and ultimately Trench call good business. Despite this treatment, the maid is the only servant who will stay with the Sartoriuses, which suggests the masochism inherent in the poor who know the brutality of landlords but have nowhere else to go except another equally vicious capitalist's house. As Mearns explains in "The Bitter Cry of Outcast London," "the information given does not refer to selected cases. It simply reveals a state of things which is found in house after house, court after court, street after street," just as in the immoral slums where "the vilest practices are looked upon with the most matter-of-fact indifference."[19] Would the parlour maid, or the slum tenants, be better off on the streets beyond the "benevolent" grasp of this class?

Shaw's next dramatic effort also taught by negative example, separating the would-be ingenue character of Blanche into two pure strains: the widowed Grace Tranfield, who represents feminism's New Woman, and her rival Julia Craven, who aspires to similar "unwomanliness" but cannot give up the theatrics that go along with possessiveness, jealousy, and the other petty tyrannies of infatuation and femininity. Grace, all the more attractive because she refuses to perform the rites of pursuit, is modeled after Florence Farr, the actress who created Rebecca West in the first English production of *Rosmersholm*, played Blanche in *Widowers' Houses*, and whose apartment ranked high among Shaw's evening destinations. Julia was modeled after Jenny Patterson, the friend of Shaw's mother whom he hotly pursued in the 1880s then tried to eschew; she occupied herself in the early 1890s with tirades about his conduct, making scenes and ambushing Shaw in precisely the way depicted in the first moments of his new play. In the midst of this was the philandering socialist himself, renamed Charteris.

CHARTERIS. Listen to me. Am I a particularly handsome man?

GRACE (astonished at his conceit). No.

CHARTERIS (triumphantly). You admit it. Am I a well dressed man?

GRACE. Not particularly.

CHARTERIS. Of course not. Have I a romantic mysterious charm about
  me? do I look as if a secret sorrow preyed on me? am I gallant to
  women?

GRACE. Not in the least.

CHARTERIS. Certainly not. No one can accuse me of it. Then whose fault
  is it that half the women I speak to fall in love with me? Not mine: I
  hate it: it bores me to distraction. At first it flattered me—delighted
  me—that was how Julia got me, because she was the first woman
  who had the pluck to make me a declaration. But I soon had enough
  of it; and at no time have I taken the initiative and persecuted women
  with my advances as women have persecuted me. Never. Except, of
  course, in your case. (CPP 6: 730)

By his own account, Shaw was meddling with many more women than just Patterson and Farr—May Sparling née Morris (daughter of the socialist artist), Janet Achurch, and Bertha Newcombe—so the play had considerable personal topicality.

The Philanderer's topicality extends beyond Shaw's relationships with women, inventing an Ibsen Club where characters of advanced views (unwomanly women and unmanly men) socialize by the credo of individualist self-fulfillment. "The usual tone of the club is low, because the women smoke, and earn their own living, and all that" (CPP 6: 755). Grace and Charteris are members in good standing, and Julia's sister Sylvia is so thoroughly assimilated that she wears mountaineering breeches and goes by her surname in the best old clubman style. Julia was admitted under false pretenses but is tolerated as long as she does not show signs of womanliness. With an ironic twist he no doubt enjoyed, Shaw drew Cuthbertson (Grace's father) after the most powerful anti-Ibsenite theatre critic, Clement Scott, "the leading representative of manly sentiment in London," who joined the club in order to see his daughter from time to time and thereby salvage a bit of family life (CPP 6: 745).

Cuthbertson's life is lived in theatrical clichés which Charteris (and Shaw) enjoy playing up. Cuthbertson happens to come across his oldest friend at the theatre, apparently an indispensable acquaintance lost sight of since Cuthbertson came out the victor dozens of years before in a contest for a woman's hand. This old friend happens to be Jo Craven, Julia's father. Cuthbertson and Craven happen to walk into Julia's fervent tête-à-tête with Charteris, whose explanation is proffered in the most perfunctory critical plot synopsis:

CHARTERIS. Julia wants to marry me: I want to marry Grace. I came here tonight to sweetheart Grace. Enter Julia. Alarums and excursions. Exit Grace. Enter you and Craven. Subterfuges and excuses. Exeunt Craven and Julia. And here we are. Thats the whole story. Sleep over it. Goodnight. (He leaves). (CPP 6: 749)

The club expounds a topsy-turvydom of sexual mores, while Cuthbertson propounds conventional matches. Dr. Paramore, a balding physician whose sinister appearance is counteracted by an irrepressible bedside manner, aspires to woo Julia. Cuthbertson goads him on, redolent in clichés:

CUTHBERTSON. He hangs about after her; but he's not man enough for her. A woman of that sort likes a strong, manly, deep throated, broad chested man.

PARAMORE (anxiously). Hm! a sort of sporting character, you think?

CUTHBERTSON. On no, no. A scientific man, perhaps, like yourself. But you know what I mean: a MAN. (He strikes himself a sound blow on the chest). (CPP 6: 753)

This play takes up a lot of issues, rather haphazardly, though in isolation some passages are thoroughly engaging. Shaw is at his best when deflating bitter foes, not only Patterson and Scott but also medical doctors. Craven is diagnosed with Paramore's Disease, a liver ailment requiring an extreme ascetic regime. However, during the course of the play, Paramore's diagnosis and scientific validity are punctured by better funded foreign researchers with more numerous laboratory subjects than Paramore's mere three canines and a monkey. Shaw's wit shines brightly in a passage where Craven unknowingly exposes what he sets out to condemn, a tactic lasting a moment in *The Philanderer* which stretched out for an entire act in *Widowers' Houses*.

CRAVEN. Come, Paramore! I'm not selfish, believe me: I can feel for your disappointment. But you must face it like a man. And after all, now really, doesnt this shew that theres a lot of rot about modern science? Between ourselves, you know, it's horribly cruel: you must admit that it's a deuced nasty thing to go ripping up and crucifying camels and monkeys. It must blunt all the finer feelings sooner or later.

PARAMORE (turning on him). How many camels and horses and men were ripped up in that Soudan [*sic*] campaign where you won your Victoria Cross, Colonel Craven?

CRAVEN (firing up). That was fair fighting: a very different thing, Paramore.

PARAMORE. Yes: Martinis and machine guns against naked spearmen.

CRAVEN (hotly). Naked spearmen can kill, Paramore. I risked my life: dont forget that.

PARAMORE (with equal spirit). And I have risked mine, as all doctors do, oftener than any soldier.

CRAVEN (handsomely). Thats true. I didnt think of that. I beg your pardon, Paramore: I'll never say another word against your profession. But I hope youll let me stick to the good oldfashioned shaking-up treatment for my liver: a clinking run across country with the hounds.

PARAMORE (with bitter irony). Isnt that rather cruel? a pack of dogs ripping up a fox? (CPP 6: 773–74)

This idea may have been more organically integrated in the original four-act version. An Act III subplot involving the delivery of Julia's long-lost dog to Dr. Paramore as a research specimen was abandoned. In what remains, Julia, severely hurt by Charteris but flattered enough by the adoring Paramore to accept his marriage proposal, later uses vivisection as a metaphor of Charteris's behaviour. Idealism and philistinism fuse with villainy, in both the alluring unintentional suavity of Charteris and the uncompromising diagnostics of the doctor.[20] In this, *The Philanderer* and *The Quintessence of Ibsenism* meet.

The Philanderer utterly rejects conventional femininity and marriage "as a degrading bargain, by which a woman sells herself to a man for the social status of a wife and the right to be supported and pensioned in old age out of his income" (CPP 6: 733). As such it was impractical for the British stage. It was even more so in its original format: Shaw was persuaded to drop the final act as too inflammatory. It depicts Paramore and Julia several years later, utterly bored with each other. They agree to go to South Dakota, where divorce is expeditious, but when Julia discovers her husband is in love with Grace, the plan is jeopardized until Charteris agrees to accompany Julia to America. While all four acts focus on Charteris's fundamental inability to commit himself, the last shows relentless pessimism on the subject of marriage. Even without the last act's structural resolution worthy of the old dramatists and amoral cynicism worthy of the degenerates, Shaw could not find a producer. This is not surprising, considering that the play is in part a corrective reaction to Ibsenite critics who failed to rally round *Widowers' Houses* when produced by the ITS. He tried Grein, Elizabeth Robins, and Charles Wyndham—a West End producer way beyond his present connections—and was forced to shelve the play. In the future, he also retreated from such transparently autobiographical subjects.

In an unfinished essay of 1889, Shaw delineated two criteria by which novels or plays may be critiqued: "the documentary and the artistic."[21] Both serve the didactic purpose yet both failed him in *The Philanderer*. His next effort, begun just weeks after the last, harmoniously subsumed artistic concerns in the interest of documenting social realities and his own hard-biting philosophy.

Shaw's third full-length play was considered unproducible for very different reasons. *Mrs. Warren's Profession* deals with the sociological dimensions of sexual prostitution, questioning just what the precise nature of prostitution is in a society where women have so few economic choices. Shaw refused to comply with the Victorian conventions for writing about bad women and dispensing with their ruined souls, mixing up the brothel keeper Mrs. Warren's reconciliation with her university-educated daughter Vivie both structurally and circumstantially, and portraying Vivie's decision to make an absolute break from her mother because living idly on her wealth would make her complicit with the reprehensible exploitation that propelled her mother into prostitution in the first place. The play is about the women and men behind the gorgeous magdalens and sallow wretches of the stage and literature. The Lord Chamberlain, official licensor of drama in England, refused to sanction the play for performance. It was eventually seen by a private audience at the Stage Society in 1902 (see Illustration 2) and in an ill-fated American production in 1905, but did not overcome the licence prohibition in Britain or France for several decades.

For Victorians prostitution was a topic almost as urgent, taboo, and politically heated as AIDS is in the 1990s. The spread of venereal disease made prostitution of urgent concern to the military, resulting in several Contagious Diseases Acts allowing the routine forced examination and hospitalization of women in proximity to various barracks towns. The taboo on discussing prostitution in polite society resulted in an ingenious set of theatrical codes allowing "a woman with a past" and "a fallen woman" to precisely signal indiscretions without having to mention sex. Shaw is even more circumspect. He never uses the word prostitute or even a synonym. Mrs. Warren communicates her chosen profession by describing how, when she was young, her sister Lizzie simply vanished until she serendipitously reappeared at the bar where Mrs. Warren was employed: "One cold, wretched night, when I was so tired I could hardly keep myself awake, who should come up for a half of Scotch but Lizzie, in a long fur cloak, elegant and comfortable, with a lot of sovereigns in her purse" (CPP 3: 66). This is sufficient to communicate to Vivie that her aunt was a prostitute and her mother an instant recruit. Later, Mrs. Warren's advancement to becoming an owner of many houses on the Continent is signaled by Vivie, who calls attention to the unspeakability of the "two infamous words that describe what my mother is"—brothel keeper—which she scrawls but never utters (CPP 3: 94–99).

The subject of prostitution was highly relevant to millions of Victorian women whose financial means were insufficient to allow them to survive in comfort or even provide what was necessary for basic sustenance. Prostitutes were very visible and available everywhere except the most reform-oriented family suburbs, at prices that matched virtually every pocketbook. It is the latter point that Shaw takes up most vigorously in the play. Instead of trying to justify Mrs. Warren's choices or dramatize the consequence of her infamy, he puts the subject forward like a writer of Fabian tracts, emphasizing the similarities between prostitution and other types of business speculations, with the consequences of poor pay and high unemployment. He condemns the economic system where women find their best (and perhaps only) avenue to riches (and perhaps survival) through their sexuality. Mrs. Warren's stepsisters perished by making respectable choices, one the victim of lead poisoning and the other the wife of an alcoholic labourer whose eighteen shillings a week was insufficient to support three children. Lizzie was wiser.

MRS WARREN. When she saw I'd grown up good-looking she said to me across the bar "What are you doing there, you little fool? wearing out your health and your appearance for other people's profit!" Liz was saving money then to take a house for herself in Brussels; and she thought we two could save faster than one. . . . where can a woman get the money to save in any other business? . . . Of course, if youre a plain woman and cant earn anything more; or if you have a turn for music, or the stage, or newspaper-writing: thats different. But neither Liz nor I had any turn for such things: all we had was our appearance and our turn for pleasing men. Do you think we were such fools as to let other people trade in our good looks by employing us as shopgirls, or barmaids, or waitresses, when we could trade in them ourselves and get all the profits instead of starvation wages? Not likely. (CPP 3: 67)

For Mrs. Warren, prostitution is a business decision, not a lustful fall: she goes into it as an exercise of choice, not a consequence of seduction.

Shaw sets up for discussion the conflicts prostitution creates among women, pitting the working-class pragmatist Mrs. Warren against the analytically minded mathematician Vivie has become in ignorance of her mother's livelihood and friends. Vivie does not make moral judgements, and acknowledges the wisdom of her mother's decision. What she cannot live with is the fact that her mother continues to pursue and expand her businesses despite her wealth, and that her own allowance is from the fruits of this trade. Even her Cambridge University scholarship—the one aspect of her support not devolving from prostitution—came from an equally heinous enterprise. Her mother's business partner cuts her to the quick with this revelation: "Do you remember your Crofts scholarship at Newnham? Well, that was founded by my brother the M.P. [Member of Parliament] He gets his 22 per cent out of a factory with 600 girls in it, and not one of them getting wages enough to live on" (CPP 3: 83–84). By never having questioned the sources of her wealth and advantages, Vivie finds herself just as reprehensible as her mother and the Croftses.

This is precisely the anagnorisis Trench reached in *Widowers' Houses*: Trench and Vivie each encounter male investors utterly comfortable with their complicity in degrading the powerless, and realize that they too gain by accepting profits other than from their own labour. The difference is that Trench is squeamish on moral grounds while Vivie sees the matter more systemically. She resolves to break from the whole system, including all remnants of "family." Vivie accepts a partnership in the actuarial office of Honoria Fraser and devotes herself to work. Presumably this profession is Shaw's deliberate choice: actuaries statistically predict calamity, but they do not directly profit from or deal with its occurrence. Vivie becomes part of the competent administrative middle class Fabians needed for bringing about social change.

The social and educational advantages that qualify Vivie to take her place with Honoria are silently counterpointed to Mrs. Warren's partnership with Lizzie years before. Vivie writes to Honoria announcing that she is penniless and Honoria unquestioningly takes her in, a circumstance not unlike the brothel keeper's relationship to new recruits. The apt similarities that J. Ellen Gainor discovers between mother and daughter would astound and appall Vivie:

> Both first went into partnership with another woman already established in the business, who showed them the desirability, profitability, and suitability for themselves of the field. And both women operate within the patriarchal structure, Vivie and Honoria organizing their office along traditional hierarchical lines, with a male clerk and with no mention of their partnership as in any way distinct from that of other businessmen's, and Mrs. Warren, enmeshed in a capitalist, profit-making network recognized by, but not discussed in, good society.[22]

Vivie can take up a respectable occupation which relies on her intellectual capacities, but the mentoring relationship between Honoria and Vivie, like Mrs. Warren and her "girls," is salient even though Shaw refrains from having them say so.

Shaw does not portray Vivie as an unequivocal heroine. She rejects the sensuality, frivolity, and pretence of her mother's life and friends but proclaims her similarities with respect to devotion to work and making more money than is strictly necessary. As Germaine Greer asks, "The mystery remains—what is prostitution? What is it more than practicing upon sexuality for gain? It need not involve indiscriminacy, or even sexual intercourse, or even money, but simply gain."[23] She sees this as a failing in Shaw's analysis:

> It is not vice at its worst or virtue at its best which exploits men and women, but the profit motive, which is indifferent to ethics and has no sex at all. Shaw could get no nearer the correct etiology of whoredom than the feeble Fabian diagnosis that women were overworked, undervalued and underpaid so that they were powerfully tempted to a way of life falsely represented as easier.[24]

Greer reflects first- and second-wave feminists' concern with meticulously documenting the interconnectedness between prostitution and marriage. Frank Gardner's hopeless suit for Vivie's hand reverses the usual situation, for he would be "kept" by Vivie and (he presumes) her mother's money. The effect rendered by Shaw is substantially comic rather than political. Ultimately, *Mrs. Warren's Profession* is not about sex or even sexual politics. Prostitution is a metaphor for the Fabian "law of rent": all capitalist production is like rent in that it produces a differential advantage of one social group over another, and the exercise of this control is at everyone's expense.

On documentary criteria, *Mrs. Warren's Profession* adds a new perspective to Victorian discussions of prostitution. Josephine Butler's campaigns against the "instrumental rape" of the Contagious Diseases Acts claimed much attention in the 1880s and resulted in repeal in 1886. Just as Butler's Ladies' National Association was settling this old offence, William Stead's sensational newspaper articles likened London to a modern Babylon, where the purchase of young girls was as pervasive and reprehensible as the eighteenth-century slave trade. This provided a focus for more politically conservative reformers who believed there was a "white slave trade" among Britain, Europe, the Middle East, and North America.[25] By comparison, Shaw's evidence and tactics are mild and fulfill his preference for "pure philosophy" over "mere news."[26] His artistic achievements, apart from refining his skill at plotting and dialogue writing, include inventing a modified type of the stage prostitute (Mrs. Warren) and rejecting moral stances, which for a British dramatist was revolutionary.

Shaw's next four works, which he grouped together and called *Plays Pleasant* in an edition of 1898, show a dramatist more inclined to adopt the techniques of well-made melodrama and less determined to propagandize. As a result, the first of them actually earned Shaw £568 in performance royalties in 1894–95,[27] though its "successful" run lost about £4,000 for the backer, Annie Horniman. *Arms and the Man* employs typically improbable complications in its stock plot: a defeated soldier takes refuge in a woman's boudoir, alternately reveals vulnerability and good sense, comes out very favourably in contrast to the woman's betrothed commissioned officer, and secures her agreement to leave the hapless Balkans for what is depicted as his own eminently more sensible Swiss Alps (see Illustration 3). Shaw debunks heroism, patriotism, and equations of poetic bravery with the nobility of warfare yet also glories in making stock mountain folk settings tawdry through excessive deconstruction of the standard property lists of romantic comedy. His character sketches, such as the elaborate description of Major Sergius Saranoff in Act II, and scene settings, such as Raina's boudoir, are pure satire worthy of the melodramatic parodies in Jerome K. Jerome's *Stage-land*, a lampoon of melodrama.[28] The theatrical success of *Arms and the Man* changed Shaw's public profile, self-perception, and occupation: shortly after its run of seventy-five performances in 1894, he resigned as a music critic.

Apart from their socialist content, his plays also explore the "woman question" which urgently preoccupied Britons at the end of the century. Rather than explicitly advocating women's rights or suffrage, Shaw polemicizes gender—that is to say, the social ascription of roles, behaviours, and opportunities that tend to coincide with biological sex categories. Shaw seems to propose new types. Thus, the narcissistic Bulgarian Major Saranoff proclaims in the final speech of *Arms and the Man*: "What a man! Is he a man? following the exit of the wondrous chocolate-munching, supply-swindling, bourgeois hotelier and soldier of fortune named Bluntschli (CPP 3: 196). In *The Man of Destiny* the transmission of military and personal communiqués in the early months of Bonaparte's Italian campaign is a pretext to explore gender confusion, acuity, and brinksmanship, fabricating links between the general's personal Achilles heel and his iconoclastic genius in leadership. The unorthodox household of Candida and the Reverend James Morell allocates tasks that break gender and class norms.

Marchbanks, their aristocratic poet guest, slices onions; Candida scrubs the house clean; the reverend blacks the boots; and Morell's secretary begins her day by washing dishes. The eighteen-year-old poet is besotted with the thirty-three-year-old Candida and wishes a conventionally ladylike life for her instead of the one of household toil and marital contentment she enjoys:

MARCHBANKS (firing up). Yes, to be idle, selfish, and useless: that is, to be beautiful and free and happy: hasnt every man desired that with all his soul for the woman he loves? Thats my ideal: whats yours, and that of all the dreadful people who live in these hideous rows of houses? (CPP 3: 236–37)

The consequence of such a view is that either husband or wife must be a doll in the sense that, like Ibsen's Nora, he or she is a domesticated plaything of the spouse. In *Candida* the doll is Morell. The latter half of the play revolves around a succession of "discussion scenes" echoing Ibsen's innovation of husband and wife sitting down together and having serious talks about serious matters. Shaw wrote Candida with Janet Achurch (the first English Nora) in mind, and the connections to *A Doll's House* were strengthened for audiences seeing Achurch and Charles

Charrington performing together again in *Candida* in the late 1890s. But the play's focus on a woman's choice of male companions is totally devoid of economic critique and is separate from the socialist values ascribed to Morell. Instead, Shaw muses on a woman's enigmatic attraction for men who, like the author himself, are caught in a romantic triangle of their own making. Candida is Shaw's New Woman: incomprehensibly faithful.

The last pleasant play, *You Never Can Tell*, marks Shaw's full transition from proselytizing reformer to social satirist. Its plotting also revolves around old values supplanted by the new amidst the pernicious forces of conservatism and sentiment, most emphatically expressed in the drawing of female youth. Mrs. Clandon's eldest daughter, Gloria, groomed to succeed her mother as a proponent of women's rights, regards John Stuart Mill as appropriate seaside reading. She represents the radical liberation of gender achieved in the Clandons' twenty-year absence from England. Mrs. Clandon assumes Gloria will be regarded as a rebel; instead, her old friend and lawyer advises her that such views have been absorbed and eclipsed by even deeper reaching philosophies.

M'COMAS. You are still ready to make speeches in public, in spite of your sex (Mrs Clandon nods); to insist on a married woman's right to her own separate property (she nods again); to champion Darwin's view of the origin of species and John Stuart Mill's Essay on Liberty (nod); to read Huxley, Tyndall, and George Eliot (three nods); and to demand University degrees, the opening of the professions, and the parliamentary franchise for women as well as men? . . . My dear good lady: there is nothing in any of those views nowadays to prevent her marrying an archbishop. You reproached me just now for having become respectable. You were wrong: I hold to our old opinions as strongly as ever. I dont go to church; and I dont pretend I do. I call myself what I am: a Philosophic Radical standing for liberty and the rights of the individual, as I learnt to do from my master Herbert Spencer. Am I howled at? NO: I'm indulged as an old fogey. I'm out of everything, because Ive refused to bow the knee to Socialism.

MRS. CLANDON (shocked). Socialism!

M'COMAS. . . . (with some bitterness). We're old fashioned: the world thinks it has left us behind. There is only one place in all England where your opinions would still pass as advanced.

MRS. CLANDON (scornfully unconvinced). The Church, perhaps?

M'COMAS. No: the theatre. (CPP 6: 644–65)

The topsy-turvyness of class, both in the dignified Waiter's attitude to his Q.C. (Queen's Council) son and Crampton's horror of his estranged younger children's unconventionality, criticizes social rigidity, yet Shaw is more mocking than instructional. The impediment to producing such a play was not its socialism, for that was barely apparent. In the preface to the pleasant plays Shaw mused, "I half suspect that those managers who have had most to do with me, if asked to name the main obstacle to the performance of my plays, would unhesitatingly and unanimously reply 'The author' " (CPP 3: 118). Shaw increasingly showed the ability to write actable vivid characters, but at the same time alienated his dramaturgical sensibility from what the leading actor-managers (whose support was necessary to get a play produced) recognized as sympathetic parts for themselves.

> Far from taking an unsympathetic view of the popular preference for fun, fashionable dresses, a little music, and even an exhibition of eating and drinking by people with an expensive air, attended by an if-possible comic waiter, I was more than willing to shew that the drama can humanize these things as easily as they, in the wrong hands, can dehumanize the drama. (CPP 3: 113)

Shaw lined up a repertoire of glorious parts for women, but few women had the resources or inclination to take a risk as producers of them.

By 1890 Shaw was an accomplished social critic and political activist. He achieved, in his late thirties, a hurried apprenticeship in playwriting. As A. B. Walkley noted in his review of *Widowers' Houses*, "You have Mr. Shaw the musical critic, and Mr. Shaw the novelist, and Mr. Shaw the Ibsenite exegete, and Mr. Shaw the Fabian, and Mr. Shaw the vegetarian, and Mr. Shaw the anti-vivisectionist—and now there is Mr. Shaw the dramatist."[29] Already a prolific journalist, letter writer, diary keeper, editor, and pamphleteer, he substituted drama for the novel and wrote approximately one full-length play a year for several decades. By the standards of other Victorian dramatists such as Colin Hazlewood or H. J. Byron, Shaw's output was low. His accomplishment is more appropriately compared to his modernist colleagues Ibsen, Eugène Brieux, and Strindberg, though his working method was entirely different. Moments for playwriting were haphazardly snatched in between other activities, such as playgoing, walking, socializing, and music making. He made use of every moment he had for writing, just as his incidents from his life were heavily culled for their utility as plot and character motifs, making use of every moment he was not writing.

The autobiographical components of Shaw's first plays are legion, but he also incorporated documentation of his social circle by basing characters on his friends: the posing Raina Petkoff memorializes Annie Besant, while Mrs. Warren, it is claimed, is modelled after Beatrice Webb. Sidney and Beatrice Webb's generosity in allowing the Fabian inner circle to share their summer rental homes in the country set a rhythm both for Shaw's life and the action of visitors to Mrs. Warren's Surrey cottage: mornings were spent in writing and study, afternoons were devoted to vigorous walks, and the evenings were passed in political arguments (BS 1: 267).

In 1891–92 Shaw's life shifted focus from its previous course in four fateful ways: active involvement in a stage production, writing dramatic criticism overtly and specifically for the first time, composing and seeing produced his own first play, and publishing his first play. In the years that followed, his confidence and skill as a dramatist increased, though the theatre's indifference to this made him, for the time being, a politico who happened to write drama, rather than a dramatist who was also active politically. The public at large had no access to his playwriting apart from the ITS's published version of *Widowers' Houses* and individual editions. In 1898 the *Plays Pleasant* and *Plays Unpleasant* containing his first seven full-length plays were published, reaping a modest initial financial return. However, this was minor compared to the performance royalties for *Arms and the Man*. The incentive to persevere with the stage was considerable.

Moy Thomas and H. W. Massingham (not natural allies of Shaw) admired *Widowers' Houses* and saw promise in its author.[30] Apart from this, the record shows little direct encouragement of Shaw as a dramatist until the success of *Arms and the Man*. Nevertheless, there are excellent pragmatic reasons why Shaw pursued playwriting as a major outlet despite the string of early disappointments. Furthermore, his decision to focus principally on drama was a calculated risk: because of recent reforms in copyright law, negotiation of fair fees, and newfound respect in the profession, there was never a more auspicious moment to try the stage. Influencing public policy by reaching the influential suited the Fabian preference for gradualist and strategic reform. London Fabians were not much concerned with motivating the working classes, so it is understandable that Shaw targetted the highest ranking West End managers and performers—Irving, John Hare, George Alexander, Charles Wyndham, and Lewis Waller—to produce his plays once he despaired of making a star out of Florence Farr. He was not successful in this, but the effort is significant. He subverted well-established dramatic conventions for his own purposes, recognizing the persuasive power of oratory and debate, particularly when all the participants, pro and con, would be scripted and scored to his own tune. In contrast to the meticulously researched but ponderous prose of Beatrice and Sidney Webb's books, Shaw's plays demonstrate the utility of dialogue over narrative. Shaw's talent lay in orality, particularly speeches and drama. Even the plays' prefaces read like monologues rather than prose expositions, and this immediacy of voice—emphasized through idiosyncratic spelling and syntax as well as a ubiquitous authorial presence—came to characterize much of his writing. Nevertheless, he seized the opportunity to publish the pleasant and unpleasant volumes in 1898 as a way to reach yet another audience, the serious readers including those who bought editions of Ibsen in significant numbers. Shaw's skill as a narrativist, which shows in the lengthy description of the setting for *Candida*, suggests a timely self-apprenticeship for the cinema, though decades passed before the new medium incorporated the spoken voice. (Moving pictures were introduced into music hall programs in 1897, two years after *Candida*'s composition, and were silent until 1929.) What remained in question was whether or not Wyndham's conclusion—that the London stage would not be suited for such plays for a quarter of a century—was an accurate prophecy. If Wyndham was right, then Shaw (too early for talkies and too scenic for radio) would have nowhere to turn for a very long time.

NOTES

1. "Theatrical Gossip," *Era* (2 May 1891): 10.

2. H. A. Kennedy, "The Drama of the Moment," *Nineteenth Century* (August 1891): 258–74.

3. Thomas H. Dickinson, *The Contemporary Drama of England* (Boston: Little, Brown, 1917), 137–38.

4. Robert Buchanan, letter, *Pall Mall Gazette* (12 January 1891): 2.

5. See Shaw Diaries, 13 October 1890 (Blanch Patch's transcripts, Library of Political and Economic Science, London School of Economics); see also his letter to Alma Murray, 25 November 1890 (CL 1: 272), and Norman and Jeanne MacKenzie, *The Fabians* (New York: Simon and Schuster, 1977), 172.

6. *Quarterly Review* (April–June 1891): 305–19.

7. Herbert Beerbohm Tree, *Some Interesting Fallacies of the Modern Stage. An Address Delivered to the Playgoers' Club at St. James's Hall on Sunday, 6th December 1891* (London: Heinemann, 1892).

8. Herbert Beerbohm Tree, *Thoughts and After-thoughts* (London and New York: Casell and Co., 1913), 26–27.

9. *The Quintessence of Ibsenism*, in *Major Critical Essays* (London: Constable and Co., 1932), 22–24.

10. Ibid., 42.

11. Quoted in J. L. Wisenthal, ed., *Shaw and Ibsen: Bernard Shaw's "The Quintessence of Ibsenism" and Related Writings* (Toronto: University of Toronto Press, 1979), 20, 11.

12. "The Problem Play," *The Humanitarian* 6.5 (May 1895): 351.

13. *The Quintessence of Ibsenism*, 137.

14. J. T. Grein, "To Friend and Foe," *Playgoers' Review* (16 March 1891): 73–75.

15. Andrew Mearns, "The Bitter Cry of Outcast London," reprinted in *Into Unknown England 1866–1913: Selections from the Social Explorers*, ed. Peter Keating (Glasgow: Fontana, 1976), 94–95.

16. See Shaw's essay "The Economic Basis of Socialism" (1889), reprinted in George Bernard Shaw, ed., *Essays in Fabian Socialism* (New York: William H. Wise and Co., 1932), 1–30.

17. Some of this is expunged from later editions. See the Independent Theatre Society's original edition of *Widowers' Houses* (London: Henry and Co., 1893).

18. Martin Meisel, *Shaw and the Nineteenth-Century Theater* (1963; reprint, New York: Limelight Editions, 1984), 29–30.

19. Mearns in Keating, *Into Unknown England*, 93, 98.

20. Commentary on this point is provided in Alfred Turco, Jr., "*The Philanderer*: Shaw's Poignant Romp," *Shaw* 7 (1987): 47–62.

21. British Library Add. Ms. 50693, fols. 201–22. See also Stanley Weintraub, *The Unexpected Shaw: Biographical Approaches to G.B.S. and His Work* (New York: Frederick Ungar, 1982), 125–27.

22. J. Ellen Gainor, *Shaw's Daughters: Dramatic and Narrative Constructions of Gender* (Ann Arbor: University of Michigan Press, 1992), 38.

23. Germaine Greer, "A Whore in Every Home," in *Fabian Feminist: Bernard Shaw and Woman*, ed. Rodelle Weintraub (University Park: Pennsylvania State University Press, 1977), 165.

24. Ibid., 166.

25. Shaw supported Stead's stance until it was revealed that he had misrepresented the facts. Stead was convicted. See Judith R. Walkowitz, *City of Dreadful Delight: Narratives of Sexual Danger in Late-Victorian London* (Chicago: University of Chicago Press, 1992).

26. Weintraub, *The Unexpected Shaw*, 127.

27. Based on Shaw's income tax returns for 1894–95 (Harry Ransom Humanities Research Center, University of Texas at Austin, Ms. Shaw, G. B., Misc. Financial Records). This includes the London and New York productions (by Richard Mansfield).

28. Jerome K. Jerome. *Stage-land: Curious Habits and Customs of Its Inhabitants* (London: Chatto and Windus, 1889).

29. A. B. Walkley, *Speaker* (17 December 1892): 155; reprinted in T. F. Evans, ed., *Shaw: The Critical Heritage* (London and Boston: Routledge and Kegan Paul, 1976), 55.

30. Unsigned review [Moy Thomas], *Daily News* (10 December 1891): 5; H. W. Massingham, *Illustrated London News* (17 December 1892): 770; both reprinted in Evans, *Shaw*, 44–46, 53–54.

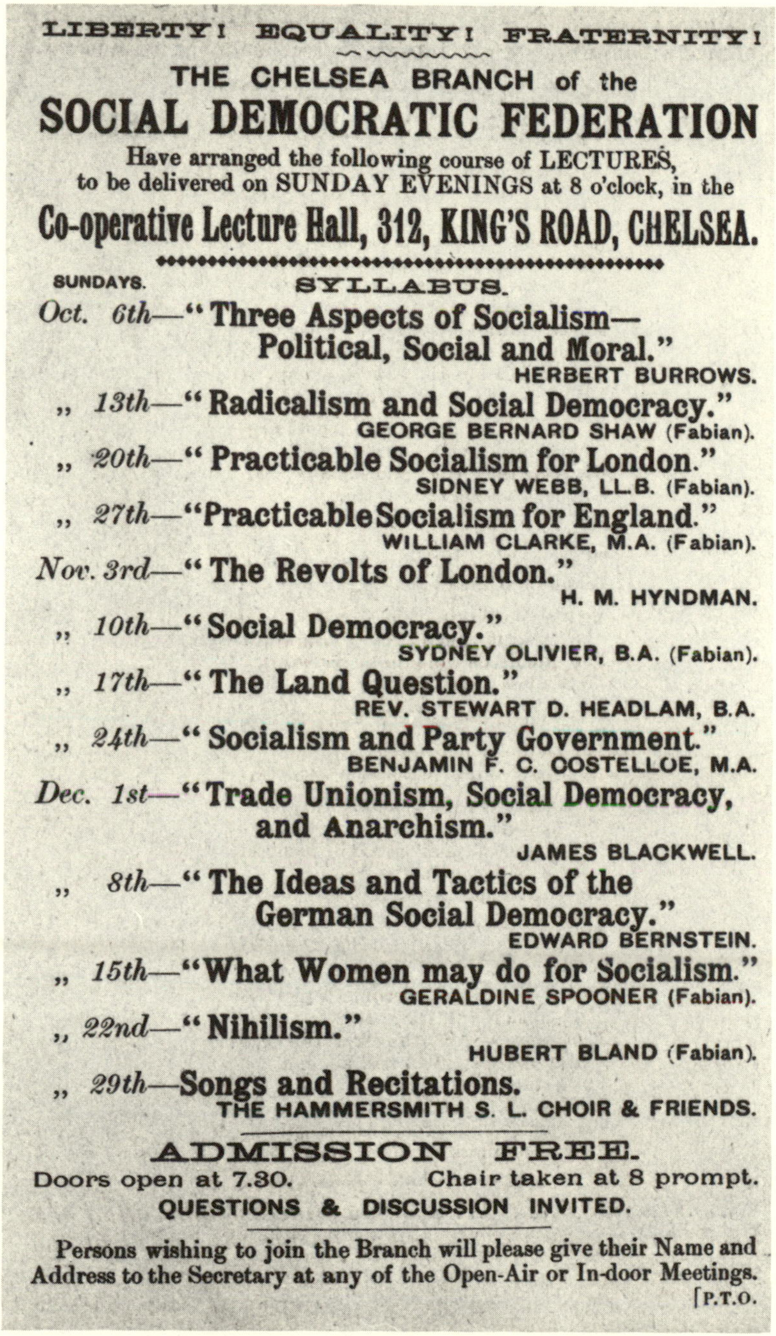

LIBERTY! EQUALITY! FRATERNITY!

THE CHELSEA BRANCH of the

SOCIAL DEMOCRATIC FEDERATION

Have arranged the following course of LECTURES,
to be delivered on SUNDAY EVENINGS at 8 o'clock, in the

Co-operative Lecture Hall, 312, KING'S ROAD, CHELSEA.

SUNDAYS.   **SYLLABUS.**

Oct. 6th—" Three Aspects of Socialism—
Political, Social and Moral."
HERBERT BURROWS.

„ 13th—" Radicalism and Social Democracy."
GEORGE BERNARD SHAW (Fabian).

„ 20th—" Practicable Socialism for London."
SIDNEY WEBB, LL.B. (Fabian).

„ 27th—"Practicable Socialism for England."
WILLIAM CLARKE, M.A. (Fabian).

Nov. 3rd—" The Revolts of London."
H. M. HYNDMAN.

„ 10th—" Social Democracy."
SYDNEY OLIVIER, B.A. (Fabian).

„ 17th—" The Land Question."
REV. STEWART D. HEADLAM, B.A.

„ 24th—" Socialism and Party Government."
BENJAMIN F. C. COSTELLOE, M.A.

Dec. 1st—" Trade Unionism, Social Democracy,
and Anarchism."
JAMES BLACKWELL.

„ 8th—" The Ideas and Tactics of the
German Social Democracy."
EDWARD BERNSTEIN.

„ 15th—"What Women may do for Socialism."
GERALDINE SPOONER (Fabian).

„ 22nd—" Nihilism."
HUBERT BLAND (Fabian).

„ 29th—Songs and Recitations.
THE HAMMERSMITH S. L. CHOIR & FRIENDS.

ADMISSION FREE.

Doors open at 7.30.   Chair taken at 8 prompt.

QUESTIONS & DISCUSSION INVITED.

Persons wishing to join the Branch will please give their Name and
Address to the Secretary at any of the Open-Air or In-door Meetings.
[P.T.O.

Illustration 1. Announcement of Fabian lecture series at Chelsea, 1889. Courtesy
of the Dan H. Laurence Collection, University of Guelph Library, and The Society
of Authors on behalf of the Bernard Shaw Estate.

Illustration 2. Fanny Brough as Kittie Warren in *Mrs. Warren's Profession*, a Stage Society production at the New Lyric Club, 1902. Courtesy of the Dan H. Laurence Collection, University of Guelph Library, and The Society of Authors on behalf of the Bernard Shaw Estate.

Illustration 3. Florence Farr and B. Gould (Bernard Partridge) as Louka and Major Sergius Saranoff in *Arms and the Man*, Avenue Theatre, 1894. Courtesy of the Dan H. Laurence Collection, University of Guelph Library, and The Society of Authors on behalf of the Bernard Shaw Estate.

Illustration 4. *Caesar and Cleopatra*, London 1913. Courtesy of the Dan H. Laurence Collection, University of Guelph Library, and The Society of Authors on behalf of the Bernard Shaw Estate.

Illustration 5. Poster for *Pygmalion* at His Majesty's Theatre, 1914. Courtesy of the Dan H. Laurence Collection, University of Guelph Library, and The Society of Authors on behalf of the Bernard Shaw Estate.

Illustration 6. Shaw in the dress circle at His Majesty's Theatre rehearsing *Pygmalion*, 1914.
Courtesy of the Dan H. Laurence Collection, University of Guelph Library, and The Society
of Authors on behalf of the Bernard Shaw Estate.

Illustration 7. Harley Granville Barker and Charlotte Shaw, c. 1905. Courtesy of the Dan H. Laurence Collection, University of Guelph Library, and The Society of Authors on behalf of the Bernard Shaw Estate.

Illustration 8. *Captain Brassbound's Conversion*, Act 2, Royal Court Theatre, 1906. Sidi el Assif (Lewis Casson) extreme left, Cadi Muley Othman el Kintafi (Trevor Lowe) and Lady Cicely Waynflete (Ellen Terry) centre, Captain Brassbound (Frederick Carr) next to Lady Cicely, Felix Drinkwater (Edmund Gwenn) and Marzo (Michael Sherbrook) right foreground. Courtesy of the Dan H. Laurence Collection, University of Guelph Library, and The Society of Authors on behalf of the Bernard Shaw Estate.

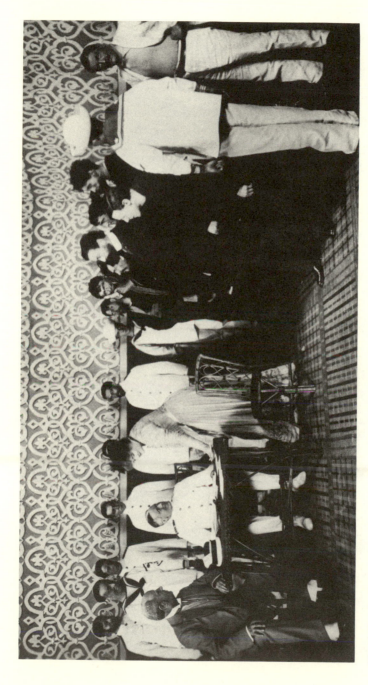

Illustration 9. *Captain Brassbound's Conversion*, Act 3, Royal Court Theatre, 1906. Sir Howard Hallam (J. H. Barnes) and Captain Kearney (James Carew) seated with Kearney's crew behind, Lady Cicely centre, Captain Brassbound and Felix Drinkwater front row right with Brassbound's crew behind and Marzo extreme right. Courtesy of the Dan H. Laurence Collection, University of Guelph Library, and The Society of Authors on behalf of the Bernard Shaw Estate.

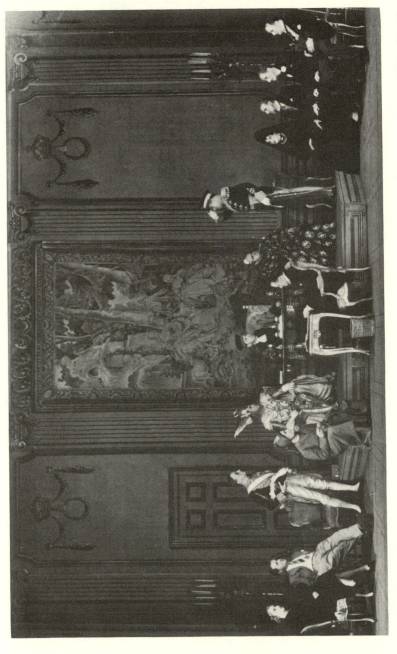

Illustration 10. *Geneva*, Saville Theatre, 1938. Centre podium, left to right: Deaconess (Olive Milbourne), Battler (Walter Hudd), Judge (Alexander Knox), Bombardone (Cecil Trouncer), and General Flanco de Fortinbras (R. Stuart Lindsell) with the Secretary to the League of Nations (Cyril Gardiner) in front. Designs by Paul Shelving. Courtesy of the Dan H. Laurence Collection, University of Guelph Library, and The Society of Authors on behalf of the Bernard Shaw Estate.

Chapter 3

Shaw's Theatrical Heyday

Delightful work may be produced under burlesque and farcical conditions, and in work of this kind the artist in England is allowed very great freedom. It is when one comes to the higher forms of the drama that the result of popular control is seen. . . . On the whole, an artist in England gains something by being attacked. His individuality is intensified. He becomes more completely himself.

Oscar Wilde[1]

Shaw's campaign on behalf of the long-suffering British playgoer and stifled true artist gained a regular platform when he became dramatic critic of the *Saturday Review*. From 1895 to 1898 he wrote a weekly column nominally noting premieres but just as noticeably expounding on the latest artistic atrocity or milestone. The theatre's faults were legion, but the gist of Shaw's complaints are succinctly represented in the following passage:

Imagine . . . the result of conducting theatres on the principle of appealing exclusively to the instinct of self-gratification in people without power of attention, without interests, without sympathy: in short, without brains or heart. That is how they were conducted whilst I was writing about them; and that is how they nearly killed me. (CPP 3: xxxix)

In some respects, the 1890s and early Edwardian years represent a period of triumph for the modernists seeking reform. Many Ibsen performances, including premieres and revivals, took place; foreign companies such as the Deutsches Theater brought their productions to London, facilitating comparisons with English efforts; and the Ibsenites' dream of a revitalized, literary, modern theatre was not quite a reality but neither were the prospects entirely bleak in several of the ITS's successors. The typical fare of the commercial stage, however, remained the musical comedies, burlesque lampoons, farces, and bloated dramas that the new generation of critics had railed at since they first saw *A Doll's House* in 1889.

In the wake of the ITS, the New Century Theatre (founded 1897), Stage Society (founded 1899), and Play Actors (founded 1907) offered the modernist repertoire on a subscription basis. As the antecedent of the professional theatre that would later keep Shaw's plays consistently before the public, the Stage Society is the most important from the perspective of literary posterity. About 150 people were invited to the first meeting, forty or fifty of whom showed up. They resolved to mount performances by and for the members one Sunday a month, in defiance of the sabbath ban on public entertainments uncontested since the reign of Charles I. Because they were a private society, this was within the scope of the law, as was their presentation of plays that had been denied a licence by the Lord Chamberlain (or would certainly have been denied if someone bothered to pay the fee and submit the text for inspection). They produced Gerhart Hauptmann, Maxim Gorky, Hermann Sudermann, Leo Tolstoy, Frank Wedekind, the first English productions (professionally but minimally staged) of six Shavian plays (*You Never Can Tell*, which inaugurated the society, *Candida, Captain Brassbound's Conversion, Mrs. Warren's Profession, The Admirable Bashville*, and *Man and Superman*), as well as works by other Fabians (Harley Granville Barker, Sydney Olivier, and Arnold Bennett). Membership grew rapidly to fifteen hundred in 1907, and the society continued producing until 1939.[2]

The Stage Society was not officially a branch of the Fabian Society, though Fabians were prominent among the members.

It was, in effect, an affiliate organization, having been formed "under Fabian influence" and depending for much of its support, in its early days at least, on a "Fabian public." According to the *Fabian News*, it was "largely officered by Fabians" as well, though this statement is something of an exaggeration. Fabians were prominent on its various committees, though not dominant in numbers. Nonetheless, close connections with the Fabian Society were reflected in its structure and its programmes as well as in its personnel.[3]

The Stage Society's work extended to the annual Fabian summer schools held in rural retreats. Artistic exposure was regularly part of the summer programs, taking the form of readings from Shaw and Ibsen by the Stage Society's stalwarts: Charrington, Shaw, and others.[4]

Acknowledgement of the links between the Stage Society and the 1904–7 seasons of the Royal Court Theatre are understated. This venture linked Harley Granville Barker, a young actor prominent in the Sunday performances, and John Vedrenne, who had worked with Frank Benson and Johnston Forbes-Robertson strictly in a managerial capacity. The Royal Court appropriated some of the repertoire the Stage Society had introduced—*Candida, You Never Can Tell,* and *Captain Brassbound's Conversion*—and Shaw never again wrote a major play for the Stage Society. They shared credit for introducing *Man and Superman,* but *John Bull's Other Island, Major Barbara, The Doctor's Dilemma,* and the older titles *The Philanderer* and *The Man of Destiny* were the Royal Court's exclusive credits. Vedrenne and Barker drew on the traditions and personnel of the Stage Society, giving greater prestige in a fully professional setting producing public (rather than subscription) performances during the week, originally as matinees but later, when box office receipts warranted, also in the evenings. As Ian Britain, a historian of the Fabians, concludes: "The Stage Society could take some credit as the testing-ground, if not the breeding-ground, of this venture, but the very success of the Royal Court's seasons inevitably robbed its prototype of the lustre and urgent vitality of lone, pioneering enterprises. It also drew off much of the talent and energy which would normally have been channelled into Stage Society productions."[5]

The Vedrenne-Barker management survived at the Royal Court from 1904 to 1907. In this management, Shaw found a congenial team that would produce his plays and find him an audience. Shaw (as director of his own plays) and Barker (as artistic director and actor) seemed to fulfill, or at least to outline, a dramatic renaissance on modernist principles.[6] More importantly, while at the Royal Court they operated autonomously in their own theatre. For three seasons, the Royal Court specialized in a repertoire of iconoclastic, socially relevant plays, most written in a realistic style, produced by a sympathetic, stable, artistic-commercial management, and performed by the new generation of actors. This signifies important progress in both the aesthetic and business spheres.

Sixteen other authors were introduced at the Royal Court, most notably
Elizabeth Robins (*Votes for Women!*), Laurence Housman and Granville
Barker (*Prunella* and Barker's own *Voysey Inheritance*), John Galsworthy
(*The Silver Box*), St. John Hankin (*The Return of the Prodigal*), and W. B.
Yeats (*The Pot of Broth*; *Where There Is Nothing* having been done
previously by the Stage Society), along with Gilbert Murray's translations
of Euripides (*Trojan Women*, *Electra*, and *Hippolytus*) and several Continental dramatists (Henrik Ibsen, Arthur Schnitzler, and Maurice Maeterlinck). The range of styles is impressive and much more adventurous than
earlier efforts by the nonprofessional societies that preceded the Royal
Court. Nearly a thousand performances were given: a third of the repertoire
and 70 percent of the performances were of Shaw's plays.[7] Shaw's
contribution to the venture's success is undeniable but the debt is mutual.

While the Royal Court Theatre seasons represent a major step forward
in English theatre, not least of all because Barker understood the plays and
gave them decent stagings, it also represents England's distinction from
the Continental modernist movement. Contemporary deviants from the
realistic play of ideas were snubbed in England, and though there was a
minor vogue for ancient Greek tragedies, they were performed at the Court
"as though they had been written for the modern stage."[8] A small amount
of interest was generated by Max Reinhardt after his 1912 visit, but the
London theatre remained far behind the vanguard producers of Germany
and Scandinavia in their exploration of proto-expressionism and scenic
stylization. While Continental producers experimented with symbolist and
mystic plays by Ibsen and August Strindberg or the anarchic work of Alfred
Jarry, the Stage Society clung to realist aesthetics. It is no wonder that
Shaw's brand of social commentary plugged into drawing-room sets and
livened up with the occasional automobile onstage or airplane crash
appealed to Edwardian audiences. They could better concentrate on the
iconoclastic ideas and onslaught of overt polemics because visually and
verbally its aesthetic was well grounded in the commercial theatre of visual
feasting, high society comedy, and well-made structure.

Prior to the Royal Court venture, it was fashionable for critics to dismiss
Shaw's dramas as amusing but unactable sermons. With each production
of a new play by Shaw, reviewers seemed to mark a strong preference for
what preceded it, yet they increasingly admitted that Shaw understood
dramatic principles. Formerly condemned even by his modernist colleagues, this wide scale acceptance of Shaw's work (albeit after a slight
interval) was partly due to a change in the reviewing corps at newspapers.
Clement Scott, who had presided at the largest circulating paper, *The Daily
Telegraph*, retired from active reviewing in 1898. The era of wholesome

Robertsonian naïveté which he championed ended, or at least its hegemony was no longer defended. Meanwhile, the genre of musical comedy flourished at the Gaiety, music halls reached their zenith of popularity and ostentation, and comedies about smart society represented a renaissance in English dramatic wit through Oscar Wilde, Henry Arthur Jones, A. W. Pinero, and J. M. Barrie. This diverse fare was sufficiently well entrenched that Shaw's work represented no threat to vested financial interests or aesthetic preferences.

It remained for reformers to generate a sustaining audience for their preferred authors. Beyond Elizabeth Robins's self-promotions and Annie Horniman's covert sponsorship of Shaw and Yeats in the experimental Avenue season in 1894, few managers dared professional productions of modernist plays, and little headway had been made to establish a serious yet popular theatre by the turn of the century. The limited audience meant limited runs, often of only one or two performances. Vedrenne and Barker envisioned a different approach. Instead of tackling the West End on its own terms, initially they hired a small theatre in Sloane Square (far to the west of the theatre district in a middle-class residential area), aimed at drawing an audience socioeconomically consistent with the area, and rejected the actor-manager system in three important ways.

They did not attempt to compete with the ostentation of commercial theatre. Their sets were shabby, and they made no apologies for them. This was not a naturalistic theatre. Making a general remark about stage practices, Shaw commented that "stage pictures are the worst pictures, stage music the worst music, stage scenery the worst scenery within reach of the Londoner" (CPP 3: xxxv–xxxvi). Strictly speaking, this was not true of all the Royal Court's commercial competitors. The Royal Court did not have the resources to keep up with the costly yet inevitably unsatisfying pictorial aesthetics of many West End theatres, and did not try. At the Royal Court, no play received more than a £200 investment, which is less than 3 percent of Beerbohm Tree's set-up costs for *Henry VIII* in 1910 and only two-thirds of what Tree took at His Majesty's box office for a single performance.[9]

Vedrenne and Barker did not invest in new plays with the hope of sustaining long runs, the financial basis of virtually all other theatres. At the Royal Court, plays were introduced in matinees (on Tuesdays, Thursdays, and Fridays so as not to conflict with the regular West End matinee days of Wednesday and Saturday) and, if successful, transferred to the evening bills. Shaw's works made the shift most often and underwrote the expenses of numerous failures by other playwrights, but even his most attractive, *Major Barbara* and *You Never Can Tell*, were allowed to hold the stage for only six weeks at a time when *Captain Brassbound's Conversion*, with Ellen Terry as the indomitable Lady Cecily Waynflete, was extended to a piffling twelve-week run. This was not the repertory system many reformers sought (for the practical reason that the Royal Court had minimal scenic storage), but it was a start. Barker recognized the value of true repertory, with several plays on the bill in any given week, but also regarded it as an impossibility in London:

> To my mind no drama and no school of acting can long survive the strangling effects of that boa-constrictor, the long run. What is needed, of course, is a repertory theatre, but the difficulty of establishing one in London would be very great. . . . As a good Socialist I am glad to be able to sum up the chief of those difficulties in the one word rent. The theatre manager cannot stand up against the ground landlord. Therefore, and as a Londoner I sincerely regret it, I think we must look for the first repertory theatre of the new order in Manchester or Birmingham, or some such centre where either the price of land is not so enormous or where the municipality or some public body will have public spirit enough to nullify this difficulty.[10]

This proved prophetic. The idea of repertory was tied up with a desire to return to an old form of theatrical organization, the stock system, that had faded out in the mid-nineteenth century. Reformers nostalgically, and to some extent correctly, believed that actors were better trained and their faculties better exercised when they were constantly challenged by different roles. The long-run system neither trained young actors to be flexible or have interpretive breadth nor allowed them to exercise creativity, for too often they were slotted into a minor role, given someone else's blocking patterns and intonations, and expected to preserve the performance intact for a period of months or years. Even with the limited rehearsal periods at the Royal Court, the acting was praised for its freshness (not broad but vibrant), well-honed talent, and ensemble qualities.

Finally, they broke from the model of the actor-manager. Vedrenne kept the books, vigilantly counting the cash flow of pounds and shillings, freeing Barker to choose the repertoire, direct, and (in the case of most of Shaw's productions) act. Barker summed up the problems with the predominant system:

> It must not be thought . . . that the actor manager is an egotistical person who stands in the center of the stage to let his company revolve

round him. More often he is so occupied in getting the best work out of other actors, and with the many troubles of a production, that he is unable to get the best work out of himself. I do not believe that it is possible for a man to play his best and produce his best at the same time. The actor manager is the victim of what is, to my mind, a vicious system.[11]

In contrast, Barker did not bill himself as star and did not take on more responsibilities that he could competently handle. Shaw's work as a director may be inferred from a didactic pamphlet describing the director's role and etiquette in the rehearsal process from start to finish. After the initial blocking is given, he advised: "Be on the stage, handling your people and prompting them with the appropriate tones, as they will, of course, be rather in the dark as to what it is all about, except what they may have gathered from your reading the play to them before rehearsal."[12] The centrality of Shaw (as director) in the early phases rather than Barker (as actor-manager) in performances is telling. The Royal Court was known for the uniform quality of its acting, and though relative newcomers attracted notice—particularly Lillah McCarthy, Dorothy Minto, Nigel Playfair, and Lewis Casson—and veterans received praise—Ellen Terry, Louis Calvert, and Rosina Filippi, to name a few—the plays, not the players, were featured. The players, in turn, had to be devoted to the cause, for their own guinea (£1 1s.) per performance salaries were trifles to such artists.

The idea of a theatre endowed by private or state funding was much on Barker's mind. In 1907 he and William Archer (who had been arguing the point since 1877) published *A National Theatre. Scheme & Estimates*, the ideas of which were eventually rejected by Parliament.[13] Every new opportunity offered to Barker proved a severe disappointment. In 1908 he and Archer sailed to New York to tend a "millionaire's theatre"; they arrived to find a behemoth of a theatre and returned on the next boat.[14] In 1909 Charles Frohman set up a repertory season at the Duke of York's with Barker, Shaw, and Dion G. Boucicault directing plays by Barker, Shaw, John Galsworthy, J. M. Barrie, and George Meredith. It did not draw the public and was cut short after just seventeen weeks (justifiably, *Peter Pan* proved a much better draw). For a few decades, the post–World War II Arts Council of Great Britain gave subsidies to a wide variety of organizations, but no British theatre of the kind proposed by Archer and Barker existed before 1976, when the National Theatre opened its complex on the River Thames's south bank.[15] By that time the absurdity of enlisting the government's help to build a national theatre while concurrently battling the authorities for defending the royal office of the play censor (the Lord Chamberlain) was finally moot: censorship was abolished in 1968. In addition to *Mrs. Warren's Profession*, Shaw's *Press Cuttings* and *The Shewing-up of Blanco Posnet* were initially banned along with Barker's *Waste*, all imbued with political criticism. The paradox of this situation was not lost on either man.

Although Barker was a Fabian and publicly identified himself as a socialist, his schemes (real and proposed) were far from the designs of either municipal socialism or a people's theatre as conceived by Continental socialists. Sidney Webb's prospectus for municipal socialism included local state control of essential services such as utilities, transportation, abattoirs, bakeries, and hospitals, as well as certain institutions central to working-class life yet of questionable benefit under the capitalist system: pawn shops, insurance agencies, and pubs.[16] The provision of "improving recreation" was allied with such proposals. Sometimes the municipality's provision of theatre and/or music was intended to create competition for the commercial establishments that were perceived as eroding or subverting working-class solidarity; other activists such as Dan Irving believed it would encourage high moral and ethical ideas through a didactic repertoire; while others hoped it would provide a realistically desirable alternative to the pub.[17] Occasionally, municipal entertainments were seen as ways for the working classes to make their own diversions, in a return to the precommercial and preprofessionalized music hall. This was a version of government *of* the people confused with the paternalism of government *for* the people.[18] Along these lines, Shaw argued for the advantages of workers making their own music in addition to being provided with quality symphonies and opera companies.[19] While the Royal Court's repertoire sometimes reflected the political concerns of the working classes, it was neither a medium for working people to express themselves nor a vehicle for improving their tastes or conditions. If anything, it replicates the Fabian preference for addressing the elite mandarin segments of the intellectually inclined middle classes.

Unlike French socialists, Britain's Labour Party did not endorse theatre or scenic spectacle as public outreach for their own policies or even as a nonpartisan educational opportunity. The Fabians unofficially sponsored the Stage Society, while in France socialist groups embraced dramatic sections as propagandists of factionalized ideology. French socialist municipalities eagerly sponsored theatrical fetes from the 1890s on, just as their unelected predecessors had staged annual May Day parades from 1878.[20] In England the idea was to make theatre less expensive, but not necessarily to make it a leveller of the classes to unify all British society in an aesthetic commensurate with a proletarian culture. As John Martin-Harvey stated before the British Drama League in 1919:

It is the most extraordinary thing that no Govt. has ever had the vision to perceive the necessity of *beauty* in the lives of the poor. . . . Who has had the vision to see that the great drama at cheap prices is the most potent instrument for the refinement of the working class? . . . Let us then concentrate upon the necessity of founding a great National Theatre, build a big one in the midst of the great labouring classes, admit them to great productions of fine work at small prices. You will have less labour unrest if you remember that man does not live by bread alone, but by beauty in his life and food for his imagination.[21]

As Loren Kruger argues, this speech seems to call for a theatre representative of the working classes yet bypasses art for the multitude as the ultimate goal. It is disturbingly reminiscent of the "rational recreations" advocated half a century before.

One can see the full import of drama as a "potent instrument." Its potency is not simply derived from a hypothetical political payoff of keeping the working class in line. Rather, by conceiving of the working class as passive recipient of beauty defined, produced, and represented by a minority, but imagining the admission of the workers at reduced cost and under the reduced circumstances of "lower caste" to the preserves of the hegemonic culture, the passage reduces the people to consumers of art whose production remains economically and ideologically beyond their reach. It also implies that the proper patrons for "fine works" are elsewhere.[22]

Had they been so challenged, Fabians could have easily deflected such criticisms.

Fabian conceptions of mass reform did not require a working-class revolution, or even the working classes' cooperation, for they did not see social change coming about through mass movements. They were not troubled by a membership exclusively of the middle-class bourgeoisie because they foresaw a state run by bureaucrats whose talents and education (rather than their birthright or political influence) led them to political and civil service offices. Fabians advocated government-sponsored recreation, but if a repertory theatre could be achieved only through private endowment, that did not trouble them: pandering to the old guard ruling bloc was acceptable in a movement built on persuasion, rather than revolution. In 1909, £70,000 were proffered by a single donor toward establishing a national theatre; in 1912 Lord Lucas was willing to put up £10,000 to start a Shakespearean repertory.[23] Shaw speculated:

> In big cities it should be feasible to form influential committees, preferably without any actors, critics, or playwrights on them, and with as many persons of title as possible, for the purpose of approaching one of the leading local managers with a proposal that they shall, under a guarantee against loss, undertake a certain number of afternoon performances of the class required by the committee, in addition to their ordinary business. . . . It will eventually become profitable for the manager to multiply the number of performances at his own risk. . . . Such a theatre would be the needed nucleus for municipal or national endowment. (CPP 3: 116)

Finally, the not inconsiderable matter of aesthetic preference—the beauty that is to be brought to the lives of the poor to refine them out of their lesser caste by exposing them to a great dramatic heritage—has nothing in common with French concepts of "people's theatre" or Bertolt Brecht's aesthetics for inciting political action. Alexis de Tocqueville noted that "the literature of the stage . . . even amongst aristocratic nations, constitutes the most democratic part of their literature," yet it was a potential that had to be realized through deliberate action. It was not an inherent force for egalitarianism.[24] If artists did not make embodiments of the new order (or represent the pathways to it), that did not trouble Fabians, because they advocated aesthetic education generally, relying on its emancipatory consequences as a matter of course. Theatre of the avant-garde in England was promoted in favour of what was strictly social(ist) theatre.

In the matter of an endowed, national, or people's theatre for the modern repertoire (such proposals went by various names), Shaw's two great passions of municipal politics and theatre coincide, linking both halves of his life during this period. Part of the incentive for Shaw and other socialists in proposing "municipal pleasures" was to wrest control of theatre from the trade in alcohol, which kept most music halls afloat, while providing a more thought-provoking repertoire. According to the *Labour Leader*, "If the joy of life is to come back to us in its fullness, the arts, too, must be rescued from the grip of callous and hateful commercialism."[25] This is not entirely an altruistic plea on behalf of the exploited working classes, for since the Fabians' strongest political base was in municipal government, producers like Charles Charrington and Granville Barker stood a good chance of gaining access to municipally sponsored theatres at favourable rates. Resolutely believing that if they provided a quality repertoire people would attend, the modernists perceived the rental costs of theatres as their greatest obstacle, for it was extremely difficult to raise the capital necessary to sublease a theatre for long enough to build an audience.

Shaw's involvement in the Royal Court is usually depicted as that of a modest author and quiet, self-sacrificing benefactor. Stanley Weintraub, for instance, relates:

> Although he hungered for commercial as well as artistic success as a playwright, Shaw (who felt the future in him) unpredictably urged the management he was quietly backing to take off his plays at the box-office peak of their runs in order to experiment with innovative new plays by other, less commercial writers; and the profits from his successes not only subsidized the others but proved the possibilities of the repertory system in England and of an English national theatre.[26]

Shaw is known to have turned back royalties when his matinee productions flopped. It is even alleged that the small profit Vedrenne and Barker took with them to the Savoy was due to Shaw's generous deed of quietly erasing the £2,000 debt that scarred the end of the Royal Court venture.[27] More likely, he put up £2,000 to guarantee Vedrenne and Barker's productions of *John Bull's Other Island* and *You Never Can Tell* at the Savoy and on tour. This was technically a loan, not a gift, and in addition to interest and royalties, Shaw had first charge on the profits after each manager withdrew a £1,000 salary.[28] After his marriage to the heiress Charlotte Payne-Townshend in 1898, Shaw could certainly have afforded such a gesture.[29] It suited his self-styled role as a champion of the new drama to have—at long last—managers whose artistic aspirations matched his and who were willing to put their convictions to the public test. When King Edward VII ordered a command performance of *John Bull's Other Island* in 1905, Shaw was suddenly news. He resolved to let his early champions, Arnold Daly in New York and Vedrenne and Barker in London, continue paying him 10 percent of the gross; all others had to pay 25 percent.[30] This was a selfish impulse, not a condition he could enforce in the long term.

Shaw's sponsorship of his champions can also be described as resistance against the large corporate managements that were springing up through amalgamations, mergers, and takeovers of individual companies. The

British theatre was rapidly becoming corporate at the turn of the century, reinforcing tendencies to present a standardized product less and less likely to challenge the status quo or promote entertainment purely for the people's joy. Shaw's views on such matters were on public record, for he wrote in the preface to *Plays Pleasant*:

> A public-spirited manager, or an author with a keen artistic conscience, may choose to pursue his business with the minimum of profit and the maximum of social usefulness by keeping as close as he can to the highest marketable limit of quality, and constantly feeling for an extension of that limit through the advance of popular culture. An unscrupulous manager or author may aim simply at the maximum of profit with the minimum of risk. These are the opposite poles of our system, represented in practice by our first rate managements at the one end, and the syndicates which exploit pornographic farces at the other. (CPP 3: 114)

The argument was also made in *An Unsocial Socialist* and *Fabian Essays in Socialism*:

> The impulse to production often takes specific direction in the first instance; and a man will insist on producing pictures or plays although he might gain more money by producing boots or bonnets. But his specific impulse once gratified, he will make as much money as he can. He will sell his picture or play for a hundred pounds rather than fifty. In short, though there is no such person as the celebrated "economic man," man being wilful rather than rational, yet when the wilful man has had his way he will take what else he can get; and so he always does appear, finally if not primarily, as the economic man.[31]

All this was penned before Shaw experienced the means to become "economic man." He was not immune from the phenomenon. He noted in 1892 that as his fame grew, he was increasingly pressed to spend his time acquiring wealth rather than writing political tracts, attending to Fabian business, or doing anything else of social utility. Young men, he noted, might be willing to forego the advantages of succumbing to pecuniary temptations but only for a time. "Now, though every clever and warm-hearted young gentleman bachelor enjoys from two to ten years of disinterestedness, during which good work can be got from him, yet in the long run he gets tired of being disinterested. *Permanently* disinterested men of

ability are very scarce."[32] Shaw was forty-eight years old when the Royal
Court seasons began. The question of whether his plays were best suited
for the stage or the study was about to be settled, yet as his fame and
resources grew, how did his resistance to "economic man" hold out?

Despite his celebrated generosity toward the managers of the Royal
Court (including Barker's and Lillah McCarthy's subsequent managements at the Savoy, Little Theatre, and Kingsway), he can rarely be accused
of being satisfied with the minimum of profit. In 1894, when performances
of *Arms and the Man* netted him £568, he discovered how profitable stage
productions could be. After years of struggling as a journalist, watching
his annual earnings creep up from £117 in 1885–68 to £329 in 1893–94,
Shaw hit the jackpot in 1898 when Richard Mansfield produced *The
Devil's Disciple* in the U.S.A.; that year his dramatic royalties alone
amounted to over £2,000. At the same time, his financial security was
guaranteed by marrying a wealthy woman. In 1904 he became truly and
irreversibly affluent in his own right as American publication royalties,
London production royalties, provincial tours, and deals for European
rights proliferated.[33] By the 1920s, when a year's typical royalties came
to £7,650,[34] Shaw had no need of parsimony, yet he resolutely refused to
engage in the kind of self-sponsorship that enabled Vedrenne and Barker
to take his works to the West End and the provinces in 1907 and give him
the exposure he so crucially needed. In 1928 he wrote to Forbes-
Robertson:

> The fact that I am not in the workhouse is due (under Heaven) to
> my iron refusal ever to put a farthing into the theatre or any other
> form of public entertainment. Let the artists contribute their talent
> and the financiers their money; all will be well. But a theatre to
> which the artists contribute their money and the financiers their
> talent is doomed. I cannot save you.[35]

Whatever the actor (retired since 1913) proposed, the truth of the matter
was that Shaw *would not* rather than *could not* assist. For decades socialists
had called for an endowed theatre, yet in 1928 (as today) they coped within
a commercially competitive system. The idea was to coax private investors, then habituate the state to invest in art, as private property was to
be eliminated under socialist reforms. Once Shaw had private property
worth counting, for the most part he held on to it and worked amicably
within the capitalist system he supposedly denounced. To be fair, however,
it must be noted that he gave generously to support the *New Statesman*, an
important socialist journal that ran at a deficit for years, and he and

Charlotte Shaw contributed generously to the various Vedrenne-Barker ventures, including £1,000 for the Haymarket season. When the Vedrenne-Barker partnership was wound up in 1911, it was in debt to Shaw for £5,250. Probably little more than two shillings in the pound (10 percent) was recovered.[36] It was as if he had taken his own advice to millionaires: target spare cash to aid propagandist societies dedicated to fleshing out the dimensions of free speech, encouraging public debate on topics of current interest, and targeting forums that would otherwise be inaccessible. The ventures were luxuries conforming to Shaw's philanthropic credo: "Never give the people anything they want: give them something they ought to want and dont."[37]

Shaw's theatrical heyday occurred in the context of a varied and robust period of play production. The decade leading up to the First World War realized the Ibsenites' dream of a renaissance in British dramatic writing. The Vedrenne-Barker management and private play-producing societies exposed English audiences to the most prominent Continental dramatists, but they also cultivated and produced John Galsworthy, St. John Hankin, John Masefield, W. B. Yeats, and Elizabeth Robins, as well as Barker. Their aesthetic styles and social agendas varied, but overall the realist English school is characterized by the desire to comment on contemporary issues and, where possible, to intervene in order to challenge individuals' practices and affect social policy. Shaw's attempts along these lines are somewhat circumspect, and rank among the less direct. Among the male writers, Galsworthy was probably the most direct and successful, particularly with the 1910 production of *Justice* in the short-lived repertory season at the Duke of York's Theatre.

For several years Galsworthy visited prisons and interviewed inmates. *Justice* implicitly questions the criminality of crimes (particularly the forgery the leading character, Falder, commits in order to emigrate with a woman married to a violently abusive drunk), though the main focus is on the implementation of prison sentences. The anguish Falder experiences during a period of solitary confinement is conveyed in one of the shortest and most poignant pantomimic scenes yet composed for the British stage. At dusk Falder waits for a sound that never comes. He makes a stitch or two in the shirt that comprises his prison labour, listens again, and paces.

> He stops under the window, and, picking up the lid of one of the tins, peers into it, as if trying to make a companion of his own face. . . . Suddenly the lid falls out of his hand with a clatter—the only sound that has broken the silence—and he stands staring intently at the wall

where the stuff of the shirt is hanging rather white in the darkness—he seems to be seeing somebody or something there. There is a sharp tap and click; the cell light behind the glass screen has been turned up. The cell is brightly lighted. Falder is seen gasping for breath.

A sound from far away, as of distant, dull beating on thick metal, is suddenly audible. Falder shrinks back, not able to bear this sudden clamour. But the sound grows, as though some great tumbril were rolling towards the cell. And gradually it seems to hypnotize him. He begins creeping inch by inch nearer to the door. The banging sound, travelling from cell to cell, draws closer and closer; Falder's hands are seen moving as if his spirit had already joined in this beating, and the sound swells till it seems to have entered the very cell. He suddenly raises his clenched fists. Panting violently, he flings himself at his door, and beats on it.[38]

Winston Churchill, the Liberal Home Secretary, was so moved by *Justice* and this scene in particular that its arguments permeate the report calling for prison reforms he wrote shortly afterward.[39] Sir Evelyn Ruggles-Brise, head of the Police Commission, also found the play an incentive to institute a series of penal reforms, especially regarding the imposition of solitary confinement.

Justice has been compared to Tom Taylor's *Ticket-of-Leave Man*, a popular mid-nineteenth-century melodrama depicting the machinations of villainy on an innocent parolee. As Jan McDonald argues, Galsworthy's work is a significant departure from the Victorian formula:

Melodrama personifies and particularises the source of evil: Galsworthy, by contrast, shows well-meaning and high-principled individuals becoming cogs in an inexorable machine. The machine of justice with its "rolling chariot wheels" rather than any individual in its service, is shown to be inflexible and, therefore, inhumane.[40]

The battered woman in *Justice* is reduced to sewing shirts (the same task given to prison inmates) when her husband turns her out of the house. Only then does she have grounds to sue for divorce from her brutish spouse. Ultimately, she resorts to prostitution to support her children, a realistic option that Taylor could not and did not opt for in his play.

Beatrice Webb admired *Justice*: "a great play, I think, great in its realistic form, great in its reserve and restraint, great in its quality of pity. Its motive, that all dealings with criminals should be treatment *plus* restraint in the interests of the community, is all worked in with the philosophy of the

Minority Report [Churchill's call for prison reforms]."[41] Her enthusiasm for this play is unmatched by any response she records to Shaw's efforts, except perhaps *Geneva*. Galsworthy's naturalism incorporates carefully honed depictions of settings operating virtually as social forces unto themselves, reinforced by well-crafted depictions of the systemic causes of characters' misfortunes. For a social scientist committed to incremental change through lobbying, permeation of government ranks, and argument, this was appealing. Shaw, in contrast, preferred to lavish verbal wit on circumstances precariously teetering on the frontiers of the farcical. Galsworthy's craft united argumentation with the manipulation of the senses and emotions; Shaw bludgeoned his spectators with ideas and left them to figure out the consequences on their own time. They had very similar views on the need for prison reforms, but theatrically only one man's formula was conducive to inspiring spectators to bring about change.[42]

Yet there are important distinctions to be drawn among Shaw, Galsworthy, and the agitprop style developed in the 1920s and 1930s by socialist and communist theatre groups. *Meerut*, which agitates against the specific case of the imprisonment of trade union organizers in 1928 and the general conditions of prisons and British rule in India, advocates revolution through a very select staged metaphor. A small chorus rushes onstage and immediately establishes the pattern of a prison grate using six sticks. They declaim a brief history of working conditions, the strike, British colonial government, and the inevitability of class-based revolution. Within minutes of the commencement, hands are thrust through the "bars," and seconds later the "bars" are thrown down, bringing the performance to its conclusion.[43] Nothing in Galsworthy is either so declamatory or so baldly polemical. Nothing in Shaw is so devoid of characterization or the well-made and motivated plot. Shaw never shouts, but he argues with bravado.

While highly personal and tinged by her rather austere aesthetic preferences, Beatrice Webb's perspective on Shaw is extremely revealing. She took Arthur Balfour, the Conservative Prime Minister, to see the premiere of *Major Barbara* days before the defeat of his government. He was "taken aback by the force, the horrible force of the Salvation Army scene, the unrelieved tragedy of degradation, the disillusionment of the Greek professor and of Barbara—the triumph of the unmoral purpose, the anti-climax of evangelizing the Garden City," but she despaired of the play's social effectiveness.

GBS's play turned out to be a dance of devils—amazingly clever, grimly powerful in the second act, but ending, as all his plays end (or at any rate most of them) in an intellectual and moral morass. . . . It is hell tossed on the stage, with no hope of heaven. GBS is gambling with ideas and emotions in a way that distresses slow-minded prigs like Sidney and I, and hurts those with any fastidiousness. But the stupid public will stand a good deal from one who is acclaimed as an unrivalled wit by the great ones of the world.[44]

This stupid public is not what Shaw sought, yet comparing the outcomes of *Justice* with *Major Barbara*—both grappling with thoroughly serious topical themes—suggests that, regardless of their collective intellect, a stupid (or stupefied) public might be precisely what Shaw engendered. *You Never Can Tell* was a perennial touring favourite in this period, curbing expectations of Shaw's serious intent even when he was at his most dour. Shaw's tendency to toss everything off with a joke cast him as a comedic dramatist. Popular audiences rejected his attempts to be serious because he conditioned them to expect comedy; even when they accepted the more serious play, they zeroed in on the comic and chose to overlook the rest.

Few spectators were as perfidious as Kate Terry Gielgud, who noted following the Stage Society production of *You Never Can Tell* in 1899: "Personally I do not care to be harrowed at one moment and in the next to be uncertain whether, given the succeeding situation, I ought not to have laughed." The problem lay in Shaw's preference for irreverence:

Mr. Shaw's sense of humour—his sense, rather, of the ludicrous in life—is, I think, his undoing. It is not that he has no serious perception, he can be as convincingly, truly tragic as anyone could wish; but only for a moment or two—he cannot hold the note, he drowns it in a chord, often enough a discord, of merriment and so spoils the effect of both. . . . This, in my humble opinion, is not good art—it may be dextrous juggling, but not polished sleight of hand.[45]

Shaw gives himself wholly over to farce only in one-act plays, such as *Passion, Poison, and Petrifaction*, where he manipulates highly theatrical media (lighting, settings, and properties) rather than his usual focus on dramatic resources (particularly the spoken word and genre blending). The full-length plays of this period invariably left audiences wondering how to respond appropriately; their concern with spectatorial behaviour rather than political follow-up is significant.

Beatrice Webb saw much resemblance between Lord Alfred Milner's administration of southern Africa (which led directly into the Boer War) and the Undershaft philosophy of "blood and money."[46] In order to fulfill Milner's policy of British supremacy, 300,000 British troops were sent in to suppress the rebellion of 60,000 to 75,000 Boers: 20,000 British lives were lost at a cost of £300 million. Nevertheless, with the Boer War behind them by the time *Major Barbara* was produced, Undershaft was instead regarded as a vaguely sketched Alfred Nobel whose great invention (dynamite) could be used for the good or the bad, according to the proclivities of individuals: the inventor could not be held accountable for abuses of power made possible by his invention. No doubt Shaw alluded to the massive buildup of armaments that the European powers engaged in between the colonial Boer War and the outbreak of hostilities closer to home in 1914, but was this what audiences were necessarily encouraged to dwell on amidst the alternatives of domestic coupling and the social amenities of the perfect garden city at Perivale St. Andrews? The play concludes with Barbara dragging her fiancé off to choose a cottage and Undershaft reminding him to show up for work at six o'clock the next morning. This is a far cry from the final moments of *Justice* (Falder's suicide), or even the ironic poignancy of willing the Zeppelins' return to the tune of "Keep the Home Fires Burning" in Shaw's darker war meditation *Heartbreak House*, a play he resisted having produced.

A few days after seeing *Major Barbara*, Beatrice Webb visited Shaw. "He argued earnestly and cleverly, even persuasively, in favour of what he imagines to be his central theme—*the need for preliminary good physical environment before anything could be done to raise the intelligence and morality of the average sensual man.*" This was precisely what Galsworthy implicated in *Justice*, yet *Major Barbara* did not inspire Balfour or any other politician to improve social amenities in the East End. Instead, *Major Barbara*'s satire on the religious, intellectual, and aesthetic amenities surrounding the munitions factory passes as an irony on the misguided alliance between capital and philanthropy as practised by the Salvation Army. Webb recorded Shaw's defence:

"We middle-class people, having always had physical comfort and good order, do not realize the *disaster to character* in being without. We have, therefore, cast a halo around poverty instead of treating it as the worst of crimes, the one unforgivable crime that must be wiped off before any virtue can grow." He defended Undershaft's general attitude towards life on the ground that until we divested ourselves of feeling (he said "malice"), we were not fit to go to the lengths needed for social salvation. "What we want is for the people to turn

round and burn, not the West End, but their own slums. The Salvation
Army in its fervour and its love might lead them to do this and then
we really should be at the beginning of the end of the crime of
poverty."[47]

As the editors of Beatrice Webb's diaries point out, the Webbs saw poverty
as a social disease with causes that should be righted; nothing was achieved
by simply ameliorating the symptoms.[48] Nor, Beatrice Webb might have
added, would anything be achieved by eliminating the poorest classes'
only opportunity for taking shelter while awaiting the welfare state. For
Shaw, however, the socialist goals of full employment, intellectual
freedom, and community harmony and cooperation could too easily be
fulfilled in Undershaft's model company town. Reminders of Perivale St.
Andrews's gruesome products and the consequences for other communities on the receiving end of the bullets are omnipresent in the last
scene; the characters must constantly negotiate their way around cannons
and straw-stuffed dummies scattered over the stage. Undershaft's solution
to poverty, Shaw seems to argue, is a socialist dystopia on a par with the
sentimentality fostered by the East End missionaries who trade contrition
for soup.

Major Barbara's first production coincided with the deliberations of the
Royal Commission on the Poor Laws, an advisory committee to the
government. The Fabians, including Beatrice Webb who was among the
commissioners, were vigorously opposed to the poor laws, which provided
relief to the most destitute members of society only after all other recourse
was closed to them.[49] By the time parishioners qualified for relief, they
were so demoralized and impoverished that there was virtually no hope of
their recovering self-sufficiency and self-respect. The recipients of Major
Barbara's charity, in contrast, achieved interim relief through active deceit.
Neither system addressed the root cause of the problem: that there were
not enough resources at the bottom of the economic pecking order. The
Salvationists' emulation of the austerity of the poor while accepting
donations that served the interests of capitalists mirrored in the private
sector what the poor laws did in the public sector. But, as Undershaft
argues: "Your pious mob fills up ballot papers and imagines it is governing
its masters; but the ballot paper that really governs is the paper that has a
bullet wrapped up in it. . . . Whatever can blow men up can blow society
up. The history of the world is the history of those who had the courage
to embrace this truth" (CPP 1: 436).

In *Major Barbara* Shaw's comprehensive attack on Victorian values is
achieved by paradoxical contrasts. J. M. Winter argues:

by dissociating the form of the ideal industrial life from its product, Shaw permitted his audience to see that to be opposed to capitalism, and the poverty it inevitably produced, was in no sense to be opposed to industry. . . . All that was needed for the transformation is the collective recognition that the destruction of the possibilities of human life by poverty was no less an obscenity than the destruction of human life in war.[50]

Shaw uses the familiar theatrical convention of a scenic transformation, switching from the squalor of the Salvation Army shelter to the picture-perfect factory town, with Lady Britomart's library serving as a fulcrum between the two. It makes for an ingenious variation on the Edwardian drawing-room "problem play," yet one drawn with larger brushstrokes and brighter colours than his naturalist colleagues used, for it includes an indispensable convention of pantomimes. In *The Voysey Inheritance*, by contrast, Barker depicts a family firm of solicitors that has been misappropriating clients' funds for two generations. The metaphors are large— the family as microcosm of a generation struggling between received and independently determined values—but the settings and small details of activity keep the play firmly rooted in naturalism. Barker, like Galsworthy, contains his work within the confines of naturalism, conducts a complex discussion without literally dramatizing debate, and suggests that after the play is over its situation will have continued life. While his colleagues mastered the naturalist aesthetic, Shaw seemed to revel in allegory. He was rarely content with an unclouded dramatization of any polemic, including those he supposedly championed. As Margot Peters points out:

He could not help seeing the ridiculous and the sham in any creed. In *The Philanderer*, seeing that Ibsen could be idealized as much as anything else, he had ridiculed the Ibsenites rather than supported them. Instead of making the servant Louka in *Arms and the Man* a working-class heroine, he portrayed her as a materialist with ultimately romantic notions about womanhood: little wonder she emerged as "enigmatic." The powers of the socialist clergyman Morell [in *Candida*] turned out to be hollow. Bluntschli, his realist hero, possessed nevertheless two hundred horses and seventy carriages—a Swiss capitalist. Marchbanks was a poet, but also the son of an earl. He intended Candida as the master of her doll's house; she emerged in some people's opinion a clever slave. Mrs. Clandon's [in *You Never Can Tell*] feminism he treated as outmoded; Gloria's lessons in emancipation as worthless.[51]

Other ventures in politically committed theatre also experimented with both generic form and presentational style. Considerable scholarly effort has recently been devoted to suffrage drama and the feminist politics that flourished with little financial means during the years that Shaw took his place on the world stage. Comparisons between these endeavours, as economic entities and as explorations of turn-of-the-century politics, are apt. Feminists, like socialist artists, felt a responsibility to fashion visions of the new order. For them, the impetus was keenest during the height of women's suffrage campaigns. Their drama aimed at persuading male citizens to extend the privilege of voting to women, preparing the populace for living in a more sexually equitable society, and forging a collectively symbolized female identity. In this feminists were very like socialists, though considerably more resourceful financially and dramaturgically.

From the outset of his career as an author, Shaw was concerned with relations between the sexes. In the novel *An Unsocial Socialist* he kills off the woman who mated for love and passion and debunked the romantic conventions of the genre by concluding the story with a marriage based on complementary geniality and admiration between helpmeets rather than lovers (rather like Shaw's own choice of Charlotte Payne-Townshend fourteen years later). In the case of another woman, however, the raisonneur Trefusis refuses to let the impoverished aristocrat Gertrude waste her life and affections on "some rich vampire of the factories or [a] great landlord"[52] for the sake of pleasing and enriching her family when a more economically humble but utterly besotted alternative hovers nearby. In Shaw's terminology this is "giving" rather than "selling" herself.[53] In the terminology of Cicely Hamilton (actress, playwright, suffragist, and author of the polemic *Marriage as a Trade*) this was "double-motived" marriage: love combined with women's unidealistic "trade" to barter themselves away in exchange for a means to exist.[54]

Marx and Engels's provocative accusations in *The Communist Manifesto* are resonant in various ways in Shaw's work:

> On what foundation is the present family, the bourgeois family, based? On capital, on private gain. In its completely developed form this family exists only among the bourgeoisie. But this state of things finds its complement in the practical absence of the family among the proletarians, and in public prostitution.
>
> The bourgeois family will vanish as a matter of course when its complement vanishes, and both will vanish with the vanishing of capital.[55]

Public prostitution, whether in the sense of preserving and reinforcing privilege through fiscally opportunistic marriages or in the sense of Mrs. Warren's profession, is eradicated at the peril of the family. Shaw describes Gertrude's family enjoying the food and good company of her humble dining table despite their initial disappointment in her marital choice; but this is utopic in the context of late-Victorian class relations. Vivie Warren is repulsed by Lord Crofts's proposals, and ultimately rejects both the capital entrenchment that would result from marriage with her mother's partner as well as any identification as either a wife or daughter. In fact, Vivie opts out of marital and familial relations in preference to a self-selected unit centered on her business partner, Honoria Fraser. Vivie has a degree in mathematics and, presumably, has studied the actuarial tables, weighed the risk, and calculated the price of the bourgeois family.

While Hamilton concentrates her argument on the "trade" connotations of marriage for women, Marx and Engels describe a similar dimension of barter amongst working-class children who are "transformed into simple articles of commerce and instruments of labor."[56] This is somewhat apparent in Doolittle's relationship with his daughter, Eliza, prior to his acquisition of wealth and her attainment of social graces in *Pygmalion*, and is explicit in the preface to *Misalliance*:

> Sometimes the family organization is as frankly political as the organization of an army or an industry: fathers being no more expected to be sentimental about their children than colonels about soldiers, or factory owners about their employees, though the mother may be allowed a little tenderness if her character is weak. . . . The farmer sees his children constantly: the squire sees them only during the holidays, and not then oftener than he can help: the tram conductor, when employed by a joint stock company, sometimes never sees them at all. (CPP 4: 86)

But for the most part, Shaw is less concerned with the economic relations of parents and children than wives and husbands. In *Passion, Poison, and Petrifaction*, *The Doctor's Dilemma*, and *How He Lied to Her Husband*, Shaw lampoons what Marx and Engels describe as the bourgeoisie's "supreme delight in seducing each other's wives."[57] *Misalliance* echoes the Communists' defence of openly legalized free love in preference to the hypocrisies of lifetime pairing of couples incompatible in every sense except the financial. *Getting Married* dramatizes what might happen when· the contractual obligations of marriage are closely scrutinized in all their legal, financial, and emotional dimensions, with an additional ironic permutation on "trade" with respect to the indomitable mayoress. Shaw argues (both through his own actions and those of his characters) that the domestic arrangements of marriage are a fundamental human need, yet everything represented by the institution must be made over if the generations enlightened to its shortcomings are to partake of it. In this regard, Shaw's views are consonant with feminists campaigning for reform since the 1860s and the formation of the Divorce Law Reform Association in 1906, leading to a Royal Commission on Divorce and Matrimonial Causes (1909–12).

Shortly after the turn of the twentieth century, feminists coalesced around the issue of suffrage and waged an all-out battle to achieve the right to vote. This was seen as a short-term measure in order to achieve a slate of objectives in the longer term. In the period from 1905 to 1914, British women became more organized than at any other time in history, before or since. The women's suffrage debate pervaded Edwardian culture: women trumpeted their cause in newspapers, at meetings, in public demonstrations, in marches, in art, and on the stage. Typically, the pro-suffrage plays can be summarized as defending the cause of suffragism (as in Evelyn Glover's *Miss Appleyard's Awakening* and *A Chat with Mrs. Chicky*, and Beatrice Harraden's *Lady Geraldine's Speech*), but for propagandists the vote was a shorthand way of encapsulating an array of desired reforms. P. R. Bennett's *Mary Edwards* argues that women are competent to manage property and their own destinies. Both Inez Bensusan's *The Apple* and Arthur H. Heathcote's *A Junction* relate suffrage issues to themes of sexual liberation and women's self-determination in both the home and marketplace. In many plays suffrage issues are related to themes of home and family in order to convince the unconverted of the importance of being pro-suffrage (e.g., H. Arncliffe Sennett's *An Englishwoman's Home*). Anti-suffrage partisans predicted the downfall of the family and Western civilization if women were allowed to partake officially in the public sphere. The women's suffrage movement amounts to a massive effort in persuasion. Men had to be made to understand the issues and take action (the purpose of both Graham Moffat's *The Maid and the Magistrate* and Cicely Hamilton and Christopher St. John's *How the Vote Was Won*), while the causes and means of suffragism also had to be justified to women (as in Gertrude Jennings's *A Woman's Influence* and Vera Wentworth's *An Allegory*).

Some suffrage plays were also explicitly educational, such as *Physical Force*, which instructed spectators in self-defence. Most served explicitly or covertly to reaffirm suffragists' stance and rehearse the arguments they were to engage in at every opportunity. Like Shaw's dramatic efforts, this should be regarded as part of a continuum including political demonstrations and marches that took the political arguments and theatrical spectacle to the streets.[58] Part of the rhetoric of women's oppression was that politics was a masculine realm that existed solely in the public arena; by refusing to stay at home, suffragists were masculinized and legitimated their claim to public spaces, such as the politicized streets, squares, and parks of London and Manchester. They simultaneously enacted their liberation and took a political role in demonstration of their commitment to participate in democratic life. If socialism was the rallying cry of young idealists in the 1880s, women's suffrage was the catalyst to organize mass movements in the early 1900s.

Because men (and men alone) formed the electorate and only men could run for parliamentary seats, suffragists' success hinged on their ability to rally the cooperation of men. Women's impact on the law was, for the time being, only indirect. The Fabians had long since endorsed women's suffrage, though the society was not officially active in the struggle. Shaw could not be expected to leave the topic alone. In one instance where suffragism was not an intended reference, an audience nevertheless insisted that they saw it. In Barker's 1912 production of *Androcles and the Lion* at the St. James's,

> feminists took the persecution of the Christians as a direct reference to their own cause. Christians, says the Roman Captain, have only their "own perverse folly to blame" if they suffer. Since a Christian need only perform a simple ceremony to the gods in order to be freed, "every Christian who has perished in the arena has really committed suicide." When Ben Webster delivered these lines, the play was interrupted by "suffragette cheers from the gallery."[59]

Shaw is more deliberately on course in *Getting Married* (1908), where he argues in favour of sexually equitable and liberal divorce laws, and most particularly against the bondage and economic dependency of marriage.

All his novels and most of his plays are concerned with the question of marriage—usually as a metaphorical pairing of complements. Until 1907 they were generally treatises validating monogamy no matter what lapses may be contemplated along the way (as in *The Doctor's Dilemma* and *Passion, Poison, Petrifaction*) by one sex or both. In *Getting Married* a bishop's daughter unexpectedly refuses to go through with her marriage ceremony moments before it is scheduled to occur. Both she and her fiancé mysteriously received pamphlets entitled "Do You Know What You Are Going to Do? By a Woman Who Has Done It," laying out all the case law on sex-based inequalities in English marriage. The fiancé, Cecil Sykes, realizes that Edith Bridgenorth's public outspokenness about factory owners might cause him to be sued for thousands of pounds in slanderous damages. Edith, the fiancée, learns that even if her husband commits a murder and is condemned to a lifetime in prison, she would not be able to obtain a divorce. Women take husbands "for better or worse" and can sue for divorce only if their spouses are adulterous, and only then when adultery can be proved. If marriage is to be acceptable, it must be on even grounds and it must be voluntary. The ideal—recognizable in the Shaws' own marriage during this period—is represented through the mayoress, Mrs. George, who flirts with St. John Hotchkiss (recently the co-respondent in Edith's aunt's divorce case) but will stand by her coal merchant husband.

MRS. GEORGE. Oh, I dont know that I love him. He's my husband, you know. But if I got anxious about George's health, and I thought it would nourish him, I would fry you with onions for his breakfast and think nothing of it. George and I are good friends. George belongs to me. Other men may come and go; but George goes on for ever. (CPP 4: 464)

With even less orthodoxy Shaw has another of Edith's aunts, a spinster long pursued by a priggish general, advocate state support of unmarried mothers. The argument has remarkable currency in the late twentieth century:

LESBIA. I ought to have children. I should be a good mother to children. I believe it would pay the country very well to pay ME very well to have children. But the country tells me that I cant have a child in my house without a man in it too; so I tell the country that it will have to do without my children. If I am to be a mother, I really cannot have a man bothering me to be a wife at the same time. (CPP 4: 403)

The following year Cicely Hamilton lamented in *Marriage as a Trade*: "How many children, I wonder, are born each year merely because their mothers were afraid of being called old maids? One can imagine no more inadequate reasons for bringing a human being into the world."[60] Lesbia prefers perpetual independence from men even if this means she will be childless. Her challenge to "family values"—so resonant over eighty-five years later—sets the terms for debate on an issue that has racked social policymakers for decades and now remains as controversial and socially divisive of the left and right on the political spectrum as it was in 1908.[61]

Another Shavian parable for the suffragists' cause, *Fanny's First Play*, was enormously successful when first produced by Lillah McCarthy in 1911. When the children of two respectable business partners are briefly jailed for public high jinks, propriety suffers the first of a series of calamitous decays. Parental despotism is defied, the partners' firm begins to put corset advertisements in its shop window, the jailed son marries a prostitute, and the jailed daughter marries the footman (who, as anticipated by the prostitute, is really the brother of a duke, self-exiled to domestic service to atone for an injustice he once dispensed toward one of his own staff). This is the gist of the play-within-the-play, framed by another plot wherein a young Cambridge Fabian, Fanny (supposedly watching the production of her first literary attempt), forces a gaggle of theatrical critics to witness the play without having knowledge of its true author. This is an allusion to the forcible feeding imposed on fasting jailed suffragettes: the play will be forced down the throats of critics just as food was so painfully pumped into the stomachs of feminist dissidents. The presence of several members of the Actresses' Franchise League in the cast reinforced the connection.[62]

In these plays Shaw mirrors the tactics of several brands of suffragists. The liberal feminists attempted to win converts by force of logic, also a staple of Shavian comedy. The radicals in the Women's Social and Political Union (the only group correctly called "suffragettes") believed that extreme injustice called for extreme actions, including guerrilla acts of sabotage. Though Shaw does not, in these plays, advocate violent means, they are somewhat akin to the elaborate subterfuges of suffragists' disguises in escaping the legal system when temporarily freed from jail (the "Cat and Mouse Act") to recover from bouts of fasting. In *Press Cuttings*, set in General Mitchener's office, the Prime Minister disguises himself as a suffragette chained to the boot scraper outside Mitchener's door in order to gain passage to his colleague's premises without harassment from women. The play addresses two coincident phenomena: demands for female suffrage and the implementation of male conscription as well as civil rights (including enfranchisement) for the armed forces. Here a joke based on identity reversal sets off more profound proposals, though the play conforms to the typical pattern of the farcical genre, namely that an anti-suffrage advocate convinces a man to be pro-suffrage by her sheer extremism and illogic. Yet, in this respect, it also differs markedly from suffrage plays written by women, such as Joan Dugdale's *10 Clowning Street*.[63]

With the outbreak of the 1914–18 war, the suffragists laid aside their grievances and for the most part offered themselves in service to the nation.

Suffragist playwriting, like the nascent women's theatre movement sponsored by the Actresses' Franchise League and Pioneer Players, dissolved. The nation's attention shifted back to macro-politics in gruelling territorial battles abroad.

Sheila Stowell argues that in Elizabeth Robins's character Vida Levering (of *Votes for Women!*, a Royal Court production of 1907), there is "a new voice, that of politicised woman".[64] *Votes for Women!* draws on Robins's experience—including her own speeches—in the women's movement.[65] This degree of commitment and personal involvement echoes the earlier years of Shaw's playwriting career but, as Beatrice Webb noted, Shaw experienced a withdrawal from political involvement in the years leading up to 1914. To a great extent, he substituted the theatre for politics to the detriment of his Fabian liaisons and, Webb believed, his powers of rational argument:

> He used to be a good colleague, genuinely interested in public affairs and a radically kind man. Now he is perverse, irate and despotic in his relations, and he is bored with all the old questions. And the quality of his thought is not good. . . . The literary quality is not distinguished enough to carry the poor and petulant reasoning, the lack of accuracy, logic and dignity. For the last year or so we have found it increasingly difficult to discuss with him; he no longer tries to meet another person's points. He merely orates, and all his talk revolves round persons and not ideas. In political theory he is inclining towards Belloc and Chesterton, and the propaganda of revolt. Now and again he has a brilliant flash of illuminating thought, but it is over before one has had time to fit it in to the rest of his philosophy of conduct.[66]

The evidence for this complicated complaint is woven throughout Webb's diaries, with instances drawn from Shaw's social and romantic encounters as well as each new dramatic work. From her insightful perspective, Shaw was glorying in the "rabbit-warren" philosophy of life: centered on the sex instinct solely, without anything morally or socially uplifting to redeem the metaphor. The impetus for *Misalliance*, though attributable to the scandalous affair between H. G. Wells and Amber Reeves and thus founded on empirical observation, was merely erotic farce unredeemed even by the "intellectual brilliancy" of the dialogue.[67] This is a marked departure from the feminist plays combining new character models with dramaturgies designed to instigate social change. It is also indicative of the wide gulf between socialist aesthetics and Shaw's own techniques.

Joan Scott's reading of Emile Veyrin's *La Pâque Socialiste*, a warhorse of the socialist theatre in France, provides a useful contrast with Shaw's nonrevolutionary and increasingly classless dramatizations. The play has a Christian overtone, but then so did much socialism in the 1890s.

> The major themes of the play are represented in the two tableaux vivants. The first (act 4) centers around Micheline, an inspirational figure who articulates and incarnates the dream of the future new society. The second (act 5) involves Gilbert. It depicts the passage of history, the transfer of the ownership of the means of production from capitalist to worker. (At the end of this act Gilbert, having fulfilled his historic mission, dies.) The tableaux visually symbolize what the characters have articulated verbally in earlier acts. The play is about the transforming power of ideas in history. Micheline symbolizes the idea, the dream which Veyrin depicts as the leading force for social change. "It is often forgotten," she says early in the play, "that each time humanity has advanced a stage, a dream has led the way." And, of course, she literally leads all the action in the play.[68]

Micheline reinforces Gilbert's courage to take action, so the female represents the ideals and the male represents the enactor of the ideals. Through her, his sensibility is transformed from an individualistic personal feeling to a collective goal transferred thereafter from Gilbert to the workers.

> The dream inspires and gives larger significance to individual action. It at once infuses history with meaning and interprets it. That is why Micheline's tableau precedes Gilbert's. The tableaux juxtaposed depict the inevitable passage from capitalism to socialism, informed by the inspirational and directional force of the eternal ideas of human love and social justice.[69]

Like many of Shaw's plays, the outcome (in socialist terms) is negative yet Veyrin casts it as a morality tale to strengthen the people's resolve to persevere despite setbacks. Micheline's goodness and vision transcend the circumstances of politics, implying that if her ideals can survive then so can the people's cause. In contrast, Shaw's solution is more often than not to conclude with an ambivalent or even dystopic vision for the future.

In the years between the world wars, this set Shaw further apart from the bona fide socialist drama of the Unity Theatre, Theatre of Action, and other pan-national participants in the workers' theatre movement. Aesthetically and philosophically there could be no reconciliation. Shaw addressed the habitual theatregoing middle classes with realist aesthetics and philosophical conundrums, while the worker's theatre took drama to the factory gates and union halls with stark "poor" resources and unambiguous political propagandizing. Shaw's plays were demanding examples of the visually rich professional stage. They required actors of the highest order, with multiple sets and luxurious costumes. Comparisons between the Workers' Theatre Movement and *Saint Joan* quickly illustrate the point: while Shaw calls for seven settings, dozens of period costumes (designed by Charles Ricketts), and actors of the first rank, *Meerut* needs only a few props and explicitly exists to put the words in the mouths of amateurs undifferentiated in skill from the spectators. This leftist theatre was counteracted by dramatized denunciations of communism, particularly in the aftermath of the 1917 Russian Revolution,[70] yet this served to make it even more integrated into the political debates of Britain, while Shaw moved further and further away into his own singular school of writing. Shaw may have been fully cognizant of this divergence. Margery Morgan argues that Shaw's portrayal of the Fabians' influence on the Labour Party and the foundations of the welfare state are exaggerated, if not mythical constructs deliberately engineered by Shaw.[71]

Bourgeois drama is based on the soulful examination of the individual in a highly individualist manner. In Shaw's plays which takes precedence: overarching social concerns or the dilemmas of an individual? In most of the critically revered plays both are important, and critical emphasis can fall on either aspect. In many respects the plays encourage dealing with these factors simultaneously. Compare this description of Shaw's lecturing style to his play structure:

> When lecturing, Shaw habitually threw out an axiom designed to shock and annoy; next, by offering a series of paradoxes, he goaded the audience to discard hidebound theories and prejudices in order to examine the proposition from the opposite point of view; finally, he would demonstrate that what his original statement had implied to them was not what it really meant to him. After a certain amount of discussion, the audience would depart, refreshed by having been forced into some lateral thinking and at least three-quarters convinced that what the great man had said was right.[72]

Shaw adapted this formula for dramatic debates (such as Undershaft's self-explanations in Act III of *Major Barbara*) on a conversational scale as well as in the overall organization of his plays. The extraordinary individuality of characters in his full-length plays of the Royal Court pre–World War I years and the tour de force debating style adopted by iconoclast and raisonneur characters alike reorients the soulful examination of bourgeois drama toward explorations of individualism per se and its function as a social catalyst. This is particularly evident in Shaw's articulation of the Life Force and the concept of creative evolution.

Shaw's theory of creative evolution brought about through the will is worked out in the mature plays of the early twentieth century. Usually described as a Nietzschean philosophy, it is also possible that Shaw's early contact with Henry George molded his theory of the Life Force. This is from George's last chapter on "The Problem of Individual Life":

> When we see that social development is governed neither by a Special Providence nor by a merciless fate, but by law, at once unchangeable and beneficent; when we see that human will is the great factor, and that taking men in the aggregate, their condition is as they make it; when we see that economic law and moral law are essentially one, and that the truth which the intellect grasps after toilsome effort, is but that which the moral sense reaches by a quick intuition, a flood of light breaks in upon the problem of individual life. These countless millions like ourselves, who on this earth of ours have passed and still are passing, with their joys and sorrows, their toil and their striving, their aspirations and their fears, their strong perceptions of things deeper than sense, their common feelings which form the basis even of the most divergent creeds—their little lives do not seem so much like meaningless waste.[73]

The purpose of human life, according to this creed, was to improve human society; the improvement of humanity itself would be taken care of by nature. Unless human beings are the agents of improvement, their existence is inexplicable. Shaw focused on the working out of this creed insofar as it was manipulated by individuals (particularly men) or worked out as an unconsciously wielded instrument of the will (particularly in women).

In the plays the inexorable sex instinct pairs women and men; their attraction/repulsion acts like planetary orbits' gravitational pull, and most of the works conclude with the distinct implication that they will mate and breed. Under the guise of the Life Force or "evolutionary appetite" (CPP 5: 612), Shaw compounds a quasi-mystical explanation of sexual desire with a eugenically evolutionary thesis about the new breed of beings that will combine intelligence, vitality, uncluttered morality, and socialist ideals to bring about the new millennium. This sexual choreography is most clearly demonstrated in *Man and Superman* and *Major Barbara*, though it is also prominent in *Arms and the Man, Misalliance, Back to Methuselah, On the Rocks*, and *The Millionairess*, elusive in *John Bull's Other Island* and *The Doctor's Dilemma*, and thwarted in *Pygmalion* and *The Simpleton of the Unexpected Isles*.

Although *Man and Superman* played well in its original shortened version, the work was incomplete without the third act (the so-called "Don Juan in Hell" scene). Beatrice Webb believed it to be Shaw's best work, perhaps because it melded the genres in which he excelled and was unobjectionably expressed in the philosophizing manner that was his forte. To her it was "a play which is not a play; but only a combination of essay, treatise, interlude, lyric—all the different forms illustrating the central idea, as a sonata manifests a scheme of melody and harmony."[74]

As Margot Peters notes, "in *Man and Superman*, Shaw had managed to have it both ways: in the comedy proper, Jack Tanner succumbs to mating; in the philosophical dream sequence, Don Juan does not."[75] In Jack's conscious life he can no more resist Ann Whitefield's allure than she can turn it off. It is a sexist mating ritual, and one that accords with Shaw's perceptions of his own attraction to a host of women. Jack stages his desire to flee—and a spectacle of cross-Europe motoring ensues—but he cannot escape the Life Force's design. Shaw's version of the New Woman is not of someone intellectual in her own right or someone whose sense of self allows her to chart her own course in life, but rather she is so irresistible that a man who is her match in terms of will (but can also intellectualize the rationale of socialism) cannot ultimately resist her. Ann's "powers of fascination" are likened to "rent," the principle by which one extracts money and extorts a whole system of behaviours from another class (CPP 3: 677). Jack condemns the institution of marriage in the same breath as announcing his own wedding plans.

Shaw's version of the New Woman, without whom the intellectual Life Force has no embodied complement, relegates the debate about women to the private realm of sex and reproduction rather than the public realm suffragists claimed through the struggle for enfranchisement. For Jack/Don Juan marriage is a sexual relation that exists to propagate the species with supermen. For Ann/Doña Ana marriage is the most personal relationship possible, and a mate must be sought who is both worthy and companionable for raising the new generation of supermen.

DON JUAN. To a woman, Señora, man's duties and responsibilities begin and end with the task of getting bread for her children. To her, Man is only the means to the end of getting children and rearing them.

ANA. Is that your idea of a woman's mind? I call it cynical and disgusting animalism.

DON JUAN. Pardon me, Ana: I said nothing about a woman's whole mind. I spoke of her view of Man as a separate sex. It is no more cynical than her view of herself as above all things a Mother. Sexually, Woman is Nature's contrivance for perpetuating its highest achievement. Sexually, Man is Woman's contrivance for fulfilling Nature's behest in the most economical way. (CPP 3: 624)

Women are essentialized by their biological functions, men by their economic roles in the conventional family under bourgeois capitalism. Ann is endorsed as the psychic irrational in a dualistic system; in so doing, Shaw *seems* to depict her as a disruptive agent "normalizing" Jack (the wayward masculinism) back into a family unit, whereas in fact it is she who is ultimately absorbed into *his* system. This reinforces rather than disrupts the ideology of women domesticated as the caretakers of the home and family. But, as the brigand Mendoza states, "a movement which is confined to philosophers and honest men can never exercise any real political influence: there are too few of them" (CPP 3: 594).

The play's other couple—Violet Robinson and the American Hector Malone—have concealed their marriage in order to protect his relationship with his father, who promises to disinherit him if he marries anyone lesser than an aristocrat. As Malone, Sr., says, a marriage must benefit someone, and mixing with the middle-class Violet would not change status relations in any way. Wanting a daughter-in-law with a decrepit country estate to mate with his drawling nouveau riche son is Malone, Sr.'s idea of revenge on England for starving his forebears out of Ireland. Following a small display of filial disobedience, Malone, Sr., makes a pact to defer to Violet in all matters and not only restore but incresae his son's allowance. Hector may be won over by love, but his father (the family chequebook) is cowed merely by female assertiveness:

TANNER (drawing Ramsden's attention to Malone's cringing attitude as he takes leave of Violet). And that poor devil is a billionaire! one of the master spirits of the age! Led in [*sic*] a string like a pug dog by the first girl who takes the trouble to despise him! I wonder will it ever come to that with me. (CPP 3: 668)

Don Juan's understanding of the perils of a philosopher in the grip of the Life Force is mere theory; the Malones' deferral to Violet and Jack's capitulation to Ann illustrate creative evolution in practice.

In *Major Barbara* three couples are contrasted. The parental generation of Lady Britomart and Andrew Undershaft represent the ideological impasse reached between the upper-class liberal who shuns association with the work ethic yet wants to live well off its fruits, and the working-class millionaire adopted into a long-established manufacturing enterprise because he is a foundling untainted by the corruption of do-gooder palliatives. The offspring of Britomart and Undershaft come in three forms. Their obedient but useless son, Stephen, adopts his mother's high-minded outlook without inheriting her backbone. He is destined for a career in politics because, as his father perceives, "he knows nothing and he thinks he knows everything" (CPP 1: 415). There, he will simply do the bidding of the capitalists, creating wars and quelling civil unrest in order to provide dividends. The status-conscious daughter, Sarah, will mate with a ludicrous specimen of the brainless upper crust whose imbecility is apparent to all, including himself. The third child, Barbara, has a calling to ameliorate the wants of the poor by serving in the Salvation Army, and she scruples to resign her commission when she discovers that the capitalists not only cause the plight of the poor but sustain and underwrite charitable palliatives such as the Salvation Army according to their own self-interests. Her bleak East End missionary centre is scenically contrasted with Undershaft's rural munitions factory, a beautiful garden city as replete with excellent social services and religious ecumenicalism as it is with the instruments for global destruction. Shaw's recurrent paradoxes of idealism versus realism, both in the moral and political senses, are embodied in these two settings.

The intertextual layerings of *Major Barbara* are legion: Thomas Paine's *Common Sense* and *The Rights of Man*, Charles Bradlaugh's secularist lectures, Machiavelli's unscrupulous *Prince*, and particularly Euripides' *The Bacchae*. The Undershaft family represents the diversity of the body politic in a single family. Significantly, Barbara's fiancé, Adolphus Cusins, who qualifies as a foundling, elects to succeed Undershaft as the world's leading armourer. As a professor of Greek and translator of Euripides, he represents the melding of the old-school trained mind with the spirit of joyous revelry. Like Tiresias in Euripides' play, Cusins is simultaneously the sophisticate and primitive who appreciates the power of both; in combination with Barbara, he will settle down in a cottage and produce the new line of supermen that merge ability, rationality, art, and conscience in a socialist future. This is the evolutionist objective of Shaw's Life Force. Salvation is not granted by another on the basis of a conversion experience, repentance, and grace. Salvation is not the personal goal of the individual but the objective of the race. Few are called, few will serve, yet the many will benefit. Lady Britomart/Agave, locked in the ecstasy of her caste's delusions, will metaphorically tear her son limb from limb. The future lies not in Agave's male progeny or the masses at the mercy of their corporeal desires. Hope rests in the progeny of Barbara and Cusins, inheritors to the significantly named firm Undershaft and Lazarus, which has an efficient and conscientious work force that may turn this epitome of capitalism against its own interests and toward a more productive and peaceful future. Humanity will come back from its death-like state. It was a dystopic vision at the brink of transformation, an optimism rooted in 1905 following the Boer War but no longer possible a decade later.

The Euripidean quotations and allusions in *Major Barbara*—somewhat obtuse today—were highly topical in 1905. The concurrent production of two Euripidean plays translated by Gilbert Murray (the model for Cusins) at the Royal Court rounded out the intertextuality of *Major Barbara*. The audience, by implication, sided with Cusins, for they were privy both to the ideas of this radical among the ancients while recognizing the rot at the core of their own system. The Royal Court was to be the catalyst converting them away from the vacuousness of Stephen, the self-interestedness of Sarah, Barbara's delusion that change comes by first addressing the needs of the working classes, and Undershaft's creed (like Jack Tanner's) of being "unashamed" in all circumstances. But it was not to seriously challenge the institution of marriage or the "womanly" roles middle-class society traditionally dictated. For women the "creative" part of evolution was a biological function, augmented occasionally by being a muse for men. Eliza Doolittle in *Pygmalion* literalized this metaphor in the case of her "sculptor," Higgins, as well as in the man whose backbone she "sculpts," her husband, Freddy.

Much scholarly attention has focused on the real women in Shaw's life who were the prototypes for characters in the plays. As a friend, flirt, and paterfamilias, he had an early and abiding preference for creating ménages à trois in which he could move in and out of couples' domestic situations without fear of engendering abiding commitments. With Jenny Patterson, Bertha Newcombe, Florence Farr, Janet Achurch, and Ellen Terry he enjoyed the relationships as long as he could woo *almost* to the point of seduction, parlay his wit, and avoid commitments. This was all very well while he was a single man, but after his marriage to a woman who had grown "indispensable" to the routine execution of his work, he stood on a new corner in his habitual ménages à trois—husband, rather than suitor—and the repartee of words and parlaying of physical desire took on new connotations.

Some of these flirtations were work-related, such as the prolonged epistolary exchange with Ellen Terry, culminating in a role for her in *Captain Brassbound's Conversion,* or the earlier tête-à-têtes with Achurch and Charrington, intended to promote her in *Candida* and a variety of other roles. These women were not only the prototypes of characters but also the intended actresses for them. Margot Peters describes how careful attention to Shaw's relationships with women keyed her into a new perception of Shaw. It was not favourable.

> Listening to the voices of the women who had known him, I found it impossible to retain my original view of Shaw as woman's champion, even though I could account for some of the negative reaction— Elizabeth Robins: feminist resentment of his gallantries; Beatrice Webb: jealousy; Virginia Woolf: snobbery. I could no longer trust the man. Could I trust the works? I returned to them, and found I could not. The same ambiguous attitudes toward women Shaw displayed personally are present in his art, where, although ambiguity might be expected, it has often been overlooked.[76]

Shaw increasingly built his plays around women who were stars but not actress-managers, rather than men who were actor-managers but—at least in England—not predisposed toward Shaw. He needed women as go-betweens to advance his interests with men. He knew he could be more effective in persuading women, and did not hesitate to flatter, cajole, and mislead them for his own ends.

In the first years of his marriage, Shaw's calendar of engagements became less harried as he liberated himself from the grind of theatregoing, reviewing, and socialist stumping. He moved out of his mother's house, hired a secretary, and adopted a more regular routine; for these and a variety of other reasons he was better able to concentrate on major works. As a Fabian and benefactor of the London School of Economics, his new wife, Charlotte, was thoroughly integrated in his socialist network of friends and colleagues. She had no connections to the theatre, nor did she desire to cultivate them. That, paradoxically, became Shaw's "private" realm. Narratives (such as Margot Peters's) of Shaw's relationships with actresses have more fodder before his marriage, but there is one very important assignation that preoccupied him in the years 1912–14.

He was fifty-six when he fell "head over ears in love with her—violently and exquisitely in love," and she was forty-seven.[77] Mrs. Patrick (Stella) Campbell's greatest successes in the modernist repertoire were behind her, yet she was as alluring as ever and commanded celebrity status. They had met years before, and Shaw had already modelled at least one play for her, *Caesar and Cleopatra* (1898), though Johnston Forbes-Robertson had to find another leading lady when it was eventually given a few performances in London in 1913 (see Illustration 4). His later, intense infatuation was cultivated alternately at her bedside while she recovered from an illness and the bedside of Shaw's sister Lucy, whose tuberculosis was in the final stages; Shaw and Campbell could meet there without attracting Charlotte Shaw's suspicion. On the occasions of other rendezvous, Charlotte Shaw thought he was attending rehearsals for *John Bull's Other Island*. He always caught the last train home, but just barely.

The wooing had *Pygmalion* as its pretext: Shaw wanted Campbell for Eliza, she wanted the role, but a leading man and manager had to be found. The liaison was persistent and, evidently, more serious than usual. Shaw tried to minimize the consequences at home, but Charlotte felt compelled to seek advice from Beatrice Webb, who had been witness to virtually all of Shaw's assignations. It seems that in middle life Shaw regressed to the flirtatious manner that characterized his earliest years as a socialist:

> One used to watch these faults leading to all sorts of rather cruel philanderings with all kinds of odd females. But I had certainly thought he had outgrown this business. Though I was alarmed by it as a symptom of intellectual deterioration, it never occurred to me that it meant emotional disturbance.

Shaw's friendship with the Webbs was severely strained during this period, and Beatrice was not disposed to be unnecessarily kind to either of the Shaws.

> From what I recollect of GBS's chatter about Mrs. Pat the relationship is one of gross mutual flattery, each pandering to the other's morbid craving for the recognition of unique genius. It is remarkable how long Charlotte has kept his volatile nature attached to her. . . . The present obsession, reacting on declining vigour, may be more serious. Formerly he was always quite detached and he could pull himself up when he chose. He allowed himself to be adored, I never knew him adore. In this case I gather that he is the fly and the lady the spider.[78]

The liaison grew into a serious threat to the Shaw's marriage—at least as far as the husband was concerned. When Campbell sought some privacy to study her part in Barrie's *The Adored One*, Shaw followed her uninvited to the south coast, attempting to engineer the consummation of his lust.

She beseeched him to leave her alone, but he was heedless to hints and ultimata alike. She escaped by giving him a false rendezvous time, and he returned to London, thoroughly routed.

The Adored One was a failure, and Campbell quickly picked up *Pygmalion* (see Illustrations 5 and 6). A production at His Majesty's Theatre with Herbert Beerbohm Tree was arranged for the spring of 1914. Any romantic aspirations on Shaw's part were irrevocably ruptured when Campbell eloped with George Cornwallis-West just a few days before *Pygmalion* was scheduled to open.[79] They disappeared the very day his divorce from Lady Randolph Churchill was finalized. Altogether, Shaw's experience was painful and possibly humiliating, but it was extremely fruitful from the artistic point of view. He functioned as Higgins, the self-styled benefactor of Campbell/Eliza, thwarted by her preference for a younger, less intellectual man, Cornwallis-West/Freddy.[80] The relationship also inspired *Overruled, The Music Cure, Heartbreak House*, and *The Apple Cart*, all meditations on adultery. Shaw's only serious flirtation after this was with the American actress Molly Tompkins, a May-November romance.

With *Pygmalion* Shaw resorted to having plays produced in the actor-manager system he professed to detest. It should be emphasized that though he railed against actor-managers, he sought their support from the outset and would not have garnered half his fame so quickly without them. His worst fears were realized at His Majesty's, for Tree took tremendous liberties with the text and hammed unrestrainedly, but Shaw counted his royalties and stayed away from the theatre. He knew the cost of dealing in the mainstream and quietly bore the burden. The day after *Pygmalion* opened, Ernita Lascelles, whom Shaw and Barker had coached for Grace Tranfield in a New York production of *The Philanderer*, paid a visit to Shaw. He recorded that she "reviled & spat on me for rolling out to the enemy of the theatre, as she calls Tree. She is not altogether wrong" (CL 3: 228). The play was a resounding success among the playgoing public that preferred Shaw the Comedian; the focus on Eliza's "bloody" expletive (in the third act) in preference to all the social and political matter demonstrates the point most vividly. Expectation of the promised foul word was intense, and the reaction on the first night had not been exceeded since Bill Walker smashed Jenny Hill in the face during *Major Barbara*, a grievous deviation from the gender protocol of violent stage expression.

Shaw's comfort (or at least resignation) in this situation reflects the changes in his life since the mid-1890s. While the Shaws luxuriated in their money, Elizabeth Robins used the profits of *Votes for Women!* to buy a farm in Sussex; it became a haven for recovering suffragist hunger strikers and women medical students, as well as a cauldron of feminist sympathy. Had he the means two decades earlier, Shaw might have done something comparable, but no longer. *Pygmalion* rails against the constrictions of a classed society, yet since his marriage Shaw spent much of his time meandering between town place and country place, and on the holidays and purposeless peregrinations his wife adored. He lived the life of a leisured gentleman—except for the fact that he loathed leisure—and enjoyed all the privileges of high caste. It was extremely comfortable and precisely the life he had been brought up to believe he deserved. When a socialist critic noted that at the first matinee of *Major Barbara* "there were almost as many carriages and motor cars outside the theatre at the first performance as there are in the Mall on a Drawing-room day"[81] (a Buckingham Palace event at which society was introduced to the monarch), Shaw was attracting an audience of his social peers. He had always aligned himself with the upwardly mobile middle classes, and now he was more upward then most.

In 1903 his second term on the St. Pancras local government came to a close. He had been an effective and diligent vestry councillor, attending fortnightly meetings as well as serving on committees. He showed particular interest in issues implicated in the Fabian platform of municipal socialism (such as socialized insurance), advised on the introduction of electricity, and stood up for ancient rights-of-way on public land.[82] In 1904, when he failed to be elected to the London County Council, he terminated his career in formal public service to allow for greater involvement in the theatre. By the end of the decade Shaw had achieved genuine fame and wealth, and proceeded to enjoy both. Beatrice Webb registered the changes with evident disapproval. In her view, his enjoyment of indulgence was impeding the socialist cause.

He and Charlotte are getting every day more luxurious and determined to have everything "just so" without regard to cost or fitting in with other people's convenience. But they are neither of them quite satisfied with their existence. GBS is getting impatient and rather hopeless of his capacity to produce anything more of value; Charlotte is beginning to loathe the theatrical set and is even turning to us to try and interest GBS again in socialism. He and Sidney really like and appreciate each other and they might be, as they have been, of great value in mutual [stimulus?] and criticism. But GBS is bored with discussion; he won't give and take; he will orate and go off on to the sex question, which does not interest Sidney as GBS has nothing positive to propose.[83]

Evidently their friendship was at risk of dissolving along with others in the old Fabian enclave, including Graham Wallas and Sydney Olivier; Granville Barker, who had been so intimate with both Shaws (see Illustration 7), grew estranged after his second marriage. The Webbs grew increasingly despairing over Shaw. Their collaboration in creating a journal, the *New Statesman*, was fleeting. He refused to sign his pieces. "GBS has in fact injured the *New Statesman* by his connection with it; we have had the disadvantage of his eccentric and iconoclastic stuff without the advantage of his name. Lots of people will think any article brilliant that they know is by him, whilst dismissing his anonymous contribution as tiresome and of no account, or as purely mischievous."[84] He made matters worse by writing letters to the *Nation*, the new journal's rival, whenever he was dissatisfied with his colleagues. His participation in the new venture was, necessarily, short lived, though the infamous 1914 composition "Common Sense about the War" was originally published as a supplement to it. Perhaps Shaw sensed the malaise, for soon after he became very attentive at Fabian lectures and business, and offered financial help to the *New Statesman* even though he was no longer a part of it.[85]

His success with *Pygmalion* on the eve of World War I was soon curbed in the United Kingdom and the United States by two factors: wartime preferences for lighter theatrical fare and perceptions of GBS's professed views about the conflict as unpatriotic. He felt strongly about the question of fighting in a just cause and explored the theme in *Androcles and the Lion* (1912) while all Europe armed itself and a conflict grew inevitable. With "Common Sense about the War" his magnificent public esteem was shattered. His contemporaries had an equally profound awakening, leading them to reassess everything they had presumed about Shaw as a political figure. In 1898 Shaw had noted that "public and private life become daily more theatrical: the modern Kaiser, Dictator, President or Prime Minister is nothing if not an effective actor" (CPP 3: 115). Extending this analogy, Shaw went overnight from being a superstar of public commentary to a blacklisted bit player.

NOTES

1. Oscar Wilde, "The Soul of Man Under Socialism," *Fortnightly Review* 49 (1891): 192, 313; reprinted as *The Soul of Man Under Socialism* (Boston: John W. Luce, 1910), 38–9, 43.

2. Ian Britain, *Fabianism and Culture: A Study in British Socialism and the Arts c. 1884–1918* (Cambridge: Cambridge University Press, 1982), 174. This upsurge in membership was probably due to the controversy generated by Barker's *Waste*, which was produced unlicensed at the Imperial Theatre.

3. Ibid., 173–74.

4. Ibid., 187.

5. Ibid., 175.

6. In drama, modernism connotes the experiments in form and style encompassing realism, naturalism, and symbolist abstraction beginning c. 1880. At first rejecting the artifices of the well-made play and extreme theatricalism, by the Royal Court years modernism's attack on bourgeois moral and social values also allowed for patently unreal and subjective visions in styles as disparate as August Strindberg's *Dream Play*, Afred Jarry's *Ubu Roi*, and episodes in Shaw's *Major Barbara* or *Man and Superman*, as well as realism.

7. This is over the two-and-a-half-year period from 18 October 1904 to 29 June 1907 and does not include the proto-season of *Candida* in April and May 1904. See Desmond MacCarthy, *The Court Theatre 1904–1907: A Commentary and Criticism*, ed. Stanley Weintraub (Coral Gables, Fla.: University of Miami Press, 1966), 107–8.

8. Ibid., 19.

9. Production costs for *Henry VIII* were £7,204 (£2,756 was spent on costumes alone), returning a gross profit of approximately £20,000 after 254 performances. See Michael R. Booth, *Victorian Spectacular Theatre, 1850–1910* (Boston and London: Routledge and Kegan Paul, 1981), 158–59.

10. Barker's remarks were made at the dinner in his and Vedrenne's honour at the end of their Royal Court tenancy, 7 July 1907. Reprinted in MacCarthy, *The Court Theatre*, 162–63.

11. Ibid., 163–64.

12. Originally a letter to Matthew Edward McNulty, it was revised and printed in *Collier's Weekly* 69 (24 June 1922); reprinted in Shaw, *The Art of Rehearsal* (New York and Los Angeles: Samuel French, 1928), 6.

13. See William Archer and Harley Granville Barker, *A National Theatre. Scheme & Estimates* (London: Duckworth, 1907), based on a privately printed version, *Scheme & Estimates for a National Theatre* (1904); William Archer, *Henry Irving, Actor and Manager* (London: Field and Tuer, 1883); the introduction to William Archer, *The Theatrical "World" of 1896* (London: Walter Scott, 1897); and "National Theatre in London," *Parliamentary Debates*, Commons, ser. 5, vol. 52 (23 April 1913): 454–95.

14. Dennis Kennedy, *Granville Barker and the Dream of Theatre* (Cambridge: Cambridge University Press, 1985), 99.

15. Arguably, the Royal Shakespeare Theatre predates this. It branched out from a strictly Shakespearean repertoire in the early 1960s but did not have a permanent London home until 1982. Though not strictly "national theatres," the repertory movement fulfilled part of Archer and Barker's vision. See George

Rowell and Anthony Jackson, *The Repertory Movement: A History of Regional Theatre in Britain* (Cambridge: Cambridge University Press, 1984). The Arts Council still exists, though its brief is no longer so comprehensive.

16. Sidney Webb, *Socialism in England* (1889; reprint, London: Carl Slienger, 1977).

17. See Chris Waters, *British Socialists and the Politics of Popular Culture, 1884–1914* (Manchester: Manchester University Press, 1990), esp. 131–55.

18. See George Haw, *Today's Work: Municipal Government, the Hope of Democracy* (1901), cited in ibid., 154.

19. Shaw, *Shaw's Music: The Complete Musical Criticism in Three Volumes*, ed. Dan H. Laurence (New York: Dodd, Mead and Co., 1981), 1: 198, 625–28, 651; 3: 733–39. This theme is introduced very early in Shaw's opus. See *The Irrational Knot* (1880), which opens with a rather dismal demonstration of "top down" musical provisioning; reprinted in *Selected Novels of G. Bernard Shaw* (New York: Caxton House, 1946).

20. Joan Wallach Scott, "Popular Theatre and Socialism in Late-Nineteenth-Century France," in *Political Symbolism in Modern Europe: Essays in Honor of George L. Mosse*, ed. Seymour Drescher, David Sabean, and Allan Sharlin (New Brunswick, N.J.: Transaction Books, 1982), 200. See also Loren Kruger, *The National Stage: Theatre and Cultural Legitimation in England, France, and America* (Chicago and London: University of Chicago Press, 1992), 38.

21. Quoted in Kruger, *The National Stage*, 124.

22. Kruger, *The National Stage*, 125.

23. *Bernard Shaw's Letters to Granville Barker*, ed. C. B. Purdom (New York: Theatre Arts Books, 1957), 154, 182.

24. Alexis de Tocqueville, "Some Observations on the Drama amongst Democratic Nations," in *Democracy in America* (1835); reprinted in Eric Bentley, ed., *The Theory of the Modern Stage: An Introduction to Modern Theatre and Drama* (Harmondsworth and New York: Penguin, 1968), 479.

25. Langdon Everard, "Socialism and the Theatre," *Labour Leader* (30 October 1908): 689; quoted in Waters, *British Socialists*, 136–37.

26. Stanley Weintraub, *The Unexpected Shaw: Biographical Approaches to G.B.S. and His Work* (New York: Frederick Ungar, 1982), ix.

27. Ibid., 147.

28. Shaw Papers, draft memorandum of agreement between Vedrenne, Barker, and Shaw, September 1907, Harry Ransom Humanities Research Center, University of Texas at Austin. The salaries allowed Vedrenne and Barker were almost twice what they earned at the Royal Court. There, they agreed to take just £20 a week. See also the letter from Shaw to Vedrenne dated 27 July 1907 in Purdom, *Bernard Shaw's Letters*, 91–92.

29. Technically, they separated their estates, though the cushion of her wealth allowed Shaw to make financial speculations for the first time in his life.

30. Theodore Stier, *With Pavlova Round the World* (London, n.d.); cited in Weintraub, *The Unexpected Shaw*, 141.

31. Shaw, *Fabian Essays in Socialism* (London: Walter Scott, 1889), 25.

32. Shaw, "The Fabian Society: Its Early History. A Paper Read at a Conference of the London and Provincial Fabian Societies at Essex Hall on the 6th February 1892," *Fabian Tract* 41 (1899): 27.

33. Royalties from the Vedrenne-Barker seasons contributed little to this windfall. In 1906 Shaw wrote to Barker that the matinees of *Major Barbara* brought him about £11 a week for three performances. See Shaw's letter to Barker, 21 August 1906, in Purdom, *Bernard Shaw's Letters*, 68–69.

34. Based on figures from 1920–27, after U.S.A. income taxes were deducted, for English language rights only. From Shaw's Diary and Personal Accounts, vol. 2, Harry Ransom Humanities Research Center, University of Texas at Austin.

35. Shaw, letter to Johnston Forbes-Robertson, 15 November 1928, Crane Collection, Theatre Arts Collection, Harry Ransom Humanities Research Center, University of Texas at Austin.

36. Purdom, *Bernard Shaw's Letters*, 171.

37. Shaw, "Socialism for Millionaires," *Contemporary Review* (February 1896); reprinted in *Fabian Tract* 107 (1901): 12, 14.

38. John Galsworthy, *Justice*, in *Galsworthy: Five Plays* (London: Methuen, 1985), 103.

39. Kennedy, *Granville Barker*, 106.

40. Jan McDonald, *The "New Drama" 1900–1914: Harley Granville Barker, John Galsworthy, St. John Hankin, John Masefield* (London and Houndsmill: Macmillan, 1986), 139.

41. Beatrice Webb, entry dated 15 March 1910, *The Diary of Beatrice Webb*, 4 vols., ed. Norman and Jean MacKenzie (Cambridge: Belknap Press of Harvard University Press, 1982–85), 3: 138.

42. In 1922 Shaw wrote the preface to the Webbs's *English Prisons under Local Government*, opening with the statement: "Imprisonment as it exists today is a worse crime than any of those committed by its victims; for no single criminal can be as powerful for evil, or as unrestrained in its exercise, as an organized nation." Reprinted in Shaw, *On Imprisonment* (Chislehurst: Kenion Press, 1944), 7.

43. The text of *Meerut* and production notes by Charlie Mann are reproduced in Raphael Samuel, Ewan MacColl, and Stuart Cosgrove, eds., *Theatres of the Left 1880–1935: Workers' Theatre Movements in Britain and America* (London: Routledge and Kegan Paul, 1985), 106–8, 114–17.

44. Webb, entry dated 29 November 1905, in MacKenzie, *Diary*, 3: 13.

45. Kate Terry Gielgud, *A Victorian Playgoer*, ed. Muriel St. Clare Byrne (London: Heinemann, 1980), 87–88.

46. Webb, entry dated 4 September 1906, in MacKenzie, *Diary*, 3: 49.

47. Ibid., 2 December 1905, 3: 14.

48. Ibid., 3: 10.

49. When the Royal Commission's report came down in 1909, Beatrice Webb wrote a minority report with counterproposals. It advocates the elimination of

parochial relief and both the class and condition termed "pauperism," and recommends much wider powers for central authorities in guaranteeing child welfare, public health, old-age pensions, and assistance for the unemployed. "The Charter of the Poor" (London: Christian Commonwealth Co., [1909]).

50. J. M. Winter, "Bernard Shaw, Bertold Brecht and the Businessman in Literature," in *Business Life and Public Policy*, ed. Neil McKendrick and R. B. Outhwaite (Cambridge: Cambridge University Press, 1986), 197–98.

51. Margot Peters, *Bernard Shaw and the Actresses* (Garden City, N.Y.: Doubleday, 1980), 220.

52. Shaw, *An Unsocial Socialist*, in *Selected Novels of G. Bernard Shaw*, 719.

53. Ibid.

54. Cicely Hamilton, *Marriage as a Trade* (1909; reprint, London: The Women's Press, 1981).

55. Karl Marx and Friedrich Engels, *The Communist Manifesto*, trans. Paul M. Sweezy (New York: Washington Square Press, 1964), 87–88.

56. Ibid., 88. The point is further developed vis-à-vis Shaw in Norbert Greiner, "Mill, Marx and Bebel: Early Influences on Shaw's Characterization of Women," in *Fabian Feminist: Bernard Shaw and Woman*, ed. Rodelle Weintraub (University Park: Pennsylvania State University Press, 1977), 90–98.

57. Marx and Engels, *Communist Manifesto*, 89.

58. See Lisa Tickner, *Spectacle of Women. Imagery of the Suffrage Campaign 1907–14* (London: Chatto and Windus, 1987).

59. From the *Manchester Guardian*, quoted in Kennedy, *Granville Barker*, 171; c.f., Shaw's *Androcles and the Lion* in CPP 4: 594–95.

60. Hamilton, *Marriage as a Trade*, 29.

61. In the context of the U.S.A., the issues are well laid out in Rickie Solinger, *Wake Up Little Susie: Single Pregnancy and Race before "Roe v. Wade"* (New York: Routledge, 1992).

62. See Katherine E. Kelly, "George Bernard Shaw and Suffrage: A Minor Player on the Petticoat Platform," *Shaw* 14 (1994).

63. Sheila Stowell, *A Stage of Their Own: Feminist Playwrights of the Suffrage Era* (Ann Arbor: University of Michigan Press, 1992), 62–64.

64. Ibid., 19.

65. Ibid., 29.

66. Webb, entry dated 13 July 1913, in MacKenzie, *Diary*, 3: 190.

67. Ibid., 27 December 1909, 3: 133.

68. Scott, *Popular Theatre*, 203.

69. Ibid., 204–5.

70. Steve Nicholson, "Responses to the Revolution: The Soviet Union Portrayed in the British Theatre, 1917–29," *New Theatre Quarterly* 8.29 (February 1992): 62–69; and "Bolshevism in Lancashire: British Strike Plays of the 1920s," *New Theatre Quarterly* 8.30 (May 1992): 159–66.

71. Margery M. Morgan, "Edwardian Feminism and the Drama: Shaw and Granville Barker," *Cahiers Victoriens et Edouardiens. Studies in Edwardian and*

Anglo-Irish Drama 9–10 (October 1979): 63–64. Her argument is a development of E. J. Hobsbawm, *Labouring Men* (London: Weidenfeld and Nicholson, 1964), 250–71.

72. Patricia Pugh, "Bernard Shaw, Imperialist," *Shaw* 11 (1991): 102–3.

73. Henry George, *Progress and Poverty: An Inquiry into the Cause of Industrial Depressions, and of the Increase of Want with Increase of Wealth. The Remedy* (New York: D. Appleton and Co., 1881), 503.

74. Webb, entry dated 16 January 1903, in MacKenzie, *Diary*, 2: 267.

75. Peters, *Bernard Shaw*, 304.

76. Margot Peters, "The State and Future of Shaw Research: The MLA Conference Transcript. Biography," *Shaw* 2 (1982): 182.

77. Quoted in Margot Peters, *Mrs. Pat: The Life of Mrs. Patrick Campbell* (London: Hamish Hamilton, 1985), 309.

78. Webb, entry dated 13 July 1913, in MacKenzie, *Diary*, 3: 190–91.

79. Campbell wanted to publish their letters as early as 1921. The correspondence is preserved in a volume edited by Alan Dent, *Bernard Shaw and Mrs. Patrick Campbell: Their Correspondence* (New York: Knopf, 1952). Shaw would not permit publication until both he and Campbell were dead; Campbell guarded her parcel of letters as a legacy that could bring profit to her daughter. The situation was paralleled in 1928 when Edith Craig and Christopher St. John proposed publishing the correspondence between Shaw and Ellen Terry (opposed by Edward Gordon Craig, who resented Shaw's views of Irving). A volume appeared soon after, though an expurgated edition: Christopher St. John, ed., *Ellen Terry and Bernard Shaw: A Correspondence* (New York: G. P. Putnam, 1931).

80. This is explored in Morgan, *Edwardian Feminism*, 82–83.

81. Alex M. Thompson, *Clarion* (8 December 1905): 3; reprinted in T. F. Evans, ed., *Shaw: The Critical Heritage* (London and Boston: Routledge and Kegan Paul, 1976), 155.

82. Alfred D. Corrick, "George Bernard Shaw, St. Pancras Vestryman and Councillor," *St. Pancras Journal* (November-December 1950): 110–12.

83. Webb, entry dated 21 April 1911, in MacKenzie, *Diary*, 3: 157.

84. Ibid., 5 July 1913, 3: 188.

85. Ibid., 13 July and 4 December 1913, 3: 190–92.

Chapter 4

Responses to the Twentieth Century

These instances could easily be multiplied; but they are enough to shew that between a maximum of indulgent toleration and a ruthlessly intolerant Terrorism there is a scale through which toleration is continually rising or falling, and that there was not the smallest ground for the self-complacent conviction of the nineteenth century that it was more tolerant than the fifteenth.

Saint Joan, CPP 2: 303–4

At the outbreak of World War I, Shaw was fifty-eight years old and at the height of his creative abilities. *Pygmalion* was running successfully in London in one of the most commercial venues in the city. Tree's production was not exactly everything Shaw had worked for and advocated in terms of theatrical reform, but it countered decades of critical nay-saying and skepticism about the viability of Shavian plays. Abroad, Shaw had become a fixture of the American and German theatres and was gaining a reputation in a dozen other nations. As a writer, he was an international phenomenon in an increasingly factional political environment. His career seemed set to succeed indefinitely, yet a succession of miscalculations marred the reception of some well-intentioned but (from posterity's point of view) politically ill-informed writings. In his responses to the outbreak of World War I, the communist experiment under Stalin, and the rise of fascism leading to World War II can be read an intellectual history of twentieth-century Europe. On a broader scale, Shaw's writing reflects what are arguably the most significant changes in literary theory and theatrical practice of this century: feminism and postcolonial articulations inspired by socialist thought. Each of these ideas is explored thematically in the following sections, overlapping the chronology of Shaw's life in order to elucidate his various lines of thought.

The British felt the tensions of war as early as 1894, twenty years before a declaration against Germany. While some disputes regarding territories as far flung as Newfoundland, Manchuria, and Morocco were diplomatically settled, a succession of wars in Afghanistan, Korea, Ethiopia, Egypt, the Balkans, Macedonia, China, and southern Africa aligned and realigned the colonial powers of England, France, Italy, Germany, Russsia, and Japan. In 1898, largely fuelled by rivalry with England, Germany committed to plans to enlarge its navy, decisively challenging British supremacy at sea. Herbert Asquith, the British Prime Minister, recognized in 1908 that the Germans' policy made no sense unless they actually wanted war. In its attempt to keep up with the naval buildup, England was nearly bankrupted. By 1914 England (and its empire) was prepared to defend neighbouring France and Belgium against any aggressor, and France was allied with Russia which, like Japan, opposed Germany and Austria-Hungary. These allegiances were reflected elsewhere and magnified by imperialist claims on territories distant from Europe.

The global epithet of the 1914–18 war is aptly assigned. World War I was ostensibly sparked by the assassination of the Austrian Archduke Franz Ferdinand by Serbian nationalists in Sarajevo, but within weeks forces were mobilizing throughout Europe. By the end of the war fifteen European, three Asian, one independent African, one South American, and eight North American, Carribean, and Latin American states had made declarations of war in addition to the automatic entries of Australia, New Zealand, India, and Canada as British allies. War raged on the western front in defense of Belgium and France; on the eastern front in territorial grabs among Germany, Austria-Hungary, and Russia; and farther afield in the North Sea, North and South Atlantic, and Indian Ocean. Colonial properties were contested by Britain, France, Germany, and Portugal in the South Pacific, China, and throughout Africa, while other fronts opened up in the Balkans, Turkey, and the Middle East. Every inhabited continent was at war, the battle lines were drawn in regions as remote as the English Channel and Samoa, trade and shipping were disrupted around the world, while land, natural resources, and manufacturing potentials were contested with every bullet, mine, airplane, submarine, Dreadnought, mustard gas canister, coded dispatch, and propaganda campaign that was launched.

Three and a half months after England entered the hostilities, Shaw published his diatribe "Common Sense about the War" as a supplement to the *New Statesman*. His timing could not have been worse:[1] perhaps two months earlier his opinions might have carried weight, but in November 1914 indignation at the invasion of Belgium was intense; British morale was high, based on confidence that the war would be quickly won; and the day of its publication the Sultan of Turkey announced a jihad against Germany's opponents. Shaw wanted to caution against insisting on heavy war reparations at a time when no one else was even considering peace talks. In his characteristic manner, he told the thinking public what they did not want to think about, arguing that Britain's participation in the war was not just a reaction to the Belgian invasion but rather the result of decades of tension. Spurred on by jingoism on both sides, Germans and Britons alike had been duped by militaristic capitalists into doing everything they could to not honour their responsibility of maintaining the peace. Shaw's quip "the heroic remedy for this tragic misunderstanding is that both armies should shoot their officers and go home to gather in their harvests in the villages and make a revolution in the towns" did not go down well.[2] The press was full of fear and loathing for the enemy, inflating German credentials in order to stir support for British policies, whereas Shaw urged a view more proportional to the situation and the limitations of human nature:

O, my brother journalists, if you must revile the Prussians, call them sheep led by snobs, call them beggars on horseback, call them sausage eaters, depict them in the good old English fashion in spectacles and comforter, seedy overcoat buttoned over paunchy figure, playing the contra-bass tuba in a street band; but do not flatter them with the heroic title of Superman, and hold up as magnificent villainies worthy of Milton's Lucifer these common crimes of violence and raid and lust that any drunken blackguard can commit when the police are away, and that no mere multiplication can dignify.[3]

This kind of comment was widely misinterpreted as unpatriotic, and Shaw found himself in the midst of heated controversy.

In fact, Shaw was not opposed to the military buildup or resulting war. In "Common Sense" he states that Britain should have flexed its power months before and given Germany a good fright. He is almost certainly mistaken, however, in suggesting that this might have averted the conflict indefinitely. He was not opposed to war per se—urging the Anglo-French interests to resist invasion vigorously and cheering Russia's cause against

Austria—but opposed the militarism that Germany embodied in its belief that the conquest of neighbours is the "foundation of national greatness."[4] He was very critical of the British government's unpreparedness and particularly of its methods of raising and training the army.[5] He proclaimed himself in favour of compulsory service (some of which could be military)[6] but criticized the government for offering foot soldiers such low wages and their widows such pitiful pensions that no working-class person could be blamed for not signing up. "Common Sense about the War" takes some extraordinary positions, but the list of grievances on the issue of recruiting is consistently socialist: it should suffice for a soldier to swear allegiance to his country, rather than to God and king; there should be more working-class representation in the War Office; and wages should be guaranteed to demobilized soldiers until they can secure peacetime employment. His suggestion that in the future there would be only two flags, the red of socialists and the black of capitalists, is pure fantasy.

It was not the time for speculative fantasy any more than irony. Shaw's "final solution" is the driest of mocks at a situation that could so easily be reversed:

> Those Germans who took but an instant to kill had taken the travail of a woman for three-quarters of a year to breed, and eighteen years to ripen for the slaughter. All we have to do is to kill, say, 75 per cent of all the women in Germany under sixty. Then we may leave Germany her fleet and her money and say "Much good may they do you!"[7]

It is a compelling argument, rife with humanism and (allowing for irony) pacifist good sense, but one that the British were not prepared to take to heart. Instead, Shaw was condemned as a socialist who cared nothing for the success of his country's cause. By arguing that the welfare of the world was more important than that of any particular nation, he went from literary superstar to reviled traitor virtually overnight. If he was trying to find a role for himself as a socialist in the midst of international carnage, this, clearly, was not one that was going to be tolerated.

The suffragists who had been somewhat successful in attracting politicians' attention to domestic issues before the war immediately capitulated and declared a cessation of gender hostilities as soon as England entered the field. Even among the nonmilitant suffragists, extremely few declared themselves conscientious objectors. Many of the activists served with distinction on the Continent, driving supplies, tending the wounded, and carrying out logistics functions. Whether this service was rewarded by the limited franchise in 1918 or whether the government simply could not resist female suffrage any longer is not appropriately debated here. The point is that in contrast to Shaw, English feminists opposed war yet gave all their energies to their country. Christabel Pankhurst responded to "Common Sense about the War" in a *New York Times* op-ed piece, pointing out the sense of betrayal that the celebrated Irishman stirred up in his English hosts:

> Mr. Shaw is . . . in no danger whatever of being lynched. He is in far more danger of having the Iron Cross conferred upon him by the Kaiser in recognition of his attempt to supplement the activities of the official German Press Bureau. But if he were a German subject, writing on certain points of German policy as he does upon certain points of British policy, his fate can well be imagined. The only retribution that will come upon this man, who exploits the freedom of speech and pen that England gives him, is that his words lose now and henceforth the weight they used to have.[8]

J. M. Barrie, Arnold Bennett, Henri Bergson, G. K. Chesterton, Arthur Conan Doyle, John Galsworthy, Cunninghame Graham, H. Rider Haggard, Gerhart Hauptmann, Jerome K. Jerome, Rudyard Kipling, Maurice Maeterlinck, Romain Rollard, and H. G. Wells all came out in opposition to Shaw.[9] He was perceived as "bitter, extreme, and in purpose destructive" in addition to mistaken in his narration of the antecedents of the war.[10] His conceit was intolerable and his sense of comic timing reprehensible.

Excused by age for not volunteering for service, Shaw laid low in his country home north of London for most of two years. One of the comediettas of this period, *The Inca of Perusalem*, was produced in Birmingham, Dublin, and Belgium in 1916–17. The title character, also known as Allerhöchst (Highest of All), is clearly likened to the German kaiser, though the British licence forbade a close resemblance in makeup. It is a rather gentle reminder that the middle class should not take warlords seriously but should stand up to them, for the Inca's analysis of his people is very acute. They would not let him impose taxes to support life, but now that war provides all kinds of horrible deaths, they happily cooperate and display excellent morale. This makes the people as culpable as the Inca in waging war.

In another short play of 1916, *Augustus Does His Bit*, a blustering colonel is duped out of a list of antiaircraft battlements by an engaging woman who acts on a bet with the colonel's brother in the War Office. A fifty-seven-year-old clerk who sees through the whole system looks to his own advantage by joining up. It was a very thinly veiled satire of Shaw's treatment in the aftermath of "Common Sense about the War," and through a production by the Stage Society, it served as a truce between him and the government. Soon after he was invited to visit Flanders and observe the war firsthand. Another of his plays, *O'Flaherty, V.C.*, was performed in Belgium in 1917 during this visit. Dubbed by Shaw "a recruiting poster in disguise" (CPP 5: 125), it mocked English attempts to recruit the Irish by trying to appeal on all the wrong grounds. Beyond the cultural satire, the message was that the army would have no men at all if domestic life in any nation was bliss.

Shaw's most significant play of this period is *Heartbreak House*, a three-act meditation on the war. It was extremely uncharacteristic of Shaw to have stretched its composition and release over a long period (writing most of it in 1916, revising in 1917, and holding publication until 1919), indicating his determination to perfect what he hoped would be regarded as a masterpiece. It received its premiere in New York under the auspices of the new Theatre Guild which, in the 1920s, produced a succession of Shaw's plays along with some of the most significant European and American expressionist writing: Georg Kaiser's *Man and the Masses*, Elmer Rice's *The Adding Machine*, and a number of Eugene O'Neill's works beginning with *Strange Interlude*. *Heartbreak House* came early in the guild's history, and though Shaw wrote it with Chekhov's plays (the Stage Society had done *The Cherry Orchard* before the war) and the Bloomsbury set in mind, symbolist and expressionist presentational techniques are not incompatible. The New York production was successful, but the English premiere a year later was not.

Heartbreak House is prescient, reflective, comedic, and tragic in turns. A variation on the English country house weekend play (like *Misalliance*) with a matchmaking hostess, eccentric relatives, and ill-matched guests bustling around a set that resembles an old-fashioned ship, it settles down in the third act to an almost entirely static meditation of intensely metaphoric prose punctuated by "a sort of splendid drumming in the sky" produced by a German Zeppelin passing overhead (CPP 1: 577). The most profound questions of survival are tossed around in the languorous mood of stargazers at a pyjama party. Hector Hushabye, the debonair man of action devoid of anything to act upon, predicts that either humankind will soon become "history" in the scope of evolution or heaven will wreak calamity and destruction and obliterate the species. The prospects for saving the country—let alone the species—are bleak. Lady Utterword, the hostess's sister, married to a colonial governor, offers her husband's formula: "give Hastings the necessary powers, and a good supply of bamboo to bring the British native to his senses: he will save the country with the greatest ease" (CPP 1: 583). Mazzini Dunn, the go-between who makes fortunes for others but never for himself, is far too scrupulous to engineer a deus ex machina. Boss Mangan, the millionaire for whom Dunn works, is revealed as a pawn of capitalists and syndicalists with no resources of his own. Captain Shotover, the ancient mariner who presides over the house, is an ingenious inventor but derives his inspiration from rum. His miscegenated daughters, Lady Utterword and Hesione Hushabye, are fascinating and lovely but construct themselves from artificial components. The ingenue Ellie Dunn announces her marriage to Shotover, her "spiritual husband and second father," and completely deflates her fiancé, Mangan (CPP 1: 586). Secrets are told in such rapid succession that Mangan likens it to being bombarded by missiles.

The house itself functions allegorically as a ship of state, a ship of fools, or a ship floundering at sea and about to break up on the rocks. The house, like England after the war or the world devoid of its Victorian moral codes, is adrift. Shotover asks, "Do you think the laws of God will be suspended in favour of England because you were born in it?" but the question is political, not theological (CPP 1: 594). No one seems able to do anything to affect the ship's or nation's course. Mazzini gives voice to what the most discouraged Fabian, including Shaw, might have felt at the time:

MAZZINI. I joined societies and made speeches and wrote pamphlets. That was all I could do. But, you know, though the people in the societies thought they knew more than Mangan, most of them wouldnt have joined if they had known as much. You see they never had any money to handle or any men to manage. Every year I expected a revolution, or some frightful smash-up: it seemed impossible that we could blunder and muddle on any longer. But nothing happened, except, of course, the usual poverty and crime and drink that we are used to. Nothing ever does happen. It's amazing how well we get along, all things considered. (CPP 1: 592)

Just when Mazzini concludes that nothing will ever happen, they hear a dull explosion in the distance. The stage blacks out, seemingly a metaphor of apocalypse. The symbolic is quickly overturned in favour of the realistic, for the blackout is ordered by the police. The realistic is quickly overturned by the symbolic as Hector insists on turning up every light in the house and setting a beacon. The realistic and symbolic merge when it is discovered that the explosion destroyed the rectory and the rector is homeless. The servants run to the cellar and the two practical men of business—Mangan and a burglar—take cover in a nearby gravel pit. The second explosion lands squarely on the gravel pit, detonating Shotover's magazine of dynamite and utterly destroying the two parasitic men of business. Members of the pyjama party feel intense expectation, but the final explosion is more distant. Safety is equated will dullness, and Hesione and Ellie are given the last word, intensely hoping for the Zeppelin's return the next night.

Hearbreak House resists coming to firm closure on any ideas. Like Bertolt Brecht, Shaw leaves the audience thinking about the issues at hand and puts the onus on them to take action. Spectators' self-identification with any of the characters is encouraged, though the revelations of their secrets and plasticity is supposed to forestall emulation. It is a deeply pessimistic comment on the upper-middle class viewing the war as a fireworks display detonated for their amusement while others are blown to smithereens. Aestheticization of airborne carriers of destruction—or in Hesione's words, "it's splendid: it's like an orchestra: it's like Beethoven"—is satirized, for the real consequences of war are death, maimed bodies, and widespread homelessness (CPP 1: 595). Shaw relentlessly forces his audiences to watch the aesthetes, giving the barest details of horror which *must* have resonated on quite a different pitch in spectators so recently subjected to the anxiety if not the sight of war. Instead of giving the postwar playgoing public a musical or other escapist froth, Shaw gently led them through a country house weekend amidst familiar characters bumbling their way toward global calamity.

The Shaws were frequently rattled by bombs as they waited out the war, though none made a direct hit on their property. For once, in *Heartbreak House*, Shaw is not laughing off a situation and projecting an evolutionary improvement in the imagined future of an unwritten last act. Like most of his plays, it draws on real acquaintances for character sketches, but beyond that it also draws on real circumstances of war and their aftermath. *Heartbreak House* is deeply pessimistic, playing heavily on allegory and irony as in the strains of "Keep the Home Fires Burning," a sentimental World War I tune which fades in as the Zeppelin's roar diminishes.

There were good reasons to be pessimistic. By mid-1917 pacifist sentiment ran high in many countries on both sides of the conflict, but repeated attempts at peace talks led to nothing better than an impasse. In April 1917 the U.S.A. finally joined the Allies, contributing mainly to containment of the German advances on the western front. In May 1917 the Socialist Congress met in Stockholm, proposing disarmament, arbitration, freedom of the seas, and restoration of occupied territory; the pact was strongly supported by the Russians, Germans, Austrians, and Scandinavians, but England, France, and the U.S.A. refused their delegates passports so they were completely left out of negotiations. By November 1917, following the Bolshevik Revolution, Russia strongly advocated peace and restoration of territories, opening discussions with Germany and Austria-Hungary. Like Shaw, V. I. Lenin regarded the war as a capitalist and imperialist exercise. It severely hampered Lenin's ability to contain civil unrest throughout Russia and hold on to the far-flung territories. His Commissar for Foreign Affairs, Leon Trotsky, negotiated an armistice, but it failed because the Allied powers, fearing a transfer of troops from the eastern to western front, would not participate in talks. Meanwhile, several independent republics were proclaimed: Poland was released by Germany while the Ukraine, Estonia, Finland, Moldavia (later joined with Rumania), and Latvia broke from Russia.

For a time, Germany gained power and influence in the east, but by November 1918 the German fleet was mutinying, a revolution in Munich brought about the kaiser's abdication, and a Socialist leader proclaimed a German republic. The Allies forced an armistice in November 1918. Total losses were estimated at ten million people, with Russia suffering the highest numbers of dead and wounded of any combatant. At the cessation of hostilities, the Allies demanded renunciation of earlier treaties made by Russia and Rumania with the belligerents; evacuation of occupied territory including all lands west of the Rhine; transfer of 5,000 locomotives, 150,000 freight cars, 5,000 trucks, and 160 submarines and warships; and further considerations to be worked out at a later date.

Peace talks among seventy nations opened in Paris in early 1919; Germany was excluded until the terms were prepared. Shaw attempted to influence the discussions by publishing *Peace Conference Hints*, which had a relatively large print run of ten thousand copies. He opposed a number of agenda items that suggested lasting peace was not the objective of the talks. He perceived an armaments race developing between the U.S.A. and Britain, particularly through their insistence on sharing preeminence at sea. It was highly likely that other nations would rebel against such hegemony. He opposed the tendency of the Allies to demand "security" instead of disarmament, equally, from all participants in the war. Pooling of military resources for common security was, he believed, the best policy, not the maintenance of huge standing armies through conscription.[11]

The Treaty of Versailles, signed almost six months later, severely restricted Germany's right to maintain an army, navy, air force, or even merchant and fishing fleets. It dictated extraordinary reparations for civilian damage: five billion dollars were demanded from Germany in the first year, with billions more amortized over thirty years and additional burdens on Austria and Bulgaria. Before long, Germany was forced to borrow in London, precipitating a spiral of debt, neglect of its infrastructure, and economic calamity which could only be arrested by defaulting on the loans. The treaty was ratified by Germany, Austria, France, Britain, Italy, and Japan but not by the U.S.A.

As Shaw predicted in "Common Sense about the War," a congress of powers from Europe and the U.S.A. was proposed at the armistice talks. The League of Nations's aims were collective security, establishment of a world court to settle disputes through legal arbitration, and restoration of trade and prosperity around the globe.

> The Covenant provided that members should give mutual protection against aggression according to means decided upon by the Council, submit to arbitration, judicial settlement or Council enquiry into any disputes likely to lead to a rupture, and abstain from war until three months after an award. All treaties between members which conflicted with these obligations were invalid, but not "treaties of arbitration or regional understanding like the Monroe Doctrine, for securing the maintenance of peace." The League was to seek solutions to problems of disarmament, run the new Permanent Court for International Justice, to which it was hoped all nations would submit disputes, create the International Labour Organization, which non-members might also join, and direct health, educational and administrative commissions.[12]

This would have been a positive measure if all powers had been equitably represented: Germany did not serve on the council until 1926 and resigned along with the Soviet Union, Italy, and Japan seven years later; the U.S.A. never joined. It was an almost exclusively European organization, dominated by England and France.

Shaw's idea of making a committee of international cooperation a vital force in world politics was not realized until the creation of the United Nations and UNESCO in 1945 and 1946. He believed in making countries accountable to the League of Nations for armaments buildups and legislating the legality of new types of weapons, but not using it as the world's police force. His vision of replacing violence between nations with law was not realized. The League failed utterly in sanctioning through conscience because its founders were too determined to preserve the interests of the victors of World War I. In 1929 Shaw was able to express enthusiasm for the League insofar as it resembled the Fabian way of governing: "The really great thing that is happening at Geneva is the growth of a genuinely international public service, the chiefs of which are ministers in a coalition which is, in effect, an incipient international Government."[13] Nevertheless, another of his earlier predictions, that "we will endure oppressions and masteries from one another [i.e., Ireland, Scotland, and Wales under the English parliament]; but we will suffer no other state on earth to master us, or to have the means of mastering us,"[14] which applied equally to Germany's resentment of England and France, is the one proved by time. Likewise, there was enhanced nationalism in the British dominions as well as in Ireland, India, and the colonies of Egypt and Palestine, which brought additional strain on British hegemony.

The working out of these strains is amply demonstrated in the Shavian dramatic opus. Both the antecedents of World War I and its consequences are theatricalized and theorized by Shaw in his twentieth-century writings. In dramatic form, these enormously complex situations somehow become manageable. In *Too True to Be Good* (1931), for example, Shaw sets out several relationships usually taken as hierarchical distinctions but instead depicts them as mere role-play situations. This allows him to question the basis of the social order after World War I, propose what is most likely to produce change commensurate with the priorities of the left, and set an agenda for literati and politicians to rationalize twentieth-century culture. Three of the relationships are servant and master, implicating the responsibilities of indentured labourers under capitalism; soldier and ranking officer which, unlike servant and master, maintains authority under compulsions other than economic (Shaw also questions the likelihood of competent individuals rising to the top and wanting to stay there); and English and "native" Other, usually likened respectively to the "higher" intellectual and "lower" sexual centers supposed to exist in everyone to one extent or another, commensurate with individuals' "advancement" or societies' "civilization," with implications for entitlement to the fruits of capitalism. Shaw does not break down these binaries, but he does demonstrate their hypocrisy by inverting the casting in *Too True to Be Good*: when everyone is stripped of the lies that determine their hypocritical behaviours, they find that the world is opposite to what they were led to expect by Western instruction and conditioning. This realization parallels Shaw's metaphor of individuals and societies going from sickness to robust good health. It is, in many respects, Shaw's overarching agenda for both his political and dramatic writing in the twentieth century. It is implicit everywhere in his critiques of imperialism, nationalism, and the struggle toward postcolonial status for the remnants of empires struggling toward self-determination. Each term is discussed in detail in the following section.

As popular as socialism had been in everyday discourse from 1885 to 1895, imperialism took the focus from 1895 to 1905. Fabians did not agree on the desirability of imperialism—the economic and political colonization of Africa, Asia, and the Americas by "first" and "second world" highly industrialized states—or how it aided or impeded socialist change, though the predominant opinion was that imperialism worked as an instrument of capitalism. In 1896 a Fabian report asserted that when armies are deployed in order to preserve imperial interests, it is speculators who benefit most. Citizens in the imperialist nations put up with this because war is popular. Nationalization of industries at home, according to the report, would reduce if not eliminate the possibility of such speculation, particularly if the major industrialized nations (at that time the U.S.A., England, Germany, and France) nationalized industries simultaneously. This would also serve to reduce friction between these nations, and hence the possibility of war at home and in their colonies.[15] Fabians did not have the opportunity to prove the second part of the analysis, though the first part was amply tested in the Boer War of 1899–1902. The war fueled intense jingoism and patriotic bluster on behalf of the military actions to preserve British dominance of southern African territories in the face of Boer and Afrikaner settlers' desire for autonomy. The militarist mood that pervaded England at the beginning of the new century was not conducive to furthering socialist reforms. The Fabian Society debated the Boer War, and Shaw, who sat on the executive committee and sided with the majority, was accused of focusing too exclusively on the political aspects at the expense of ethical and economic considerations.[16]

During this period the meaning of "imperialism" was far from universally agreed upon, and it is essential to check the context of its use. It appears in economic arguments, positively contrasted with the "sordid interests" that dominate jingoist attitudes. It appears in racialist arguments of evolutionary superiority whereby Europeans, but particularly the English, justified their domination of other peoples because, it was supposed, what was good for England was good for the world. This is wittily debunked in *The Simpleton of the Unexpected Isles* (1934) when various sectors of the British Empire dispatch opinions of the polygamous marriage of a Church of England minister back to his remote Pacific colonial home:

HYERING [the governor]. Number one from the English admiral. "If the polygamist-adulterer Hammingtap is not handed over by noon tomorrow" that is today "I shall be obliged to open fire on Government House." Number two, from the commander of the Bombay Squadron. "Unless an unequivocal guarantee of the safety and liberty of Mr. Hammingtap be in my hands by noon today" that came this morning "I shall land a shore party equipped with machine guns and tear gas bombs to assist the local police in the protection of his person." (CPP 6: 582)

Shaw believed in the appropriateness of giving different colonies different degrees of autonomy, depending on their degree of "civilization" (European-like qualities). His apostasy went only so far. He recognized that "we thus have two Imperial policies: a democratic policy for provinces in which the white colonists are in a large majority, and a bureaucratic policy where the majority consists of colored natives."[17] Thinking of India, an instance of the latter scenario, he predicted rebellion on the grounds of self-determination rather than Marxist revolution:

If we persist in the lazy policy of treating them like children, and adducing their submission as a proof that they are incapable of a share in government, until they rebel . . . then, after a long period of ill-will, during which they will be a menace to the Empire instead of a buttress, they *will* rebel; and their rebellion will prove our incapacity for governing, not theirs for being governed. In fact, our first duty to our subjects is to make them as independent of our guidance, and consequently as appreciative of our partnership, as possible.[18]

Not even Shaw could beat the white solipsism of the turn of the century: he was always at the centre of the universe he perceived.

Thus, imperialism projects economic, diplomatic, and military policy in tandem with nationalism, racism, and solipsistic definitions of the world order. The British Empire was indeed "something more than a geographical expression" (CPP 5: 741). In this period socialists did not necessarily distinguish between the "lofty and public-spirited" aims of societies such as the Fabians and the use of the same rhetoric in support of imperialist entrenchment abroad,[19] as if no one caught Shaw's joke of British tourists encountering vegetarians and a unisexual clergy (married, no less) in *The Simpleton of the Unexpected Isles*:

THE YOUNG WOMAN. I have eaten so much fruit and bread and stuff that I dont feel I want any meat.

THE PRIEST. We shall not offer you any. We dont eat it.

THE Y.W. Then how do you keep up your strength?

THE PRIEST. It keeps itself up.

THE Y.W. Oh, how could that be? (*To the priestess*) You wouldnt like a husband that didnt eat plenty of meat, would you? But then youre a priestess; so I suppose it doesnt matter to you, as you cant marry.

THE PRIESTESS. I am married. . . . I could not be a priestess if I were not married. How could I presume to teach others without a completed human experience? How could I deal with children if I were not a mother?

THE Y.W. But that isn't right. My sister was a teacher; but when she married they took her job away from her and wouldnt let her teach any more.

THE PRIESTESS. The rulers of your country must be mad.

THE Y.W. Oh no. Theyre all right: just like other people. (CPP 6: 553)

Lenin popularized the interpretation of "financial imperialism" whereby imperialism was seen as an economic exercise involving the exploitation of raw materials and labour by capitalists in collusion with their government and its interests. He observed that capital was invested in foreign holdings when the possibility of return on home investments became too marginal. And where capital went, governments went: the French to Tunisia, the British to Egypt, the Germans to Venezuela, and the U.S.A. to Central America. Ultimately, in the Leninist scheme of things, this was a revolutionizing factor for the countries experiencing foreign capitalist exploitation. By 1921 Soviet policy looked to the whole colonial (or "third") world—Asia, Africa, and Latin America—as proto-revolutionary allies. During the Cold War this put the U.S.S.R. at odds with the capitalist strongholds of Europe and the U.S.A. on ideological grounds implicating economic as well as political systems. According to the superpowers' rhetoric, the U.S.A. and U.S.S.R. were each engaged in a battle to liberate developing nations, yet from the perspective of the "liberated," this quest to influence the widest sphere resulted in puppet regimes, extraordinary oppression, and economies geared to foreign needs just as under the colonial masters of the nineteenth century.

Shaw develops the dependency-independence nexus somewhat differently. In plays dating back to the turn of the century, he depicts the constant military threat maintained by the industrialized nations over their colonies, highlighting the strategies that keep even semiautonomous peoples from rising definitively against oppressors. In *Misalliance*, for example, Shaw relates Lord Summerhay's stories of his governorship of the colony of Jinghiskahn, allegorically linking the governance of colonies to the play's main theme, the raising of children. In both instances the child and the native Jinghiskahnians desire to "affirm their manhood." As governor, Summerhay sat back, let the Jinghiskahnians become so irked that they transgressed the colonial law, then had the police exercise the full force of their authority, making prisoners out of citizens. Like so many parents, his governance by force or fraud was perfectly acceptable to him when law and persuasion were less efficient. Through this allegory Jinghiskahnians are infantilized both by their similarities to the children actually portrayed in the play and by their subjection to the colonizers' power (CPP 4: 189–91). It is significant, however, that the power is vested in men, and thus the colonized are not only infantilized but feminized circumstantially. This is the classic formula of male-as-colonizer and woman-as-colonized exposed by feminist critics.

Captain Brassbound's Conversion depicts the same suturing together of colonizing, infantilizing, and feminizing elements. In 1899, when Shaw struggled to persuade Ellen Terry to accept the role of Lady Cicely Waynflete (which he had written expressly for her), he proclaimed that as Lady Cicely she would stand at the border of colonist and colonial. His plea, contained in an 1899 letter to Terry, includes a character study setting Lady Cicely in the context of world politics:

I—poor idiot!—thought the distinction of Ellen Terry was that she had this heart wisdom, and managed her own little world as Tolstoy would have our Chamberlains & Balfours & German Emperors & Kitcheners & Lord Chief Justices and other slaves of false ideas & imaginary fears manage Europe. I accordingly give you a play in which you stand in the very place where Imperialism is most believed to be necessary, on the border line where the European meets the fanatical African, with judge on the one hand, and indomitable adventurer-filibuster on the other, said ind-adv-fil pushing forward 'civilization' in the shape of rifles & pistols in the hands of Hooligans, aristocratic *mauvais sujets* and stupid drifters. . . . I try to shew you fearing nobody and managing them all as Daniel managed the lions, not by cunning—above all, not by even a momentary appeal to Cleopatra's stand-by, their passions, but by simple moral superiority. It is a world-wide situation, and one totally incomprehensible to

Cleopatras of all sorts and periods. . . . Here then is your portrait painted on a map of the world—and you prefer Sargent's Lady Macbeth! [the portrait of Terry based on Irving's production] . . . Here is a part which dominates a play because the character it represents dominates the world—and you think it might do for Mrs P[atrick]. C[ampbell].! . . . In every other play I have written—even in Candida—I have prostituted the actress more or less by making the interest in her partly a sexual interest. . . . In Lady Cicely I have done without this, and gained a greater fascination by it. (CL 2: 98–99)

The opening sentence casts Terry as the supreme commander of her own empire at a point in time when her acting partnership with Irving and the Lyceum company was most uncertain, calling her livelihood into question for the first time since 1875. Irving needed an ingenue, not a mature actress as experienced as himself and in full command of her abilities. Shaw urged Terry to strike out on her own—in his play—and establish a theatrical empire in her own right. *Captain Brassbound's Conversion* is set in Morocco and depicts the values of an intrepid "lady traveller" amidst European and African hosts. She is accompanied by her brother-in-law Sir Howard Hallam (an aged English judge accustomed to dispensing justice) and Brassbound (the disreputable captain of the ship *Thanksgiving*) on an excursion into the Atlas Mountains. Unbeknownst to anyone but Brassbound, he is Sir Howard's nephew; he seeks revenge on Sir Howard for neglectfully allowing his deceased brother's Brazilian property to fall into the hands of a land agent rather than Brassbound's widowed mother and for subsequently (when Sir Howard's professional situation allowed him to travel to Brazil) securing the estate for himself rather than enquiring whether his brother might have an heir. Brassbound arranges with Sheik Sidi el Assif to ambush the party and ransom Sir Howard on the pretext that he is an infidel. Back on the coast, Lady Cicely's host hears of the plot and persuades an American man-of-war to anchor in Mogador harbour. Sidi's superior, Cadi Muley Othman el Kintafi, bears the news of the threatened gunboat diplomacy to the mountain hideaway, where the captors comply with the demand that the hostages be returned to Mogador lest the man-of-war devastate the Moroccan coast.

Shaw's reference to Lady Cicely's "simple moral superiority" equates to her staunch belief that by treating everyone in the same polite manner—greeting them with a handshake and a "Howdyedo?"—they will welcome and respect her. She believes herself welcome in everyone's house and levels all classes and races with her behaviour. Shaw does not portray her interacting with women—she is the only female character in the play—but this serves doubly to emphasize the idea that her unorthodox predilection to travelling alone throughout Africa makes her neither exactly masculine nor feminine, while she bears the power to emasculate, feminize, and infantilize others. Her open-mindedness and lack of racial bias suggest she supersedes the constructs of colonialism practised by men (particularly Sir Howard, who frequently invokes the wrath of the Colonial Office when he is threatened, and the captain of the man-of-war, who first turns his guns toward Morocco then represents Justice presiding over the legitimately vengeful Brassbound), while she simultaneously imposes a form of inter-personal colonialism on the men around her. She plays the Great White Nurse when one of Brassbound's sailors is shot, treating his wounds, stitching him a sling, then without hesitating repairing Brassbound's jacket and reducing him to childlike status. Lady Cicely accepts none of the class-bound prejudices of English society and sees no need to perpetuate them in Africa, yet she orders the sailors to wash the ingratiating Cockney Felix Drinkwater, transforming him from mud hues to a flaming redhead, as readily as she dresses Brassbound in her diplomat brother's formal wear in preparation for his trial. She would have the same scrubbing down and dressing up done to the Moorish castle in which she is temporarily housed. There is no escaping the commands for cleanliness and order from this thoroughly British eccentric.

Lady Cicely is Shaw's reading of Terry's essential self, intended to be complimentary at a point when their flirtation was most intense. The last passage of the letter is noteworthy, for Shaw claims that Lady Cicely is the only female role he had written up to that time that did not deploy an actress's sex appeal to hold the stage. Lady Cicely believes her "How-dyedos" elicit the best in people:

LADY CICELY. Why do people get killed by savages? Because instead of being polite to them, and saying Howdyedo? like me, people aim pistols at them. Ive been among savages—cannibals and all sorts. Everybody said theyd kill me. But when I met them, I said How-dyedo? and they were quite nice. The king always wanted to marry me. (CPP 1: 617)

Relying on the "natural gentility" of men with kind faces, she has seen much of the world and written about it for the *Daily Mail*. But Shaw's characters do not agree with their creator about Lady Cicely's allure. Indeed, Sheik Sidi is instantaneously fascinated by Lady Cicely while

Captain Brassbound (not exactly a king, yet commander of a ship) in the last moments of the play makes a pitch to marry Lady Cicely, and she nearly agrees. Like other Shavian heroines embodying the Life Force, she pulls men in by fascinating them, which is a sexual attraction above all else. The sound of gunfire from the *Thanksgiving*, the signal that the crew is ready to sail, pulls them both back to reality. Brassbound admits that in his temporary infatuation he "blundered somehow on the secret of command at last," restoring and correcting his "power and purpose" in compromise to something other than the solipsistic masculine (CPP 1: 687). If only Lady Cicely could deploy the same kind of heterogeneous worldview on racial issues.

In *Captain Brassbound's Conversion* Shaw partially reverses the usual formula of male-as-colonizer and female-as-colonized. The white males still colonize the Africans and dispense foreign justice, but the sole female in the play deploys some of the practices of colonialism onto white men while retaining her independence. She is marked strongly by "Englishness" and "femininity," yet she is self-determining and exerts agency according to her own will. The plot and (if illustrations 8 and 9 are anything to go by) the staging emphasize Lady Cicely's pivotal role in interracial relations and the dispensation of justice. In Act II the Moroccan characters wear blackface in keeping with theatrical conventions of the period, just as Marzo makes up with a "swarthy" Italian complexion. This might have eluded interpretations of insidious racism if Brassbound, whom Shaw specifies is "an olive complexioned man with dark southern eyes and hair," had not been played by Frederick Carr as a fair-skinned European (CPP 1: 620). Brassbound is the son of an English father and a Brazilian mother, a person of mixed race sailing autonomously in northern seas, reputed to be a slave trader, tried by a Yankee naval captain, and acquitted solely because Lady Cicely deleted his revenge plot from her testimony. He does not get legal or mercenary satisfaction from his uncle, is "tamed" first by Lady Cicely's sewing then her loan of diplomatic clothes, and is almost seduced by her. In other words, the one character who represents a merging of the European and "savage native" (like Shotover's daughters in *Heartbreak House*) is not allowed to be the Other. As long as he tyrannizes his crew, he commands respect in the mythologized persona of "Black Paquito," but once he comes into contact with Lady Cicely, he is whitewashed, made respectable, and obedient. He functions like Caliban in *The Tempest* whom Laura E. Donaldson describes as "the 'native' Other suffering from the cultural deracination which serves as the intellectual and emotional counterpart to economic enslavement." At least Brassbound manages to escape the firm sense of closure that marriage brings to a text and the projectory of a character's future, avoiding the "order, definitiveness, and stability" that might otherwise be imposed.[20]

Time and again, history has demonstrated how colonized people fear extermination above all else. Faced with extermination to the last child, woman, and man, many native peoples of the Americas and Australia agreed to live on reservations, trading real death for a kind of psychological and emotional death. Anything, even cooperation with their colonizers, was preferable to extermination. It may be that Brassbound represents something of this phenomenon. His way of life, if not his very life, is irrevocably changed, and he returns to the ship with a name synonymous with a legend about native and colonial cooperation resulting in the colonists' preservation by New World plants in New England. The only other model for surviving was one that did not catch the world's attention until 1919: Mahatma Gandhi's campaign of passive resistance and non-cooperation with the British, which Shaw greatly admired. It served to unite disparate Indian peoples against a single colonizer, eventually making independence possible.

Gender analysis of *Captain Brassbound's Conversion* reveals two forms of imperialism: the formal assertion of colonial power by British diplomacy and the U.S.A.'s gunboats, and the informal rule of Lady Cicely over all the men she encounters. Usually, in England's colonies, the colonial governor maintained power by informal means such as liaison with local rulers and maintenance of indigenous judicial systems. In the opening moments of the play, Lady Cicely's host (the Scottish missionary Rankin) admits that despite many years of evangelizing in Africa the Cockney Drinkwater is his only convert, so evidently the mere invitation to assimilate European customs and institutions is not at all effective. Brassbound maintains an economic relationship with Sheik Sidi provided he does not escort Christian men through the inland territory. This is neither control nor occupation on Brassbound's part, and the Moroccans gain without losing. Shaw constructs this as a balanced stasis among religions, races, and finances. The woman, Lady Cicely, creates a temporary diversion largely because she does not possess the passionate nature ascribed to women by Christian and Muslim cultures. Sheik Sidi exempts women from his travel ban on the grounds that women have no souls so cannot be infidels. He does not reckon on a woman like Lady Cicely. Ironically, she is also the only traveller not seeking to create change. Morocco's escape from her, like Brassbound's escape from marriage, is "glorious."

Like an imperialist power, Lady Cicely exercises control over men even when she seems to defer ultimate legal authority to a figure such as the American gunboat captain. But despite the Moroccans' being played in blackface, it is not they but Lady Cicely who is "othered": she is the exotic, unfathomable, irresistibly alluring creature whose values neither the European nor Moroccan men can comprehend. Despite Shaw's challenge to the formula—particularly in his depictions of a woman in control—Woman once again becomes the object of colonization. The whites in *Captain Brassbound's Conversion* are not successful colonizers in terms of religion, but with military might they hold the balance of power and the arbitration of law. Lady Cicely controls the controllers, yet still she becomes the object of mystery and attraction that perpetuates the cycle of imperial conquest.

Nationalism is one of the forces that helps the oppressed resist colonialism and attempt to forge a *post*colonial identity and governance. For the Dutch-descended Boers and Afrikaners seeking autonomy from British rule in southern Africa, the nationalist impulse was temporarily defeated in the Boer War, while Indians were entirely successful in gaining home rule after World War II. Despite the fact that the Boer War was based on one set of colonial descendents battling a more recent immigration wave, whereas India's independence was advocated by indigenous peoples of the Asian subcontinent, nationalism is the common principle. Like imperialism, however, the meaning of nationalism was in dispute in the early twentieth century. Between the two world wars it tended to operate in Europe as a justification for totalitarianism and violence, hence the fascists' choice of "National Socialist Party" (elided to "Nazi") to connote their desire for pan-German unification into both a political and ethnic identity. While in some areas of the globe—such as India and Shanghai—nationalism connoted positive qualities of self-determination and national self-fulfillment, in other areas—such as Germany—it was manifest in the negative extremes of demagoguery and ethnic intolerance. The same racist and evolutionist rationalization for colonizing and controlling "lesser" peoples abroad applied to glorifying unconditionally the "master race" in Germany.

Between the two world wars Shaw deployed the concept of nationalism in two contexts, overlapping their referentiality and letting the events of five centuries impinge on his early-twentieth-century message. The contexts are the struggle for home rule in his native Ireland and the canonization of Joan of Arc, a mystic visionary who led the French to victory against imperialist English occupiers at Orléans in 1428.

In Shaw's view early-twentieth-century Ireland existed in much the same mode and circumstances as in the seventeenth century: religious divisions, living conditions, and preindustrialism (ensured by English suppression of any nascent Irish enterprise) were conditions he grew up with and found unchanged on visits in 1905, 1913, and five more times between 1918 and 1923. Very strong individualism, a national mania for litigation, and deep respect for the law suggested to Shaw that a strong government was wanted and would succeed.[21]

Characteristically, Shaw saw the problems stemming from land owner- ship and the solutions resting in modifications of Henry George and state socialism. Ireland was largely agricultural, and it was on small family holdings that the attention focussed. In 1881 William Gladstone's land act tried to make joint ownership between landlord and tenant possible, but this did not encourage industriousness and maximum productivity. The second land act, in 1903, encouraged tenants to purchase land, while the government contributed the difference between the tenants' purchase offers and the landlords' prices. This proved to be an idealistic and impermanent solution. Shaw discovered on his early-twentieth-century travels in Ireland that

fellows come here and stand a lot of beer and make themselves popular. Then, of course, a good many of these people have got land and they dont know how to manage it. They sell it to anybody who comes along. These fellows come and buy and buy, and the old process [of absentee ownership] is beginning again. The estates are getting re-integrated, and if matters go on as they are at present it is only a question of time when you will have all the old landlordism, but with a new set of landlords.[22]

This is part of the premise behind *John Bull's Other Island* which attracted attention from King Edward VII and the Prime Minister when produced at the Royal Court in 1904–5.

In the years leading up to World War I, many European countries stood at the brink of civil strike, but few so explosively as Ireland. The third Home Rule Bill was introduced to the English parliament in 1912, passed in 1914, but immediately suspended. By that time, conservative Unionist forces had equipped a volunteer army of 100,000 men in the largely Protestant-controlled area of Ulster (the northern counties). In the south arms were collected in preparation for civil war. The Ulster Unionists were determined to maintain political dependency on England, while the Catholics were equally stirred by nationalist impulses to evict the "foreign" colonizers, government, and church that had been present in Ireland for centuries. The bloody 1916 Easter Rising in Dublin launched the inde- pendence movement and the Anglo-Irish War. As Shaw observed, at the end of World War I, "every second street in Europe now contains men who have found out how easy it is to get rid of an opponent by thrusting a bayonet through him or throwing a bomb at him, and are well practised in both operations," and Irish cities were no exception. "To glorify such methods when the practitioners were in the trenches, wholly preoccupied with the Germans, was common prudence: to do so now when they are face-to-face with the hegemonists of their own country is rash madness."[23] He generally regarded civil war as the only justifiable kind of war, yet in this instance nationalist causes resulted in the rending apart of, rather than unification and self-determination for, the whole island. A treaty was drafted in 1921 proposing an Irish Free State in twenty-six out of thirty-two counties, with the remaining six in northeast Ireland under the control of the English parliament. A year of civil war ensued, yet the separation of Eire (the southern republic) from Northern Ireland (Ulster) was finalized in 1925. Shaw predicted as early as 1919 that the partitioning of Ireland would not be tolerated by either side. He preferred a federation between the islands of Great Britain and Ireland that allowed each to form a parliament and manage its own affairs. Domestic governance would reside in each country, though imperial and regional security matters could be the purview of a higher body. He believed Ireland should be a part of the Commonwealth on the same terms as Scotland, or perhaps Canada; though it could not have the geographical independence of Canada or Australia, it could be federated with England.[24]

In his views Shaw was noticeably out of sync with his compatriots, even though his sympathies tended to align with Irish Catholics rather than the misguided Liberals he portrays in Broadbent, the Englishman who proposes to "take Ireland in hand, and by straightforward business habits teach it efficiency and self-help" in *John Bull's Other Island* (CPP 2: 605). He rejected nationalism outright: Ireland for the Irish no matter what the consequences was neither a practical nor desirable slogan, not least of all because it contradicted the inevitability that Ireland would remain beholden to the Catholic church in Rome to rule on issues of birth control and censorship. On economic grounds he believed that home rule per se would not work because once Ireland became prosperous, it would be too tempting for England to reconquer it, just as in the Jacobite Revolt of 1745.[25] He likened the racist rationale of Westerners who feared and oppressed hardworking, prosperous Chinese immigrants to the inevitability of English reconquest of an independent flourishing Ireland, accepted it, and recommended a modified course. He opposed the partitioning of Ireland, as of Jerusalem, and believed—so far, wrongly— that it would not last (CPP 3: 751–53). He had no sympathy for those who sought to renew the Gaelic language and so found himself equally alienated from many of the Irish politicians, artists, and intellectuals who flourished in the early part of the century,[26] yet declined nomination to serve in the Irish Senate. Throughout, it is evident that Shaw identifies *as* an Irish national (albeit an expatriate living abroad) but not strongly *with* the Irish people who must cope with the political solutions that are derived. He recognizes English imperialism, rejects nationalism as a resistive response, and so does not assist in forging a vision of a postcolonial Ireland. He is capable of topical satire, as in *John Bull's Other Island*, and insights into the national psyche, as evident in numerous articles and speeches from the interwar years, but does not break the literary or intellectual mold. Thus, through Ireland he made an attempt to bring some of the colonial circumstances "home" to the centre of the imperialist culture, but manages to make it a very Anglocentric exercise. A similar pattern is evident in *Saint Joan*.

Much of *Saint Joan* was written while Shaw vacationed in Ireland in the early 1920s. "The Troubles," as the manifestations of Irish nationalism and English domination were known, saturate the text. Shaw's precise impetus for dramatizing Joan's life in 1923 is debatable,[27] but the contemporary precedents for this portrayal are not. The two most significant influences are Mary Hankinson and T. E. Lawrence, figures inextricable from feminist and nationalist thought and action. Hankinson was a Fabian, organizer of the summer schools, founder of the Fabian Women's Group in 1906 (an organization in which Charlotte Shaw was also active), and lifelong campaigner for women's rights. Joan may have been the consummate rational dresser of her century, but her desire for reform went much deeper than the sartorial or cosmetic. Her greatest benefactor, Charles VII, after being crowned, speaks the all-time classic speech of the sexist: "If only she would keep quiet, or go home!" (CPP 2: 383). She would not, of course, go home. Like the English suffragists who were granted the right to vote in national elections in 1918 (yet not on equal terms with men until 1928), Joan insisted on enacting her beliefs in the public realm. Like the suffragettes, she was imprisoned and tortured. Shaw relied on the translations of Jules Quichert's transcripts to compose the trial scene, yet recommended Sylvia Pankhurst's experiences to anyone wanting to understand a modern Jeanne d'Arc: by reflecting on the suffragette "you will understand a great deal more about the psychology of Joan, and her position at the trial, than you will by reading the historical accounts, which are very dry."[28]

From his close friend T. E. Lawrence, famous as "Lawrence of Arabia" for his service during World War I, Shaw sketched an unorthodox military leader brought down by narrow-minded superiors and a visonary who foresaw creating a modern state out of feudal holdings, united by a single monarchy. Shaw's Joan, like Lawrence, was a champion of nationalism: in the one case French, in the other Arabian. Whereas Lawrence studied the history, politics, and languages of the Middle East in a university before lending his knowledge to the English Army, Joan studied the ways of the peasant farmers and village artisans, ascribing to God her vision for uniting French speakers to a common cause and expelling the English. In the fourteenth and fifteenth centuries the English sought to maintain control of France in order to dominate its commerce and prevent embargoes on exports from England. Like most wars, the cause of the Hundred Years War between France and England was economic, yet to Shaw's Joan it was to be fought and fuelled by nationalism: "JOAN. They are only men. God made them just like us; but He gave them their own country and their own language; and it is not His will that they should come into our country and try to speak our language" (CPP 2: 329). Her rationale is not shared by the ruling classes, for when the English chaplain Stogumber remarks that Charles (the dauphin) is "only a Frenchman," the Earl of Warwick recoils:

THE NOBLEMAN. A Frenchman! Where did you pick up that expression? Are these Burgundians and Bretons and Picards and Gascons beginning to call themselves Frenchmen, just as our fellows are beginning to call themselves Englishmen? They actually talk of France and England as their countries. Theirs, if you please! What is to become of me and you if that way of thinking comes into fashion? . . . Men cannot serve two masters. If this cant of serving their country once takes hold of them, good-bye to the authority of their feudal lords, and goodbye to the authority of the Church. (CPP 2: 357)

In his astute self-interested analysis, Warwick realizes that Joan would make the king the absolute ruler, centralizing power and weakening the peerage. Secular and religious factions from both sides of the Channel unite to condemn Joan—common enemy of all aristocrats and bishops—for if feudal lords are no longer to be the intermediaries between the people and the monarch, then, by the same logic, priests as the intermediaries between Christians and God are redundant. Her nationalism would lead to a profound social reorganization.

WARWICK. These two ideas of hers are the same idea at bottom. It goes deep, my lord. It is the protest of the individual soul against the interference of priest or peer between the private man and his God. I should call it Protestantism if I had to find a name for it. (CPP 2: 368–69)

Cauchon, the Bishop of Beauvais, sees the parallel:

CAUCHON. As a priest I have gained a knowledge of the minds of the common people; and there you will find yet another most dangerous idea. I can express it only by such phrases as France for the French, England for the English, Italy for the Italians, Spain for the Spanish, and so forth. It is sometimes so narrow and bitter in country folk that it surprises me that this country girl can rise above the idea of her village for its villagers [i.e., communism]. But she can. She does. . . . To her the French-speaking people are what the Holy Scriptures describe as a nation. . . .

WARWICK. Well, if you will burn the Protestant, I will burn the Nationalist [i.e., Pro*test*ant and *Nat*ionalist]. (CPP 2: 369)

There is a limit to cooperation between the various interests: the same competition that inspires all imperialists. Stogumber solipsistically sees that while "England for the English goes without saying" as a "law of nature," so any attempt to deny "to England her legitimate conquests, given her by God because of her peculiar fitness to rule over less civilized races for their own good" must be stopped (CPP 2: 369–70).

Shaw's purpose was neither to set the record straight on events that were five centuries old nor to justify the Catholic church's decision to elevate Joan to the status of the Venerable and Blessed saints. That would be merely didactic time travelling. Instead, he emphasized the congruity among questions common to the fifteenth and twentieth centuries. As he remarks in the preface, "the Reformation, which Joan had unconsciously anticipated, kept the questions which arose in her case burning up to our own day (you can see plenty of the burnt houses still in Ireland)" in sectarian warfare flying in the face of fundamental similarities between Protestants and Catholics (CPP 2: 308). The epilogue which critics find so contentious is the key to Shaw's modern referentiality, for it emphasizes that Joan's history did not end with her execution but rather *began* twenty-five years after her death, with the annulment of her sentence.

In the epilogue Joan and a host of her persecutors and champions appear in Charles VII's dream. They praise her and bemoan their own follies. A messenger from 1920 announces her canonization, whereupon she proposes to come back alive in the twentieth century. The consternation that ensues, with rapid closure on the play, unambiguously places Shaw's contemporaries on the same ground as Joan's: genuinely fearful of a powerful yet humble woman. She is like Trotsky, Stalin's defeated rival for power in the 1920s, whom Shaw knew "we dare not allow . . . to come to England, not so much because we are afraid of him making war here, but because his own country is so afraid of him that we feel that any hospitality we extended to him would be almost interpreted as an attack on the Russian Government. You may think of Trotsky as being a sort of male St. Joan, in his day, who has not been burnt."[29] Joan could be redeemed in death but not in life, just as Trotsky could be preferred by foreign governments but not welcomed.

In the published preface Shaw cautioned that the events of *Saint Joan* should not be dismissed as the acts of superstitious medieval bumpkins. He takes care to depict Joan's "miracles" ambiguously as coincidences, yet admits that in the twentieth century we are still susceptible to tales of miracles posing as science, and take a lot on faith because of what "experts say," no less so than in the fifteenth century.

> The medieval doctors of divinity who did not pretend to settle how many angels could dance on the point of a needle cut a very poor figure as far as romantic credulity is concerned beside the modern physicists who have settled to a billionth of a millimetre every movement and position in the dance of the electrons. Not for worlds would I question the precise accuracy of these calculations or the existence of electrons (whatever they may be). The fate of Joan is a warning to me against such heresy. (CPP 2: 310)

Perhaps the most vivid example of this is the modern practice of inoculating children against virulent diseases—a practice Shaw opposed—as an act of faith and superstition akin to the medieval insistence on baptism (CPP 2: 302). Shaw was determined to avoid depicting the events in the manner of old melodramas: the inexorable contests between villain and hero. The decision to burn Joan was "purely political" (CPP 2: 424), just as her preference for execution over lifelong imprisonment was a calculated choice to remain faithful to her own belief system and what she regarded as a quality life. She was burned for doing what women must not do—innovate in war, religion, dress, and statecraft—linking the causes of nationalism to personal freedom.

The first production was mounted in New York by the Theatre Guild, following on the artistic if not commercial success of *Back to Methuselah*. It opened to mixed critical reaction but gained momentum and played 214 performances before going on tour. Three months after the New York opening, in March 1924, it opened to acclaim in London. In contrast to *Back to Methuselah*, this was indisputably a play for the stage. Lillah McCarthy offered to go back into management if she could play Joan, but Shaw gave the play to Lewis Casson to produce with his wife, Sybil Thorndike, in the title role. Casson and Shaw ostensibly codirected. Charles Ricketts's designs facilitated the sense of compression and simplicity in tension with grandeur, and fully dispensed with the painterliness of Victorian spectacle. No real water, kingfishers, cathedrals, or mounted horses, no mock battles, crackling bonfires, or staged ascensions. The play of ideas had an environment far from the Victorian drawing room, closer to the unit set of Shakespearean histories, and yet exalted in the ultimate illusionary disruption when the papal messenger from 1920 bantered about which contingent was really in fancy dress. Shaw, who had been nominated for the Nobel Prize for Literature on several previous occasions, was finally made a laureate in 1925.

The novella *The Adventures of the Black Girl in Her Search for God*, written in South Africa in 1933 while Shaw waited anxiously for his wife to recover from an automobile accident, is his most explicit suggestion of how to break from the molds of sexism, racist imperialism, and capitalist deadlock depicted in *Heartbreak House*, *Captain Brassbound's Conversion*, *John Bull's Other Island*, and *Saint Joan*. Reminiscent of Voltaire's *Candide* and Bunyan's *Pilgrim's Progress*, the Black Girl sets out on a quest to meet God, encountering many challenges to her faith along the way. She is first instructed in Christianity by a white female missionary who, in her self-indulgent love of suffering, has gone to Africa to devote herself to saving others' souls despite the obvious fact that her own is hardened against love (she is based on Mabel Shaw, one of the author's acquaintances). In the 1938 play *Geneva*, Shaw likens communist agents to the missionaries of bible societies: just as the British fear that Russians dispense propaganda amidst democracies, the infiltration of missionaries is resented in non-Christian cultures. The Black Girl does not resent the missionary's presence, but when parted from her do-gooder converter, she finds the missionary's influence quickly waning. In the book's first episode she encounters a vengeful white Old Testament God; when the Black Girl goes to smite him as mercilessly as he has killed a snake, her Bible begins to disintegrate. When she next encounters another white god who delights only in arguments about his evident malevolence, more of the Bible disintegrates. Her subsequent encounters with prophets and preachers provide opportunities for her to measure her values against those of contemporary and ancient cultures. She is particularly loath to accept the doctrine of a shortsighted scientist (Ivan Pavlov) who insists that knowledge is empirically derived and does not hesitate to test hypotheses at the expense of animals' suffering. She finds less cruel ways to demonstrate his hypothesis that the universe is a system of conditioned reflexes, frightening him into climbing a tree by declaring he is seated upon a crocodile and then just as effectively proving that he can descend from the tree by claiming a vicious snake hovers at his shoulder. His belief in science and conviction that it has nothing to do with either faith or the soul drives her away. Another scientific metaphor is dismissed in the encounter with the "Caravan of the Curious," consisting of a group of white explorers served by fifty or so black bearers. The Europeans discuss the history of believing, concluding with Darwin's theories of natural selection. The Black Girl astutely ascertains the significance of this reversal, for it may well suggest that Africans are superior: "The missionaries teach us to believe in your gods. It is all the instruction we get. If we find out that you do not believe in them and are their enemies we may come and kill you. There are millions of us; and we can shoot as well as you."[30] The Europeans demonstrate how they continually take new ideas without throwing out the old ones. This stops progress in both science and politics. Like Shaw, who in 1923 called South Africa a slave state (BS 3: 275–76), the Black Girl concludes with a stinging rebuke of the white enslavement of blacks formerly in harmony with nature.

> Lion and elephant shared the land with us. When they ate or trampled on our bodies they spared our souls. When they had enough they asked for no more. But nothing will satisfy your greed. You work generations of us to death until you have each of you more than a hundred of us could eat or spend; and yet you go on forcing us to work harder and harder and longer and longer for less food and clothing. You do not know what enough means for yourselves, or less than enough for us. You are for ever grumbling because we have no money to buy the goods you trade in; and your only remedy is to give us less money.[31]

She concludes that it must be because they "serve false gods," clearly pointing to capitalism and imperialism. For this a white woman threatens to shoot her; the Black Girl retaliates in self-defence, despite knowing that the justice system will not protect her fairly.

In an encounter with Jesus Christ she refuses to acknowledge God as a father, either literally (for her own father beat her until she was big enough to fight back) or figuratively. Her culture is matriarchal, and the most she will concede is to honour her grandfather. She rejects Christ's "cheap cure-all commandments," asserting that she seeks *God*, not commandments.[32] Her decision is reinforced by the encounter with Peter, laden down with the Church on his back; others, similarly burdened with *their* true churches, parade by him. On a second encounter with Christ she finds him posing on a cross while an artist carves his image. Christ and Mohammed debate the theological imputations against graven idols while the Black Girl asks why the idols never represent women. This sparks a discussion on the different faiths' views of polygamy, which the Black Girl abandons, saying, "I shall not find God where men are talking about women."[33]

Finally, she arrives at a garden tended by an old wise man. His message is to let God come to you in his own way and time, cautioning the Black Girl against hoping for an audience with God's full, unmediated presence. She concurs and joins the old man in his labours. A socialist Irishman, not recognizing private property, lets himself into the garden. He proclaims that God is just an unfulfilled purpose. The old man and Black Girl gradually teach and refine the socialist's manners and speech. This all goes for nothing when the Girl, persuaded by the old man, declares that she will marry the Irishman. He flees, protesting, "Is it me marry a black nigger-woman?,"[34] a clear indication that the efforts to reeducate the racist are not necessarily successful. But they do marry and have a brood of children. In rearing them and tending her husband's needs, the Black Girl becomes so busy she leaves off her search for God. By the time she has enough leisure to renew her quest, "her strengthened mind had taken her far beyond the stage at which there is any fun in smashing idols with knobkerries [her girlhood weapon]."[35] Instead of crashing through the jungle, she (like Voltaire's Pangloss) chose to settle down and cultivate her garden, and thence came wisdom. Having debunked the rhetoric of Christianity, Judaism, and Islam, she nevertheless ends in a (holy) family tableau. She had misheard one of the explorer's questions about $\sqrt{-x}$ (an allusion to the key to the universe) as something multiplied by itself, constituting a woman named Myna's sex.[36] In other words, instead of contemplating the mathematical abstraction separately from lived reality, she thinks Myna finds fulfillment in and of herself rather than necessarily as a married pair. Yet only through procreation does the Black Girl achieve the same kind of satisfaction.

The Black Girl represents a colonized people breaking through to a postcolonial consciousness, yet her achievement is contradicted in myriad ways. On the first page of the novella, by insisting that she go beyond the teaching of the white missionary and find God for herself, she thinks she seeks the God of Europeans. Indeed, she encounters this deity many times in many forms, yet never accepts his truth. It is a powerful metaphor of the postcolonial subject rejecting the solipsism of white identity and refusing to collude with racist (and capitalist) culture passively. Shaw sets her up in the classic formula of female-as-colonized, lets her break out of it, yet also depicts her settling down to domesticity in the midst of a tidy cultivated garden plot. J. Ellen Gainor argues that in this conclusion, "Shaw imposes on this story of religious exploration in a more primitive world the pattern of a young, unlearned, female character who is to be educated to function independently in her society but also to embrace the Victorian tradition of marriage and family for women."[37] She becomes a wife, not a mate. Becoming a wife, particularly in the final moments of a Western-authored text, inevitably suggests an elaborate complex of social significations and constraints. This puts Shaw's ostensible agenda of liberation at odds with the rhetorical traditions of novelistic discourse.

Reading intertextually, it is important to realize that the sources (*Candide* and *Pilgrim's Progress*) begin with domesticity and send the male heroes in search of something else. Having the Black Girl settle down in a thoroughly domestic setting—her socialist racist husband and her own refusal to wear clothes notwithstanding—calls the story's radicalism into question. The gendering and domestic entrenchment of the figure is crucial in the final moments, despite the upstanding articulations of antiracism and anti-imperialism. It demonstrates the truth claims of Donaldson's maxim: "If Marxism ignores the gender-saturated nature of all class relations, then feminism often ignores the racially saturated nature of all gender relations."[38] Despite her prodigious feats of breaking through the inflated rhetoric of scientists crushing the religious delusions of thousands of generations, the African "girl" (by the end of the story actually a matron) entraps a racist and breeds a new generation distinctive only by its modified skin colour. Her mind is "strengthened" in domestic routines: in other words, she turns away from all intellectual quests. This is despite her earlier prediction that the next great civilization will be black. Perhaps Shaw is admitting the impossibility of returning to a "pure" past unsullied by colonialism. But is the best alliance for the future truly between a black, female freethinker and a socialist Irishman? This has more than a hint of autobiographical egotism.

In addition, Shaw puts himself in an untenable position vis-à-vis a postcolonial text. Except with regard to Ireland, he postulates the post-colonial from the position of the colonizing power. He is not inventing the postcolonial text, but reinventing the colonial text. He was neither Christian nor a great enthusiast of British foreign policy, which may mitigate the presumptuousness somewhat, as may his sympathy with communism in this period. The critique was strong enough for the book to be banned in Ireland for "indecent and obscene" tendencies, though arguably more offence was taken at the woodblock illustrations relentlessly depicting the nude heroine than the political implications. It was a best-seller elsewhere, quickly reprinted and translated.

For six years after World War I, Shaw confined all his travels to the British Isles. In the late 1920s he sojourned in Italy and Yugoslavia. He was more adventurous in the next decade, travelling not only in Europe but also in the Middle East, India, South Africa, New Zealand, East Asia, and Central America, making his first visit to the U.S.A. in 1933 and taking advantage of the long sea journeys to write under relatively unmolested circumstances. By 1936 this globetrotting, which had largely been instigated by Charlotte Shaw, came to an end. The most significant of all the journeys from a political standpoint was the trip to Russia in 1931, on invitation from the Soviet government.

While it struggled to repulse encroachments at its borders by other European and Asian powers during the 1914–18 war, Russia also slid toward war internally. Germany gambled that by facilitating the return of exiled Bolshevik leaders, Russia would more quickly break down into disorder. Lenin, exiled in Switzerland, was allowed to pass through Germany in a sealed railroad car. After an aborted attempt in July 1917, the Bolshevik Revolution succeeded in November with the support of the war-weary masses. Under Lenin's leadership the new government instituted policies that resembled some staples of the Fabian platform: nationalization of all theatres, land, banks, and factories (which were turned over to the workers); government control of trade unions; suppression of private trading; rationing; and confiscation of church property and abolition of religious instruction. Two years later the Bolsheviks (renamed the Communist Party) backed off and lifted some of the restrictions on banking and private trading in surplus food production. The Union of Soviet Socialist Republics was organized in 1922 with the federation of Russia, the Ukraine, White Russia, and Transcaucasia (Georgia, Armenia, and Azerbaijan) centralized in Moscow; the Baltic states remained independent, while some Far Eastern territories were challenged by Japan.

Lenin's death in 1924 sparked a period of factionalist power struggles culminating in Joseph Stalin's complete victory in 1927, the year Britain severed diplomatic relations. Stalin bears the brunt of historical blame, yet in both his reign and Lenin's the nation experienced desperate famines, brutal suppression of intellectuals and political dissidents, and profound disorganization and corruption. Stalin's decision to exile Trotsky, his chief political rival and an outspoken critic, was perhaps the kindest of all the actions he took against free speech. Trotsky subsequently denounced Stalin as betraying the revolution and the cause of international communism, and to many socialist sympathizers outside the U.S.S.R. the revolutionary experiment was awry.

In the late 1920s Stalin instituted his policy of rapid industrialization and collectivization of agriculture. The first Five Year Plan (1928–32), also known as the second Bolshevik Revolution, aimed to destroy the village system in communities where collectivization was resisted. The methods were far from gentle, as suggested by the fact that the country's rate of population growth dropped from 3,000,000 a year in 1928 to 100,000 in 1933. Instead of improving productivity, farm output dropped in the same period by 15 percent.[39] In the manufacturing sector Stalin's reforms emphasized productivity, particularly of armaments and steel, without necessarily equipping the new factory buildings with machinery or trained workers. Production of consumer goods was virtually unknown, causing high inflation in retail goods and basic foodstuffs in the state and private markets alike and a dangerous degree of unrest in the population. Increases in industrial production in the first Five Year Plan met only 60 percent of the goal. Target levels for the second Five Year Plan (1933–37) were not met until the early 1950s.

The U.S.S.R. desperately needed to improve its balance of trade and diversity of trading partners. Stalin broadcast an official policy of wanting to strengthen trading relations with capitalist nations; he needed goodwill and even better press abroad. Britain resumed diplomatic relations in 1929, followed by the U.S.A. in 1933. Shaw's nine-day invited tour in July 1931 was in the company of a small entourage including his close friend Lady Nancy Astor (a flamboyant American and the first woman to be elected to the British Parliament), the Marquis of Lothian, and J. W. Mallin (head of London's Toynbee Hall Social Welfare Centre). Soviet authorities recognized Shaw's worldwide infamy as a socialist writer and were determined to cash in on the propaganda value of his goodwill, should they be able to secure it, including in the itinerary a face-to-face meeting with Stalin. Shaw, who on his seventy-fifth birthday was treated to a horse race (a form of entertainment he condemned), liked to think he was on a serious fact-finding mission and boasted of wandering away from his compatriots and guides to investigate whatever took his fancy. He was taken to the theatre, but his real interests centered on politics and the standard of living of ordinary citizens. He claimed to have seen the real Soviet Union and to have found it free of the starvation and discontent that was rumoured, countering H. G. Wells's damning report from 1920 detailing rampant mismanagement.[40] His itinerary was tightly controlled, yet Shaw repeatedly claimed that he was not—and could not possibly have been—duped by the authorities.[41] Nevertheless, the introduction to a collected volume of Shaw's writings about this trip makes it clear that while in the U.S.S.R. Shaw and his entourage saw what the Soviets wanted them to see—no more, no less—and went where they were taken. In public Shaw said very supportive things and, much to the relief of his hosts, remained on his most austere good behaviour; perverse Shavian logic and aphorism were confined to more private encounters.[42] It adds up to counterpropaganda, much like Beatrice and Sidney Webb's *The Truth about Soviet Russia*—a defence of the Soviet political system, asserting that it was the freest democracy to date, reproducing and contextualizing the New Constitution of 1936[43]—yet there are also indications that the *pretenses* and performances of the Perfect Communal Society did not fool Shaw.[44] The socialist theatre was no longer something confined to a few small independent stages: it was a set of performances of national and world dimensions.

Michael Holroyd accounts for the enthusiastic response to Soviet life as if Shaw was a starving idealist banqueting on nutritious dishes of the practical working socialist model which had hitherto been merely untried recipes:

> When Shaw travelled to Moscow he was chiefly interested in Soviet methods of social and economic reconstruction; by the time he had left he had been converted to the religion of communism. Here was a creed, in practical operation and with a clear-cut code of morals, that could restore his homogeneity of thought and feeling. From Darwin to Einstein, the landscape of knowledge had been broken up during his lifetime, destroying many idealized and apparently absolute values that he had attacked, but leaving no solid ground of morality from which to survey the past and future. . . . This was the appeal in the 1920s and 1930s of autocracies such as Mussolini's fascists and Hitler's Nazis whose dogmatic myths and parades of order gave Italy and Germany a sense of definite national purpose. (BS 3: 243)

Shaw was also attracted to the simplicity of design and undeniable initial effectiveness of fascist states in their earliest days. Shortly before setting out to Moscow, he openly praised Benito Mussolini, who was granted dictatorial powers in 1922, banned labour strikes in 1926 (shortly before the General Strike in Britain), abolished women's and much working-class suffrage, and was in the process of reconstructing Italy's air and naval power. By the early 1930s Mussolini's government was in almost complete control of finance and industry in a "corprative state."

Conflating Italy's gargantuan feat of infrastructure building with the Soviet Union's ideological origins, Shaw regarded Stalin as the executive of Lenin's idealist plans and the veritable Life Force of socialism. His defences of Soviet tactics are elaborate, laying bare the implications for his personal project of self-justification. He accepted, for example, that

> the persecution of the intelligentsia in Russia did not last very long. It was, I think, justified at the time when it was not yet perceived to be impracticable. I have often said myself that if I were a revolutionary dictator my first care would be to see that persons with a university education, or with the acquired mentality universities inculcate and stereotype, should be ruthlessly excluded from all direction of affairs, all contact with education especially with their own children, and, if not violently exterminated, at least encouraged to die out as soon as possible. Lenin shared my views and attempted to carry them into action.[45]

This is a far cry from Fabian socialism of the 1890s, yet Shaw uncritically observed the U.S.S.R.'s move from government by a class of highly skilled mandarins to totalitarian rule by an ideologist. He proclaimed the importance of a class that performs the "higher brain work" in Fabian socialism yet callously accounted for the demise of noncommunist Russians as a necessary expedient for reform.[46] Vigorously defending his own fortune against the ravages of postwar taxation, he hated paying his burden of income tax yet consistently claimed he was a communist. He railed against the class that expected to inherit without doing anything to deserve its riches, advocated a common wage, yet defended the prerogatives of a genius such as himself to live in relative luxury. In all, he envied the Soviets for the chance to implement theories, while the British—it was abundantly clear—were not going to achieve a fraction of Fabian reforms at the pace the Labour Party was setting, even after being elected to power a second time. For whatever its flaws, the Soviet Union was trying out ideas that Shaw had advocated for more than fifty years.[47] His enthusiasm for postrevolutionary Russia comes about from a combination of blindness to Soviet failings or abuses and the selective belief that its system reified his own agenda.[48]

Shaw's frequent reiteration of the story of F. E. Djerjinsky (Dzerszhinski)—originator and head of the Cheka secret police, who, as transport commissar in 1921, summarily shot two railway workers for allegedly treating their government jobs like sinecures—is a classic example of the purge epidemic as well as Shaw's selective processing of details. The Djerjinsky story serves as a parable for other workers tempted to slackness on the job. Shaw *admired* this managerial style, without irony.[49] In the preface to *The Simpleton of the Unexpected Isles*, he postulates a post-apocalyptic world in which there are no more button moulders (a character in Ibsen's *Peer Gynt* who claims the remains of human lives for shredding and recycling) or heavenly tribunals to judge the worthiness of individuals. In the Djerjinsky parable there is a mechanism of earthly judgement where individuals are assessed according to their record of either creating things of social value or parasitically consuming and destroying them. "The essential difference between the Russian liquidator with the pistol . . . and the British hangman," according to Shaw, the staunch opponent of capital punishment, "is that they do not operate on the same sort of person." One compunction is evident: "Has Russia, then, in adding exploiters and parasites to the stock list of the undesirable, taken a step in advance of Europe or merely made a mistake?"[50] When, in the coup of 1991, Djerjinsky's statue was among the first communist icons to disappear, the Russian people gave their verdict.

From 1920 Shaw was increasingly pessimistic that Fabian gradualist democratic techniques would bring about massive social change. Major changes were not going to be driven by the populace, at least in Britain, so they would have to be imposed by legislators. Invention of the British welfare system was a far cry from the picture coming into focus in Germany and the Soviet Union. Shaw remained rather blind to the totalitarianism that united Stalin's and Hitler's systems, preferring to emphasize the achievements of their public welfare measures. In Holroyd's words, "Shaw let his imagination play round Lenin's revolution until it flowered into a thoroughgoing Fabian event. For if words did not have the power to initiate political change as simply as he had once believed, they could still encircle events and change them mythologically" (BS 3: 229). Fabians waited hopefully for the U.S.S.R. to demonstrate the efficacy of socialism to the world. In his 1897 chapter for *Forecast of the Coming Century* and again in the 1928 *Intelligent Woman's Guide to Socialism and Capitalism*, Shaw warned against regarding all socialists as united in philosophy as well as tactics. He was always prepared to diverge from the party line, admitting for example that "Socialism will not prove worth carrying out in its entirety," but described this as a shortcut possible after socialism was firmly entrenched as a worldwide political system, rather than out of expedience for short-term goals to get socialism off the ground. In 1897 he predicted "that Socialist States will connive at highly undemocratic ways of leaving comparatively large resources in the hands of certain persons, who will thereby become obnoxious as a privileged class to the consistent levellers,"[51] but in the early 1930s he praised such developments. His gesture of recommending Stalin for the Nobel Peace Prize was a serious embarrassment to other socialists.

Up to 1933 Russia and Germany were close allies and trading partners, but when German militarization stepped up, it forced Russia to increase defensive air and naval power and to regard Germany as a potential aggressor instead of an ally. The U.S.S.R. joined the League of Nations in support of the ideal of collective security. In 1935 the Third Communist International proclaimed fascism a greater enemy than capitalism, advising communist states to ally with democratic nations and support military buildups. This recommendation was insufficiently heeded by the Soviet government, for in 1939, when Germany attacked Poland, the U.S.S.R. was party to a nonaggression pact with Germany, making if officially neutral. But in 1941, when the Soviet Union was invaded, it switched allegiance to Britain and its allies. The text of Shaw's banned radio broadcast from the previous year shows a new deployment of pro-Soviet rhetoric:

> If you want to blow off steam by calling Mr. Hitler a blood-stained monster do so by all means: it won't hurt him, nor need you care if it does. But if you call Stalin a blood-stained monster you must be shot as the most dangerous of Fifth Columnists; for the friendship of Russia is vitally important to us just now. Russia and America may soon have the fate of the world in their hands: that is why I am always so civil to Russia.[52]

A second global war came as no surprise, though its justification was other than Shaw anticipated. In 1929 he predicted that "the next war may not be a war of conquest or self-defence or revenge, but a crusade: a crusade for Internationalism against Nationalism and Imperialism, for Socialism against Capitalism, for Bolshevism against Liberal democracy."[53] With Germany occupying most of Western Europe and pushing at the borders of Russia, Soviet Communists allied to British Conservatives, and the Germans wreaking military revenge against its former victors, it is no wonder that Shaw admitted confusion. At any rate, he admitted it to himself, though he was banned from saying it on the radio: "This war was unpopular at first, and is so still, because nobody seems to know exactly what we are fighting for. . . . What is the Big Idea that we are to risk our lives for?"[54]

Rather than going to war *for* an idea, it was as if Britain warred *against* one: fascism. In the 1940s Shaw called fascism " 'State financed private enterprise' or 'Socialism for the benefit of exploiters.'. . . 'I advocate national control of land, capital, and industry for the benefit of us all. Fascists advocate it equally for the benefit of the landlords, capitalists and industrialists' " (BS 3: 113). Like his friend Nancy Astor, the fascist dictators represented a triumph of will over circumstances. Like Shaw, they were self-made men rising to eminence despite their modest origins. The paradigm is dramatized in *The Millionairess* (1934): The Astor-like Epifania exhibits a genius for business organization, and through exercise of laissez-faire economics amasses a fortune in six months. She is willing to take calculated risks and so rises above the struggling horde. Highly educated figures of the colonized world, represented by an Egyptian physician, cannot resist Epifania's modus operandi, her pace of development, or (literally) the lifeblood pulsing through her veins. This is how fascist dictators build their empires.

The other part of the equation is depicted in *On the Rocks* (1933): Set in the offices of the Prime Minister, the unemployed masses (unseen and offstage) represent the British nation on the brink of despair during the Great Depression. These are the circumstances under which the working classes could become fascist. The play concludes with the unemployed breaking the windows of 10 Downing Street while singing "England Arise" to the beat of police batons. Revolution, however, is not projected: the song announces the day of revolt but nothing is actually *done* to make radical change, for the extremes of left and right maintain the delicate political impasse. Shaw parallels the disorder of the Prime Minister's family with the disorder in the nation and the world, like a refrain of *Misalliance*: intermarriages between the classes and repudiation of upper-class privileges are two solutions to make the nation understand its problems better. Racism must also be curbed: the imperialists are reminded that the conquered civilizations enjoyed a heritage of art and philosophy when Britons "were naked savages worshipping acorns and mistletoe in the woods." A careless insult hurled at the fabulously wealthy Sir Jaffna Pandranath will cost the allegiance of India, and then the empire, for "how are we to hold the empire together if we insult a man who represents nearly seventy per cent of its population?" (CPP 5: 599, 601).

As the 1930s wore on, Shaw came to distinguish between the accomplishments of Mussolini in the first years of his administration and the excesses. In the preface to *The Millionairess* he depicts Hitler as a scheming opportunist who weighed the intentions of World War I's victors astutely against what was merely blustering rhetoric. And at home, "Hitler was able to go further than Mussolini because he had a defeated, plundered, humiliated nation to rescue and restore, whereas Mussolini had only an irritated but victorious one" (CPP 6: 189).

> Mr. Hitler did wonders for his country by his National Socialism, and then threw it all away to turn his workers into soldiers and his factories into munition works when they might have been making themselves happy and comfortable as sensible welfare workers. Heaven defend us from Governments who can think of nothing but the next war and do nothing but prepare for it![55]

There were aspects of this that Britain could use to improve democracy, but the rest—particularly racism—should be thrown away.

Nazi racism is the pretext most often used to express condemnation for Hitler and his regime. Albert Einstein is Shaw's constant example. Shaw, the conspicuously Nordic/Celtic specimen, unambiguously refused "to claim moral superiority to him and unlimited power over him; to rob him, drive him out of his house, exile him, be punished for miscegenation if I allow a relative of mine to marry a relative of his, and finally to kill him as part of a general duty to exterminate his race."[56] Shaw vigorously denied any validity to the concept of pure racial strains. He did not condemn Nazi racism without qualification, frequently alluding to English treatment of Ireland, but insisted that anti-Semitic policies were a serious issue requiring all nations' response (CPP 6: 189–92; see also 5: 631).

After the outbreak of war one of Shaw's most effective rhetorical techniques against British overreaction was to humanize the enemy. He leads his compatriots away from categorizing Hitler in a fascist bestiary, demonstrating that

> I have no prejudice against him personally: much that he has written and spoken echoes what I myself have written and said. He has adopted even my diet. I am interested in his career as one of the great psychological curiosities of political history; and I fully appreciate his physical and moral courage, his diplomatic sagacity, and his triumphant rescue of his country from the yoke the Allies imposed on her after her defeat in 1918.

Instead of condemning Britons for blockheadedness and inviting wrath on himself, as in the 1914 "Common Sense about the War," he demonstrates similarities between himself and Hitler and the advantages of an impassioned examination of the man. The inevitable twist in the argument is an assertion of the backwardness of Britons when compared to the German leader, for "his mind is a twentieth century mind, and . . . our governing class is mentally in the reign of Edward the Third, six centuries out of date."[57] Shaw's solution is only half a century behind the times: dictators are like bosses, Fabians effectively curbed some of the bosses' abuses by implementing the Factory Acts, so the equivalent of a Factory Act should be imposed on Hitler—as if the problem could be legislated away.

Shaw missed the chance to stage a confrontation between the persecuted Jewish people and Hitler in his topical play *Geneva* (1936). Nations reached a point where they recognized war was utterly ruinous, but "War and imperialist diplomacy persist[ed] none the less" (CPP 5: 632). Its incidents lead up to a trial of dictators (Hitler, Mussolini, and Franco) at the international court established in conjunction with the League of Nations. A Jew asks for reparation for having been driven from Germany. Another man complains of the "Business Democrats" who prohibit the opposition from entering parliament. Thinking she is defending the interests of Britain, a young clerk deals with persecutions, revolutions, and murders, managing by the second act to propel the world into a war of sanctions. The dream of bringing nations together has backfired: for peace, Shaw seems despairingly to suggest, keep nations (and by implication *men*) apart.

The trial of the final act (Illustration 10) is relayed to televisions around the world, a futuristic projection of Cable News Network capabilities and the watchful planet. The good-willed are desperately trying to find ways to settle personal and international conflicts by arbitration and law so that blood feuds on familial and national levels can be circumvented. As the Secretary of the League of Nations states: "It turns out that we do not and cannot love oneanother—that the problem before us is how to establish peace among people who heartily dislike oneanother, and have very good reasons for doing so: in short, that the human race does not at present consist exclusively or even largely of likeable persons" (CPP 5: 741). Through the mouthpiece of Sir Orpheus Midlander, the British Foreign Secretary, Germany is warned that if it invades a lesser nation, Britain will respond militarily. As threats of escalation are bandied, the court gets word that the earth has jumped its orbit: "Humanity is doomed" in a new ice age (CPP 5: 752). Under such circumstances differences in political systems are no longer significant. Each leader has a different philosophy of dealing (or not) with the crisis. One citizen symbolically tosses her pistol into the rubbish bin, for when God's judgement is imminent, guns are useless. It all ends hopefully with a quiet tête-à-tête:

JUDGE. Can this thing be true?

SECRETARY. No. It is utter nonsense. If the earth made a spring to a wider orbit half a minute would carry us to regions of space where we could not breathe and our blood would freeze in our veins.

JUDGE. Yet we all believed it for the moment.

SECRETARY. You have nothing to do but mention the quantum theory, and people will take your voice for the voice of Science and believe anything. It broke up this farce of a trial, at all events.

JUDGE. Not a farce, my friend. They came, these fellows. They blustered: they defied us. But they came. They came. (CPP 5: 759)

It was a hopeful thought for audiences to contemplate at the world premiere in Warsaw (1938), for Germany was at Poland's borders, preparing to mobilize. Beatrice Webb disliked what she heard Shaw read of *Geneva* in 1936—"every character depraved in morals and manners and futile in intellect, with here and there a dull dissertation on public affairs"—but when she saw *Geneva* in London at the end of 1938, she found "the play has come at the best possible occasion: it relieves the terrible tension that we all feel about foreign affairs by laughing at every one concerned."[58] But its moment was very brief. It was closer to the truth, as Shaw wrote in his preface in 1945, that instead of meeting calmly over a conference table, "we are, with our incompetence armed with atomic bombs" (CPP 5: 647). The question of atomic warfare versus atomic welfare (turning ballistic science to humane purposes) in *Farfetched Fables* (1948) just increased the stakes on a game already familiar from *Major Barbara*.

In his latter years Shaw remained as active in polemical prose writing as dramatic work, though he created no explicit dramatic treatments of World War II.[59] During the Blitz London's theatres were dark, and there were no prospects of immediate production. Through the first years of World War II his wife was severely disabled, and her death in 1943 propelled him into virtual seclusion. His last decade was spent as an armchair activist as far as new creative work is concerned.

Throughout his productive life, Shaw was usually most effective in efforts that hybridized accepted genres, such as the combination of published play and preface, rather than in political treatises in the Webbs' mold or the sparse agitprop plays of the workers' theatre movement. Most of his major dramatic works are hybrids or montages of stump speech, journalistic op-ed, and thesis play peppered with jokes and lengthy diatribes. The balance between argument and plot varies, but that concern occupied all political dramatists, particularly those determined to convey a socialist message. Brecht's statement of the problem facing his particular generation is eloquent:

> Political and philosophical considerations failed to shape the whole structure, the message was mechanically fitted into the plot. The "editorial" was usually "inartistically" conceived—so patently that the inartistic nature of the plot in which it was embedded, was overlooked. (Plots were in any case regarded as more artistic than editorials.) There was a complete rift. In practice there were two possible solutions. The editorial could be dissolved in the plot or the plot in the editorial, lending the latter artistic form. But the plot could be shaped artistically and the editorial too (it then naturally lost its editorial quality), while keeping the jump from one idiom to another and giving it an artistic form. Such a solution seemed an innovation.[60]

Shaw certainly combined the idioms, but with the possible exception of *Man and Superman* does not *jump* them in the sense Brecht intends. All in all, Shaw comes out more heavily on the side of plot than editorial and was perhaps too adept at giving playgoers the option of attending to either story *or* message. The switch in idioms was an old device—as Brecht points out, it is standard in Attic choruses as well as the Chinese theatre— but what was needed to make it register as a *political* tool was Brechtian aesthetic theory or something else like it. It was a very short conceptual distance from the newspapers and ticker tape breaking the news of the angelic peril in *The Simpleton of the Unexpected Isles* to incorporation of projected text or newsreels, but Shaw did not traverse it. Shaw employed various tools theorized by Brecht—episodic plots (*Saint Joan*), cartoonish characterizations (*Buoyant Billions*, 1948), self-referentiality brought about through alienation of locale (*Too True to Be Good*), and metaphors of the capitalist system (Breakages Ltd. in *The Apple Cart*, 1928)—but tried them in isolation and never postulated or demonstrated a cogent alternative to modernist realist theory. This extreme eccentric's plays reflected the concerns of individualism and the tests of circumstance rather than theories of the drama or staging per se.

Brecht argued that "*Naturalism* and a certain type of *anarchistic montage* can be confronted with their social effects," a goal often set by

Shaw in his twentieth-century work, yet it is fair to say "that they merely reflect the symptoms of the surface of things and not the deeper causal complexes of society ... [and] can be shown to be purely reformist, merely formal efforts which supply solutions *on paper*."[61] The key point here is the effectiveness (or otherwise) of the plays as socialist propagandizing to a middle-class public. Shaw's attentiveness to political issues and theatrical drawing power are unique among topical British dramatists of the period, but it is unlikely that he swayed political opinion. His desire to politicize the theatre, though not its aesthetics, was real yet ineffective. These goals were not taken up seriously by a British successor until the late 1950s. Once again, at the Royal Court, a new generation of dramatists including John Osborne, Arnold Wesker, and John Arden dealt with the problems of the day. During Shaw's lifetime theatres dedicated to socialism sprang up in Britain and abroad, but the Shavian repertoire was no more a part of them than of the politicized literary theatre of the Cold War.

In some respects Shaw was intensely attuned to his times and his times to him. He continually sought efficiency and elegance in communicative media, embracing Pitman shorthand, the typewriter, and telephones as soon as they were available. In the early 1920s he became intensely interested in radio technology and in 1924 gave his first live reading (of *O'Flaherty, V.C.*) for the British Broadcasting Commission. Henceforth he was one of the directors of the BBC, an active promotor of spoken-word broadcasts, and an ardent fan of musical programming. He was just as interested in film technology, developing a technique of writing screenplays through trial and error. The complexity of film production corporations made such strongly opinionated authors a hazard, however, and Shaw was generally forced to leave the screenwriting to other adaptors for British, Continental, and American ventures. *Major Barbara*, ironically filmed during the Blitz of 1940, is still readily available through the video circuit. The English version of *Pygmalion*, released in 1938, was the most popular screen adaptation, garnering two Oscars.

Shaw was invited to stand for the parliamentary seats of Northampton in 1919 and West Edinburgh in 1922, but declined; he could not be lured back into elected politics. More honours came for his literary work, though he tried to avoid public accolades. In 1925, after several nominations, he was finally awarded the Nobel Prize for Literature (endowed by the dynamite manufacturer memorialized in *Major Barbara*) in recognition of *Saint Joan*. His determination to decline was thwarted; he reluctantly bore the title of Nobel Laureate and inventively used the cash to endow a foundation devoted to translating Swedish literature, most notably August

Strindberg's, into English.[62] Shaw recognized Strindberg's place in the modernist canon and believed it should be preserved, if only as a devil's advocate. Unlike some of his socialist successors, Shaw refused the knighthood offered in 1929, preferring infamy to honour.

By the outbreak of World War II more than eighty works had been published about him. Sales of inexpensive Pelican and Penguin editions—the innovators in paperback publishing—boosted Shaw to enormous popularity after 1937. On his ninetieth birthday Penguin launched the "Shaw Million" consisting of ten editions of his works at print runs of one hundred thousand each. They sold out in six weeks (BS 3: 374). From 1929, under Barry Jackson's leadership, the Malvern Festival used Shaw as a figurehead for marketing and scheduling. The first year of the festival was devoted entirely to Shaw's plays. Premiers of numerous Shavian works were given by Jackson and his successor, Roy Limbert, before the festival's demise in the early years of World War II.[63] In all, twenty Shavian plays were presented at Malvern, some of which transferred to the capital. *The Apple Cart*, originally performed in 1929, ran an additional 258 performances in London, the longest run a Shavian drama had enjoyed since *Fanny's First Play*. A historical farce, *In Good King Charles's Golden Days*, also did extremely well in Britain and the U.S.A. at the end of the 1930s. While the Malvern Festival thrived, Shaw had little difficulty getting each major new work produced. His oeuvre also provided lucrative material for revivals. He became a thoroughly established feature of the British dramatic canon, especially in the provinces (through Jackson at the Birmingham Repertory Theatre and Malvern as well as with the touring Charles Macdona Players) and abroad. The new plays of the 1920s–40s were never surefire hits, yet a reputation for "GBS" was assured and his name assumed qualities of giganticism in terms of theatrical notability, though not commercialism. He made his fortune, like his reputation, incrementally: he claimed that the terms of his royalties had not changed in fifty years.[64] In the latter part of the twentieth century the shock value of his plays is gone, though he still bears frequent revival, and several festivals are devoted to his works because of their enduring topicality and wit.

By many measurements Shaw lived far too long. His premature good-byes, in constant anticipation of his own expiration, were more than a bit reminiscent of the repeat farewell performances by Victorian grande dames of the theatre. One by one his activities decreased in variety. He was very active onstage as a director of his own work into his late seventies, but he gave up in 1934. He continued to do some lecturing in the 1930s but found it increasingly tiring and preferred to address crowds via the radio waves or, on his ninetieth birthday, in a BBC television appearance.[65] In the 1930s he and Charlotte Shaw made two circumnavigations of the earth, but by the end of the decade politics, age, precarious health, and inclination kept them in Great Britain. On his eighty-fifth birthday, two years into the Second World War, Shaw stopped attending committee meetings and retreated almost exclusively to the London area. When Charlotte died in 1943, their home and garden in Ayot St. Lawrence, a small village north of London, became the widower's nucleus and orbit. He penned the news of Charlotte's death to their pseudo-son Granville Barker, breaking two decades of silence between them, but their work at the Royal Court had long since been orphaned and taken up by others. Throughout it all, to his last days of autonomous mobility, Shaw wrote. His last big project was to publish his pseudo-autobiography, *Sixteen Self-Sketches* (1949), but he kept his hand in a lot of pies through an average of four contributions to periodicals every month of his last two years.[66]

While most of the latter half of his life—the twentieth-century sojourn—is mocked by the left and reluctantly valorized by the theatre and belles lettres, there is much that is ripe for political, dramaturgical, and historical scrutiny. Holroyd's remark that "by current standards you cannot ignore a writer whose estate makes almost half-a-million pounds a year more than forty years after his death" (BS 4: ix) highlights how, from a purely monetary perspective, Shaw is still vital. For an author to remain lucidly prolific from the age of twenty-two to ninety-six is unusual, but for him to draw such royalties in his 138th year is extraordinary.

On 2 November 1950 periodicals around the world dusted off their obituaries and announced the death of George Bernard Shaw. They span the gamut from the *New York Post* to *Coal*, the *Irish Times* to the *British Medical Journal* and *Russia Today*, each laying claim to a part of GBS by recounting "what he wrote or did for *us*," testifying to the breadth of a long and provocative life. It spanned nearly a century during a period of unprecedented change and turmoil, but while he seemed a bellwether during his lifetime, he was eclipsed by the increasing rapidity of technical—and hence social—transformation by the time of his demise. In 1856, the year of Shaw's birth, an inventor introduced the first rubber nipples for baby bottles to a world plagued by high infant death rates, post-puerperal fevers, and appalling sanitation in crowded cities of medieval dimensions. The same year Gail Borden patented condensed milk so infants had something to suck through the artificial nipples. In Shaw's youth his family's musicales were enjoyed by gaslight, then something of a novelty in Ireland, but by the time of his death scientists had begun the semiconductor revolution with the earliest use of transistors, and human in vitro fertilization was a medical goal. In 1950 Shaw took his last farewell and went out in a blaze at the Golders Green crematorium in which he had held stock. Meanwhile, President Truman instructed the U.S. Atomic Energy Commission to develop the hydrogen bomb.

Shaw was born into a world of Elizabeth Barrett Browning's *Aurora Leigh*, Gustav Flaubert's *Madame Bovary*, and Ibsen's *Feast at Solhaug*; when he died, Simone de Beauvoir's *Second Sex*, George Orwell's *1984*, and Eugene Ionesco's *Bald Soprano* affirmed the new age and portended much that was of consequence in the ensuing decades. Challenges more profound than Shaw imagined were launched on the prerogatives of cultural definition, self-government, and literary form. In the wake of de Beauvoir, Shaw's critiques are puny commentaries on sex, not gender, avoiding women's material history and the cultural constructions of difference. Shaw's portrayals of dysfunctional and dystopic twentieth-century society tend to be cautionary antimasques, highlighting through contrast the desirability of socialist choices and retaining an Einsteinian faith in human transcendence; there is rarely the unrelieved vision of Orwell, in which no humour and less hope can be summoned. Shaw's last will and testament bequeaths unprecedented bounty for the creation of a phonetic alphabet, the pet project he thought would aid international communication; he little understood the challenges to language itself that would be launched by a generation of playwrights who had already discounted him.

NOTES

1. Fred D. Crawford, "Swift and Shaw against the War," *Shaw* 6 (1986): 13–32.

2. Shaw, "Common Sense about the War," special supplement to the *New Statesman* 4.84 (14 November 1914): 3.

3. Ibid., 18.

4. Ibid., 27.

5. Ibid., 13–16.

6. Shaw, "Armaments and Conscription: A Triple Alliance against War," *Daily Chronicle* (18 March 1913); reprinted in *Bernard Shaw. Major Critical Essays*, vol. 21, *What I Really Wrote about the War* (New York: William H. Wise, 1931), 13.

7. Shaw, "Common Sense about the War," 18.

8. Christabel Pankhurst, *New York Times Current History of the European War* 1.1 (12 December 1914): 68–69.

9. Ibid.

10. Editorial, *New York Times* (5 November 1914); reprinted in *New York Times Current History of the European War*, 66.

11. Shaw, *Peace Conference Hints* (London: Constable: 1919).

12. Frank Spencer, *A History of the World in the Twentieth Century*, ed. D. C. Watt, Frank Spencer, and Neville Brown (New York: William Morrow, 1968), 301.

13. Shaw, "The League of Nations," *Fabian Tract* 226 (1929): 5.

14. Shaw, *Peace Conference Hints*, 106.

15. See "Report on Fabian Policy and Resolutions . . . to the International Socialist Workers and Trade Union Congress, London, 1896," *Fabian Tract* 70 (1896).

16. "To Members of the Fabian Society," February 1900, a minority opinion circulated to the Fabian membership (University of Guelph XZI Ms. A709010).

17. Shaw, ed., *Fabianism and the Empire: A Manifesto by the Fabian Society* (London: Grant Richards, 1900), 16.

18. Ibid., 21.

19. A. M. McBriar, *Fabian Socialism and English Politics 1884–1918* (Cambridge: Cambridge University Press, 1962), 122. See also Heidi J. Holder, "Melodrama, Realism and Empire on the British Stage," in *Acts of Supremacy: The British Empire and the Stage, 1790–1930*, ed. J. S. Bratton et al. (Manchester: Manchester University Press, 1991), 129–49; this gives a very interesting reading of the evolution of British imperialist drama, its plotting devices, characters, and historical specificity with some reference to *Arms and the Man* and *Captain Brassbound's Conversion*.

20. Laura E. Donaldson, *Decolonizing Feminisms: Race, Gender, and Empire Building* (Chapel Hill and London: University of North Carolina Press, 1992), 16, 27.

21. Shaw, "Socialism and Ireland," *New Commonwealth* (12 December 1919); reprinted in *The Matter with Ireland*, ed. David H. Greene and Dan H. Laurence (London: Rupert Hart-Davis, 1962), 214–32.

22. Ibid., 223–24.

23. Shaw, *Peace Conference Hints*, 107–8.

24. Shaw, *The Matter with Ireland*, 228–29.

25. Ibid., 230–31.

26. Ibid., 291.

27. Brian Tyson, *The Story of Shaw's "Saint Joan"* (Kingston and Montreal: McGill-Queen's University Press, 1982), 1–14.

28. Shaw, *The Listener* (3 June 1931); reprinted in *Platform and Pulpit*, ed. Dan H. Laurence (New York: Hill and Wang, 1961), 215.

29. Ibid.

30. Shaw, *The Adventures of the Black Girl in Her Search for God* (New York: Dodd Mead, 1933), 35.

31. Ibid., 39–41.

32. Ibid., 30.

33. Ibid., 52.

34. Ibid., 57.

35. Ibid., 58.

36. Ibid., 35, 48.

37. J. Ellen Gainor, *Shaw's Daughters: Dramatic and Narrative Constructions of Gender* (Ann Arbor: University of Michigan Press, 1991), 171.

38. Donaldson, *Decolonizing Feminisms*, 7.

39. Spencer, *History of the World*, 451.

40. See H. G. Wells, *Russia in the Shadows* (London: Hodder and Stoughton, 1920). Wells contrasts the conditions he observed on trips in 1914 and 1920.

41. See Shaw's letter to the editor of the *Daily Express* (25 June 1932); reprinted in *Agitations: Letters to the Press 1875–1950*, ed. Dan H. Laurence and James Rambeau (New York: Frederick Ungar, 1985), 286–89.

42. Shaw, *The Rationalization of Russia*, intro. and ed. Harry M. Geduld (Bloomington: Indiana University Press, 1964).

43. Beatrice and Sidney Webb, *The Truth about Soviet Russia* (New York: Longmans, Green, 1942).

44. Shaw, *The Rationalization of Russia*, 89–90.

45. Ibid., 80.

46. Ibid., 108.

47. Ibid., 94.

48. Shaw failed to consider the consequences of eliminating democracy in the socialist utopia; this is why Stalinism was so seductive to him, the Webbs, and other Fabians. See Peter Beilharz, *Labour's Utopias: Bolshevism, Fabianism, Social Democracy* (London and New York: Routledge, 1992), esp. 83–92.

49. Shaw, *The Rationalization of Russia*, 109–10. See also CPP 6: 538.

50. Shaw, *The Rationalization of Russia*, 113. See also Shaw, *On Imprisonment* (Chislehurst: Kenion Press, 1944).

51. Shaw, "Illusions of Socialism," in *Forecasts of the Coming Century*, ed. Edward Carpenter (Manchester: The Labour Press, 1897), 167–69.

52. Shaw, "The Unavoidable Subject," in Anthony Weymouth, ed., *Journal of the War Years (1939–1945) and One Year After* (Worcester: Littlebury, [1948]), 264.

53. Shaw, "The League of Nations," *Fabian Tract* 226 (1929): 9–10.

54. Shaw, "The Unavoidable Subject," 262.

55. Ibid., 261.

56. Ibid., 263.

57. Ibid., 262–63.

58. *The Diary of Beatrice Webb*, 4 vols., ed. Norman and Jeanne MacKenzie (Cambridge: Belknap Press of Harvard University Press, 1982–85), 4: 369–70; and *The Diary of Beatrice Webb*, holograph on microfiche, vol. 52 (Cambridge and Teaneck, N.J.: Chadwyck-Healey, 1978).

59. It took him three years to respond to his sister-in-law's request for a clear explanation of socialism, but the result blossomed into a response of two hundred thousand words: *The Intelligent Woman's Guide to Socialism and Capitalism* (New York: Brentano's, 1928). It is addressed to women who, like his sister-in-law, were from the propertied classes, and proposes positions for activism as well as explanations of concepts. Shaw felt it was necessary to be thorough in his advice for this audience, because five million women had recently been added to the voting register. It has much proselytizing verve, harking back to the earliest concepts of the Fabian tracts and reiterating Shaw's beliefs about the modern family. It had little impact in politicizing women. In the same vein but not directed specifically at women, *Everybody's Political What's What* did much better in 1944 (London: Constable).

60. Bertolt Brecht, quoted in Ronald Taylor, ed. and trans., *Aesthetics and Politics: Debates between Ernst Bloch, George Lukács, Bertolt Brecht, Walter Benjamin, Theodor Adorno* (London: New Left Press, 1977), 75.

61. Ibid., 75.

62. Apart from Strindberg, the Anglo-Swedish Foundation supported translations of works by Ingvar Andersson, Hjalmar Bergman, Erik Gustaf Geijer, Knut Hagberg (a biography of botanist Carl Linneaus), Eyvind Johnson, Pär Lagerkvist, Robert Layton (a biography of composer Franz Berwald), and Harry Martinson. It also sponsored performances of Swedish music in Britain.

63. Malvern saw the world premieres of *Geneva*, *In Good King Charles's Golden Days*, *Too True to Be Good*, and *The Simpleton of the Unexpected Isles*, as well as the English premiere of *Buoyant Billions*.

64. The truth is, I am, and always have been, the cheapest playwright in the market. I have not raised my terms for fifty years, though my living costs me so much more. My fifteen per cent operates only when the gross receipts exceed fifteen hundred dollars. When a few devoted amateurs pawn their shirts to give a performance in a village schoolhouse, and take three dollars from a crowded audience (front row twenty cents: back rows four), my competitors think it beneath their dignity to charge less than twentyfive [*sic*] dollars. I charge eighteen cents, and touch my hat, expressing a hope for future patronage. When the receipts anywhere do not exceed $250 my royalty is five per cent. I ask for no advances: if there are no receipts I get nothing. The leading playwrights of my prime would not have condescended to such popular terms. . . . I am the Cheap Jack among playwrights, and, as such, your very humble servant.

Letter to the editor, *Boston Sunday Post* (21 March 1948); reprinted in Laurence and Rambeau, *Agitations*, 344–45.

65. This was broadcast on BBC television and radio, as well as NBC radio in the U.S.A.

66. Not all, but most, were new writing.

Chronology of Shaw's Life and Writings

	Selected World Events	Selected Events in Shaw's Life	Major Plays (by date of completion)	Minor Plays	Selected Fiction and Nonfiction
1837	Victoria became queen				
1856	Steel invented	Born in Dublin			
1857	Fenians founded in Ireland				
1858	First transatlantic cable				
1859	Darwin's *Origin of the Species* published				
1861	Civil War in U.S.A. (to 1865)				
1862	International Exhibition, London				
1863	Emancipation Proclamation (U.S.A.) effective				
1864	O. Hill began slum housing reform				
1865	Salvation Army founded				
1866	14th Amendment to U.S.A.'s Constitution				
1867	Dominion of Canada created				

Selected World Events		Selected Events in Shaw's Life	Major Plays (by date of completion)	Minor Plays	Selected Fiction and Nonfiction
A. Nobel invented dynamite					
H. Ibsen's *Peer Gynt*					
K. Marx's *Das Kapital*, vol. 1					
Cro-Magnon skull found in France	1868				
Suez Canal opened	1869				
R. Wagner's *Die Walküre*	1870				
Britain legalized labour unions	1871	Began work as a clerk			
Eleonora Duse's debut, Italy	1872				
Economic crisis in Europe, America, and Australia	1873				
Factory Act (56.5-hour work week)	1874				
Public Health Act, U.K.	1875				
Telephone invented	1876	Moved to London			

Year		Shaw's life	Plays & musical works	Novels
	R. Wagner's Bayreuth Theatre opened			
1877	First Kaffir War	First musical criticism		
1878	Ellen Terry joined H. Irving's co.		*Passion Play* (fragment)	
1879	British Zulu War and massacres; H. Ibsen's *A Doll's House*			*Immaturity*
1880	Relief of Irish Distress Act, U.K.	Began self-education at British Museum		*The Irrational Knot*
1881	First electrically lit theatre			*Love among the Artists*
1882	Married Women's Property Act, U.K.	Heard Henry George lecture		*Cashel Byron's Profession*
1883	First skyscraper built, Chicago	Read Marx's *Das Kapital*		*An Unsocial Socialist*
1884	Fabian Society founded, London; Gold discovered in the Transvaal	Joined Fabians	*Un Petit Drame*; *Rheingold* (incomplete)	

	Selected World Events	Selected Events in Shaw's Life	Major Plays (by date of completion)	Minor Plays	Selected Fiction and Nonfiction
1885	Irish Land Act, U.K.	Regular music, book, and art reviewing Father died; inherited £100			
1886	*Das Kapital* published in English				
1887	Victoria's Golden (50th) Jubilee A. Antoine founded Théâtre Libre "Bloody Sunday" march, London				
1888	Kodak box camera invented Jack the Ripper murders	Read the Camelot edition of three Ibsen plays			
1889	London dock strike London County Council founded	Saw *A Doll's House*			*Fabian Essays in Socialism*

Year	World Events	Shaw's Activities	Shaw's Works
1890	First International Congress for Protection of Workers, Berlin		*The Quintessence of Ibsenism*
1891	Independent Theatre Society founded, London	Saw *Ghosts*	
1892	Keir Hardie elected to Parliament	Promoted *Rosmersholm* ITS produced *Widowers' Houses*	*Widowers' Houses*
1893	Independent Labour Party founded Irish Home Rule Bill rejected Women's suffrage granted in Spain, Belgium, and New Zealand		*The Philanderer* *Mrs. Warren's Profession*
1894	First moving pictures exhibited	A. Horniman produced *Arms and the Man*	*Arms and the Man*
1895	Gramophone disk invented Radio telegraphy invented	Became theatre critic for *Saturday Review*	*Candida* *The Man of Destiny*

Year	Selected World Events	Selected Events in Shaw's Life	Major Plays (by date of completion)	Minor Plays	Selected Fiction and Nonfiction
1896	Nobel Prizes established; Moscow Art Theatre founded		*You Never Can Tell*; *The Devil's Disciple*		
1897	Klondike Gold Rush began; Workmen's Compensation Act, U.K.	Elected to St. Pancras vestry council		*The Gadfly*	
1898	Dreyfus Affair in France; M. and P. Curie discovered radium	Married Charlotte Payne-Townshend; Last regular arts review	*Caesar and Cleopatra*		*The Perfect Wagnerite*
1899	Boer War (to 1902); Ibsen's last play, *When We Dead Awaken*, finished	Stage Society founded	*Captain Brassbound's Conversion*		
1900	Commonwealth of Australia created; S. Freud's *Interpretation of Dreams*				

1901	Death of Victoria; succession of Edward VII		*The Admirable Bashville*
1902	A. Chekhov's *Three Sisters*	Stage Society produced *Mrs. Warren's Profession*	*Man and Superman*
1903	First powered air flight; Automobiles' popularity soared		
1904	Russo-Japanese War (to 1905); Abbey Theatre founded, Dublin	First Royal Court season; First U.S.A. successes; Unsuccessfully ran for London County Council	*John Bull's Other Island*	*How He Lied to Her Husband* — *The Common Sense of Municipal Trading*
1905	Sinn Fein Party created, Dublin; International Workers of the World formed ("Wobblies"); A. Einstein's *Special Theory of Relativity*	First visit to Ireland since 1876	*Major Barbara*	*Passion, Poison, and Petrifaction*
1906	Magnetic North Pole located	Four plays open, New York	*The Doctor's Dilemma*	

	Selected World Events	Selected Events in Shaw's Life	Major Plays (by date of completion)	Minor Plays	Selected Fiction and Nonfiction
1907	New Zealand becomes a dominion Norway granted women's suffrage	Last Royal Court season		The Interlude at the Playhouse	
1908	I. Duncan popularizes modern dance		Getting Married		The Sanity of Art
1909	Cinema industry regulated in U.K.		The Shewing-Up of Blanco Posnet Misalliance	Press Cuttings The Fascinating Foundling The Dark Lady of the Sonnets	
1910	Death of Edward VII; succession of George V			The Glimpse of Reality	
1911	Rutherford's theory of atomic structure		Fanny's First Play		
1912	Wide-scale strikes in Britain S.S. Titanic sunk		Androcles and the Lion Pygmalion	Overruled	
1913	Women's suffrage agitations peaked		Great Catherine	Beauty's Duty	

Year	Historical Events	Shaw's Career	Plays	Other Writings
1914	*New Statesman* founded, London / Panama Canal opened	*Pygmalion* produced in West End / Disgraced by "anti-patriotism"	*The Music-Cure*	"*Common Sense About the War*"
1915	First World War (to 1918) / German blockade of Britain / First Zeppelin attack on London		*O'Flaherty, V.C.*	
1916	Sinn Fein Easter Rebellion / T. E. Lawrence became British liaison to Iraqis	*Heartbreak House*	*The Inca of Perusalem* / *Augustus Does His Bit* / *Macbeth* skit	
1917	Russian Revolution	Politically rehabilitated	Glastonbury skit / *Annajanska, The Bolshevik Empress* / Skit for "The Tiptaft Review"	
1918	Suffrage for British women over age thirty			
1919	Versailles Peace Conference			*Press Conference Hints*

Selected World Events		Selected Events in Shaw's Life	Major Plays (by date of completion)	Minor Plays	Selected Fiction and Nonfiction
		1920	*Back to Methusaleh*		
N. Astor elected first woman in U.K. Parliament					
League of Nations formed					
International Court of Justice formed at the Hague					
Women in U.S.A. granted suffrage					
Mahatma Gandhi leads Indian independence movement					
Anglo-Soviet trade agreement		1921		*Jitta's Atonement*	
Mussolini's Fascists in power		1922		*The War Indemnities*	
Irish Free State created					
Soviet Union founded					
BBC began radio broadcasts					

Year	Events	Works
1923	$1 U.S.A. = 4,000,000 German marks Hitler's coup d'état failed	*Saint Joan*
1924	V. Lenin succeeded by J. Stalin First live radio broadcast	
1925	Unemployment insurance instituted in Britain Nobel Prize for Literature	
1926	General Strike in Britain	First collected edition of *The Plays of Bernard Shaw: Pocket Edition* (12 volumes; later 13)
1927	German economy collapsed First talking motion picture	
1928	British women granted vote on the same basis as men	*The Apple Cart* *The Intelligent Woman's Guide to Socialism and Capitalism*
1929	New York Stock Exchange collapsed Great Depression began worldwide Malvern Festival commenced	

161

Selected World Events	Selected Events in Shaw's Life	Major Plays (by date of completion)	Minor Plays	Selected Fiction and Nonfiction
V. Woolf's A Room of One's Own				
1930 Nazis won 107 seats in German election		First collected edition of *The Works of Bernard Shaw* (33 volumes; 37 by 1951)		
1931 Empire State Building completed	Russian trip	*Too True to be Good*	*How These Doctors Love One Another!*	*Bernard Shaw: An Unauthorised Biography* (by Frank Harris, revised by Shaw)
1932 O. Mosley left British Labour Party; formed Fascist Party				*The Adventures of the Black Girl in Her Search for God*
Famine in U.S.S.R.				
30,000,000 unemployed worldwide				
1933 Japan left League of Nations	First visit to U.S.A.	*On the Rocks*	*Village Wooing*	

	Historical events	Works	
	Hitler became dictator; opposition suppressed; first concentration camps erected in Germany U.S.A. recognized U.S.S.R.		First collected edition of the prefaces
1934	Hitler elected führer by plebiscite U.S.S.R. joined League of Nations	*The Simpleton of the Unexpected Isles* *The Millionairess*	*The Six of Calais*
1935	Communist Party purges in U.S.S.R. British Council founded		*The Girl with the Golden Voice*
1936	Germany allied with Italy and Japan China and Japan at war George V died; succeeded by Edward VIII who abdicated; succeeded by George VI Trotsky exiled from U.S.S.R.	*Geneva* (revised 1939, 1940, 1946, 1947)	*Arthur and Acetone* *Cymbeline Refinished*

Selected World Events	Selected Events in Shaw's Life	Major Plays (by date of completion)	Minor Plays	Selected Fiction and Nonfiction
Spanish Civil War (to 1939)				
BBC TV inaugurated				
1937 Italy left League of Nations				
1938 House Un-American Activities Committee formed in Washington	*Pygmalion* filmed			
	Retreated to Ayot St. Lawrence			
1939 Conscription in Britain			*In Good King Charles's Golden Days*	*Uncommon Sense About the War*
London's women and children evacuated				
World War II (to 1945)				
1940 German air attacks on Britain began	*Major Barbara* filmed			
1941 Japanese attack Pearl Harbor; U.S.A. declared war on Japan, Germany, and Italy				

1942	Oxfam founded		*G.B.S.: A Full Length Portrait* (by Hesketh Pearson; revised by Shaw)
	U.S.A. scientists split the atom		
	Automatic computing technology advanced		
1943	Italy declared war on Germany	Charlotte Shaw died	
1944	T. Williams's *The Glass Menagerie*		*The British Party System*
	Women's suffrage in France		*Everybody's Political What's What*
1945	Atomic bombs dropped on Japan		
	Germany and Japan surrendered		
1946	First United Nations meetings	First TV appearance	*Buoyant Billions*
1947	Britain began nationalization of industries		
1948	Marshall Plan apportioned $17 billion aid to Europe		*Farfetched Fables*
	Israel founded		

Selected World Events		Selected Events in Shaw's Life	Major Plays (by date of completion)	Minor Plays	Selected Fiction and Nonfiction
1949	Apartheid in South Africa			*Shakes vs. Shav*	*Sixteen Self Sketches*
	Communist East Germany established				
	India's independence from U.K.				
1950	J. McCarthy began communist purges in U.S.A.	Died at Ayot St. Lawrence, Hertfordshire		*Why She Would Not*	

For more complete information, see Dan H. Laurence, *Bernard Shaw: A Bibliography*, 2 vols. (Oxford: Clarendon, 1983); and Shaw, *The Bodley Head Bernard Shaw: Collected Plays and Their Prefaces*, 7 vols, ed. Dan H. Laurence (London: Bodley Head, 1970–74).

Bibliographical Essay

When you paid the price of this book you were paying me to think for you. But I can no more do that than I can eat your dinner for you. What I can do is to cook your mental dinner for you by putting you in possession of the thinking that has been done already on the subject by myself and others, so that you may be saved the time and trouble and disappointment of trying to find your way down blind alleys that have been thoroughly explored, and found to be no-thoroughfares.

The Intelligent Woman's Guide[1]

This essay is intended to steer readers to crucial sources in Shavian scholarship as well as useful reading in ancillary topics relevant to each chapter. It cannot be comprehensive, and suggestions of where to turn for reference assistance chapter by chapter are meant to guide readers to resources that do make comprehensiveness their goal.

INTRODUCTION

Dan H. Laurence's two-volume *Bernard Shaw: A Bibliography* (Oxford: Clarendon, 1983) meticulously lists every known work edited or written by Shaw in manuscript and printed form as well as editions of his works collected by Shaw and others before and after his death. The second volume includes some intriguing categories: the stereotyped postcards Shaw had printed in bulk to answer standard queries (such as "Mr Bernard Shaw's vegetarian correspondents are reminded. . . . He does not ignore the fact that if we stop killing animals and insects they kill us," 844); blurbs for the dust wrappers and advertisements of other people's books; broadcasts with the BBC and other recordings of Shaw's voice on gramophone records and film; and recordings of Shaw's works. Final sections include a chronological list of books on Shaw and study guides to particular plays.

G. B. Shaw: An Annotated Bibliography of Writings about Him (DeKalb: Northern Illinois University Press, 1986–87) is an indispensable source containing over 8,700 articles and books published between 1871 and 1980. The three volumes, edited by J. P. Wearing, Elsie B. Adams, and Donald C. Haberman, cover criticism and commentary on every aspect of Shaw's career and reputation published in most languages, with complete bibliographical information and a brief description of the contents. Unfortunately, it does not contain an index to contents by subject so it is not easy to track entries thematically, such as sources that relate Shaw to other figures or intellectual traditions. Nevertheless, because entries are grouped chronologically, it facilitates studies of the evolution of Shavian scholarship. The index to items in foreign languages is well suited to study of the globalization of Shaw studies, while the index to primary titles of works by Shaw makes it feasible to trace reviews for a rudimentary production history or critical tradition on a particular work. For updates, see "A Continuing Checklist of Shaviana," published yearly in *Shaw*. Stanley Weintraub's *Bernard Shaw: A Guide for Research* (University Park: Pennsylvania State University Press, 1992) is a thematic bibliography, particularly useful for its lists of sources on each major play.

Other useful reference sources include Charles A. Carpenter, *Modern Drama Scholarship and Criticism 1966–1980: An International Bibliography* (Toronto: University of Toronto, 1986), updated annually in the periodical *Modern Drama. The International Bibliography of Theatre* (Brooklyn, N.Y.: Theatre Research Data Center, 1985–) is also published annually and includes a wide range of theatrical and dramatic subjects. E. Dean Bevan, comp., *A Concordance to the Plays and Prefaces of Bernard Shaw* (Detroit: Gale Research Co., 1971), is more specialized, along with Phyllis Hartnoll, *Who's Who in Shaw* (London: H. Hamilton, 1975).

Shaw studies have spawned numerous journals ranging from newsletters of nonprofessional enthusiasts to periodicals of the highest scholarly repute. The most significant journals are *The Independent Shavian, The Shavian*, and *Shaw: An Annual of Bernard Shaw Studies* (formerly *The Shaw Review* and *Shaw Bulletin*, now usually referred to simply as *Shaw*). *Shaw* publishes annually, and every other year the journal focuses on a special theme. In recent years these have included "Shaw and Politics" (1991), "Shaw Offstage: The Nondramatic Writings" (1989), "Shaw: The Neglected Plays" (1987), and "Shaw's Plays in Performance" (1983). Branch offices of the Shaw Society have spawned journals in places as far apart as Chicago (the *Shaw Society Newsletter*) and Yokohama (*GBS*), so it is worth checking locally for publications and expertise.

CHAPTER 1

Shaw never wrote an autobiography under his own name, though he did compile *Sixteen Self Sketches* (New York: Dodd, Mead and Co.) in 1949; apart from this, Stanley Weintraub's compilation *Shaw: An Autobiography 1856–1898* (New York: Weybright and Talley, 1969) is the most overt autobiographical source, and Weintraub's introduction provides a good orientation to the field of Shavian biography. A. M. Gibbs, ed., *Shaw: Interviews and Recollections* (Iowa City: University of Iowa Press, 1990), demonstrates how Shaw's contemporaries saw him and how he presented himself in interviews. Bona fide biographies are legion, but for some the circumstances of scholarly production are vexed. Until his death Shaw had a hand in the writing of each "biography," and despite the necessity to be kindly disposed to Shaw and his interventions, the extent to which some focus on Shaw as distinct from the biographer is troubling: Hesketh Pearson, *Bernard Shaw: His Life and Personality* (London: Collins, 1942; rev. ed., London: Methuen, 1961); Archibald Henderson, *Bernard Shaw: Playboy and Prophet* (New York and London: D. Appleton, 1932); Frank Harris, *Bernard Shaw: An Unauthorized Biography* (New York: Simon and Schuster, 1931); Stephen Winsten, ed., *G.B.S. 90: Aspects of Bernard Shaw's Life and Work* (New York: Dodd, Mead and Co., 1946); and St. John Ervine, *Bernard Shaw: His Life, Work, and Friends* (London: Constable, 1956). Notable biographies since Shaw's death include the memoirs of Blanche Patch, *Thirty Years with G.B.S.* (London: V. Gollancz, 1951), and works by Margot Peters, *Bernard Shaw and the Actresses* (New York: Doubleday, 1980), Daniel Dervin, *Bernard Shaw: A Psychological Study* (Lewisburg, Pa.: Bucknell University Press, 1975), Stanley Weintraub, *Journey to Heartbreak: The Crucible Years of Bernard Shaw, 1914–1918* (New York: Weybright and Talley, 1971), and the authorized biography by Michael Holroyd, *Bernard Shaw*, 4 vols. (London: Chatto and Windus, 1988–92). Stanley Weintraub's edition of *The Diaries, 1885–1897* (University Park: Pennsylvania State University Press, 1986) provides useful annotations as well as transcripts of Shaw's daily records.

Dan H. Laurence's four volumes of collected letters, *Bernard Shaw: Collected Letters* (London: Max Reinhardt, 1965–88), are indispensable, however there are also several editions of particular correspondences that benefit from being read in isolation: C. B. Purdom, ed., *Bernard Shaw's Letters to Granville Barker* (New York; Theatre Arts Books, 1957); Christopher St. John, ed., *Ellen Terry and Bernard Shaw: A Correspondence* (New York: G. P. Putnam, 1931); Alan Dent, ed., *Bernard Shaw and Mrs. Patrick Campbell: Their Correspondence* (New York: Knopf, 1952); Mary Hyde, ed., *Bernard Shaw and Alfred Douglas: A Correspondence* (New Haven: Ticknor and Fields, 1982); E. J. West, ed., *Advice to a Young Critic and Other Letters* (New York: Crown, 1955); Peter Tompkins, ed., *To a Young Actress: The Letters of Bernard Shaw to Molly Tompkins* (New York: Constable, 1961); Samuel A. Weiss, ed., *Bernard Shaw's Letters to*

Siegfried Trebitsch (Stanford, Calif.: Stanford University Press, 1986); and Stanley Weintraub, ed., *The Playwright and the Pirate: Bernard Shaw and Frank Harris, A Correspondence* (Gerrards Cross: Colin Smythe, 1982). Additional volumes of correspondence are in preparation.

For information on Fabian policies the *Fabian Tracts* cannot be outdone. In order to know what the Fabians recommended to aspiring socialists, see "What to Read. A List of Books for Social Reformers," *Fabian Tract* 29 (1896). It covers social history, economics, socialism, women's rights, and topics of reform that interested the Fabians. Some of the arguments (but not necessarily the flavour) of the *Tracts* can be gleaned from *Fabian Essays in Socialism* (London: Walter Scott, 1889), which Shaw edited. The contributors are Sydney Olivier, Sidney Webb, Annie Besant, William Clarke, Graham Wallas, and Hubert Bland as well as Shaw. This had wide circulation; the second edition (1890) had an initial print run of twenty thousand copies.

For distinctions between Fabianism and Marxism—and Shaw's stance vis-à-vis the two—Paul A. Hummert's *Bernard Shaw's Marxian Romance* (Lincoln: University of Nebraska Press, 1973) is useful. Other important studies of the Fabian milieu include Ian Britain, *Fabianism and Culture: A Study in British Socialism and the Arts c. 1884–1918* (Cambridge: Cambridge University Press, 1982), and Norman and Jeanne MacKenzie, *The Fabians* (New York: Simon and Schuster, 1977), which consists of a history and collective biography of the club's members written in a style appealing to popular readership. Chris Waters, *British Socialists and the Politics of Popular Culture, 1884–1914* (Manchester: Manchester University Press, 1990), is an important treatment of the connections among art, politics, and socialist ideals. For discussion of the connections between socialist groups and the arts see Raphael Samuel, "Theatre and Socialism in Britain (1880–1935)," in *Theatres of the Left 1880–1935: Workers' Theatre Movements in Britain and America*, ed. Raphael Samuel, Ewan MacColl, and Stuart Cosgrove (London: Routledge and Kegan Paul, 1985), 3–73.

Some of the works that impressed Shaw in his earliest contacts with political economics are also essential reading, such as Henry George's *Progress and Poverty* (1879; reprint, New York: Robert Schalkenbach Foundation, 1955) and Laurence Gronlund's *The Co-Operative Commonwealth in Its Outlines: An Exposition of Modern Socialism* (Boston: Lee and Shepard, 1884). Peter Keating, ed., *Into Unknown England 1866–1913: Selections from the Social Explorers* (Glasgow: Fontana, 1976) includes selections of the investigative journalism and social research on the poor that characterize the late-Victorian period. Jim Davis's "A Night in the Workhouse, or the Poor Laws as Sensation Drama," *Essays in Theatre* 7.2 (May 1989): 111–126, relates some of this literature to staging traditions. Essential reading on the theatre's place in the scheme of rational recreation includes Peter Bailey, *Leisure and Class in Victorian England: Rational Recreation and the Contest for Control, 1830–1885* (London: Routledge and Kegan Paul, 1978), and Robert Malcolmson, *Popular Recreations in English Society, 1700–1850* (Cambridge: Cambridge University Press, 1973).

Shaw's journalistic criticism has been grouped into several collections. E. J. West, ed., *Shaw on Theatre* (New York: Hill and Wang, 1958), includes reprinted essays from a variety of publications. Some are reviews, others are diatribes on drama and theatrical production. The complete *Saturday Review* articles are reprinted in Shaw's *Our Theatres in the Nineties*, 3 vols. (London: Constable, 1932). Stanley Weintraub, ed., *Bernard Shaw on the London Art Scene 1885–1950* (University Park and London: Pennsylvania State University Press, 1989), includes reprints of anonymous art criticism, some never before published, spanning Shaw's entire career. Weintraub has also edited *Bernard Shaw's Non-dramatic Literary Criticism* (Lincoln: University of Nebraska Press, 1972), featuring book reviews. Dan H. Laurence's edition of *Shaw's Music* appears in three volumes (New York: Dodd, Mead and Co., 1981), and Brian Tyson has edited *Bernard Shaw's Book Reviews* (University Park: Pennsylvania State University Press, 1991), reprinting Shaw's contributions to the *Pall Mall Gazette* from 1885 to 1888 on an extraordinary variety of literature and nonfiction.

Reliable introductions to the staging and literature of nineteenth-century Britain can be found in George Rowell, *The Victorian Theatre 1792–1914*, 2d ed. (Cambridge: Cambridge University Press, 1978); Clifford Leech and T. W. Craik, eds., *The Revels History of Drama in English*, vols. 6 and 7 (London: Methuen; New York: Harper and Row, 1975, 1978); and Michael R. Booth, *Theatre in the Victorian Age* (Cambridge: Cambridge University Press, 1991). More specialized treatments include Martin Meisel, *Realizations: Narrative, Pictorial, and Theatrical Arts in Nineteenth-Century England* (Princeton, N.J.: Princeton University Press, 1983); John Stokes, Michael R. Booth, and Susan Bassnett, *Bernhardt, Terry and Duse: The Actress in Her Time* (Cambridge: Cambridge University Press, 1988); and the pages of *Nineteenth Century Theatre* (formerly *Nineteenth Century Theatre Research*), *Theatre Notebook*, and other journals well indexed in the *International Bibliography of Theatre*. Eric Bentley's *The Theory of the Modern Stage: An Introduction to Modern Theatre and Drama* (Harmondsworth and New York: Penguin, 1968) reprints a number of primary documents relating to theory and practice of modernism in the late nineteenth and early twentieth centuries. Martin Meisel's *Shaw and the Nineteenth Century Theatre* (1963; reprint, New York: Limelight Editions, 1984) is particularly useful in tracing the influence of melodramatic fare on Shaw and, by contrast, his true innovations.

CHAPTER 2

Shaw's relationships with various individuals have been separated out from the chronicle and made into star turns. Such "joint" biographies for the 1890s include Josephine Johnson, *Florence Farr: Bernard Shaw's "New Woman"* (Gerrards Cross: Colin Smythe, 1975).

The English and Continental independent theatre movement is documented in John Stokes, *Resistible Theatres: Enterprise and Experiment in the Late Nine-*

teenth Century (London: Paul Elek, 1972); N.H.G. Schoonderwoerd, *J. T. Grein, Ambassador of the Theatre, 1862–1935: A Study in Anglo-Continental Theatrical Relations* (Te Assen Bij: Van Gorcum, 1963); Michael Orme [Alice Augusta Grein], *J. T. Grein: The Story of a Pioneer, 1862–1935* (London: John Murray, 1936); Anna Irene Miller, *The Independent Theatre in Europe, 1887 to the Present* (New York: Ray Lond and Richard R. Smith, 1931); and Tracy C. Davis, "The Independent Theatre Society's Revolutionary Scheme for an Uncommercial Theatre," *Theatre Journal* 42.4 (December 1990): 447–54.

J. L. Wisenthal, ed., *Shaw and Ibsen: Bernard Shaw's "The Quintessence of Ibsenism" and Related Writings* (Toronto: University of Toronto Press, 1979) reprints the variant editions of *The Quintessence* that are useful in understanding Shaw's active revisionism of his early championship of Ibsen. For an analysis of *The Quintessence of Ibsenism* and Shaw's reading of Ibsen in the context of socialism, see I. M. Britain, "Bernard Shaw, Ibsen, and the Ethics of English Socialism," *Victorian Studies* 21 (Spring 1978): 381–401.

An invaluable new resource for study of Shaw's compositional process has recently been published in the series of Dan H. Laurence, ed., *Bernard Shaw. Early Texts: Play Manuscripts in Facsimile*, 12 vols. (New York and London: Garland Publishing Co., 1981–   ). Production histories can be reconstructed through sources such as Bernard F. Dukore, comp., *Bernard Shaw's "Arms and the Man": A Composite Production Book* (Carbondale: Southern Illinois University Press, 1982). An indispensable source of information about the reception of the plays is T. F. Evans, ed., *Shaw: The Critical Heritage* (London: Routledge and Kegan Paul, 1976), which reprints selected reviews of productions and publications, as well as excerpts from retrospective essays that document Shaw's standing at various times. Raymond Mander and Joe Mitcheson's *Theatrical Companion to Shaw: A Pictorial Record of the First Performances of the Plays of George Bernard Shaw* (London: Rockliff, 1954) reproduces legions of photographs from early productions.

CHAPTER 3

Janet Dunbar's biography of Charlotte Shaw, *Mrs. G.B.S.: A Biographical Portrait of Charlotte Shaw* (London: G. G. Harrap, 1963), is the only full-length study of Shaw's lifetime partner. Biographies of other figures intimately involved with Shaw include Margot Peters, *Mrs. Pat: The Life of Mrs. Patrick Campbell* (London: Hamish Hamilton, 1985); Ellen Terry, *Ellen Terry's Memoirs* (New York: G. P. Putnam's Sons, 1932); Christopher St. John, *Ellen Terry* (London and New York: J. Lane, 1907); Lisanne Radice, *Beatrice and Sidney Webb: Fabian Socialists* (New York: St. Martin's Press, 1984); and Jeanne MacKenzie, *A Victorian Courtship: The Story of Beatrice Potter and Sidney Webb* (London: Weidenfield and Nicholson, 1979).

The endowed theatre is a subject of voluminous reflection; for this subject and any other topic relating to the theatre see John Cavanagh, *British Theatre: A*

Bibliography 1901 to 1985 (Mottisfont: Motley Press, 1989), which lists publications in the twentieth century. The most comprehensive study of the repertory concept is George Rowell and Anthony Jackson's *The Repertory Movement: A History of Regional Theatre in Britain* (Cambridge: Cambridge University Press, 1984). The repertory of the Royal Court is well served by Dennis Kennedy in *Granville Barker and the Dream of Theatre* (Cambridge: Cambridge University Press, 1985) and Jan McDonald, *The "New Drama" 1900–1914: Harley Granville Barker, John Galsworthy, St. John Hankin, John Masefield* (London and Houndsmill: Macmillan, 1986).

Heidi Hartmann's famous essay "The Unhappy Marriage of Marxism and Feminism" should be read in conjunction with the analysis of the family and Marx; it is updated and accompanied by a dozen commentaries in Lydia Sargent, ed., *Women and Revolution: A Discussion of the Unhappy Marriage of Marxism and Feminism* (Boston: South End Press, 1981). The early-twentieth-century feminist theatre has recently received considerable attention: Claire Hirshfield, "The Actresses' Franchise League and the Campaign for Women's Suffrage 1908–1914," *Theatre Research International* 10.2 (Summer 1985): 129–53; Dale Spender and Carole Hayman, eds., *"How the Vote Was Won" and Other Suffragette Plays* (London and New York: Methuen, 1985); Viv Gardner, ed., *Sketches from the Actresses' Franchise League* (Nottingham: Nottingham Drama Texts, 1985); Viv Gardner and Susan Rutherford, eds., *The New Woman and Her Sisters: Feminism and Theatre 1850–1914* (London: Harvester Wheatsheaf, 1992), especially for the reading of *Getting Married*; Sheila Stowell, *A Stage of Their Own: Feminist Playwrights of the Suffrage Era* (Ann Arbor: University of Michigan Press, 1992); Julie Holledge, *Innocent Flowers: Women in the Edwardian Theatre* (London: Virago, 1981); and Linda Fitzsimmons and Viv Gardner, eds., *New Woman Plays* (London: Methuen Drama, 1991). It is useful to draw comparisons with the suffrage dramas of the U.S.A., some of which are collected by Bettina Friedl in *"On to Victory": Propaganda Plays of the Woman Suffrage Movement* (Boston: Northeastern University Press, 1987). The history of British women's suffragism is told in Susan Kingsley Kent, *Sex and Suffrage in Britain, 1860–1914* (Princeton, N.J.: Princeton University Press, 1987), and Jane Marcus, *Suffrage and the Pankhursts* (London and New York: Routledge and Kegan Paul, 1987).

Feminist reinterpretation of Shaw's life and plays is a growing specialty. Useful examples include Margot Peters, *Bernard Shaw and the Actresses* (Garden City, N.Y.: Doubleday, 1980); Rodelle Weintraub, ed., *Fabian Feminist: Bernard Shaw and Woman* (University Park: Pennsylvania State University Press, 1977); J. Ellen Gainor, *Shaw's Daughters: Dramatic and Narrative Constructions of Gender* (Ann Arbor: University of Michigan Press, 1991); and Margery Morgan, *The Shavian Playground: An Exploration of the Art of George Bernard Shaw* (London: Methuen, 1972).

CHAPTER 4

Bernard F. Dukore has assembled *The Collected Screenplays of Bernard Shaw* (London: George Prior, 1980) and written a lucid account of *Bernard Shaw, Director* (London: Allen and Unwin, 1971). Charles A. Carpenter's bibliographic essay "Studies of Shaw's Neglected Plays and Mini-Plays," included in the special issue of *Shaw* 7 (1987): 331–50, provides details on some of the minor plays not extensively covered in this book.

Additional background on Saint Joan—the plays and the historical figure—can be found in Jules E. J. Quicherat, *Aperçus nouveaux sur l'histoire de Jeanne d'Arc* (Paris: J. Renouard, 1850), and the trial documents are translated in T. Douglas Murray, ed., *Jeanne d'Arc, Maid of Orleans, Deliverer of France* (London: Heinemann, 1902 and 1907). Brian Tyson's *The Story of Shaw's "Saint Joan"* (Kingston and Montreal: McGill-Queen's University Press, 1982) discusses the play's sources, genesis, and variations. Stanley Weintraub's *Private Shaw and Public Shaw: A Dual Portrait of Lawrence of Arabia and G.B.S.* (New York: George Brazillier, 1965) portrays one of the important contemporary inspirations for Saint Joan. Holly Hill's *Playing Joan: Actresses on the Challenge of Shaw's Saint Joan. Twenty-Six Interviews* (New York: Theatre Communications Group, 1987) is based on *New York Times* interviews with performers involved in productions in Canada, the U.S.A., Germany, and the British Isles from the 1920s to 1980s; it also includes a useful bibliography. Stanley Weintraub, ed., *"Saint Joan" Fifty Years After* (Baton Rouge: Louisiana State University Press, 1973), includes views on the play by authors as diverse as Luigi Pirandello and T. S. Eliot as well as later critics.

Explorations of postmodernism, postcolonialism, and their intersections with feminism multiply each year. Particularly readable explanations of terminology can be found in Linda Hutcheon, *The Politics of Postmodernism* (New York and London: Routledge, 1989); Bill Ashcroft, Gareth Griffiths, and Helen Tiffin, *The Empire Writes Back: Theory and Practice in Post-Colonial Literature* (London: Routledge, 1989), which also includes extremely useful reading lists on the practice as well as the theory of postcolonial literature; Homi K. Bhabha, ed., *Nation and Narration* (London: Routledge, 1990); Gayatri Chakravorty Spivak and Sarah Harasym, *The Post-Colonial Critic: Interviews, Strategies, Dialogues* (New York: Routledge, 1990); and Patricia Waugh, *Practising Postmodernism/ Reading Modernism* (London: Edward Arnold, 1992).

The indexes to *Modern Drama* mentioned earlier are excellent sources for general as well as specialized critical studies of Shaw's literary and theatrical contexts during and after his lifetime. The following monographs are excellent overviews: Raymond Williams, *Drama from Ibsen to Brecht*, rev. ed. (1968; Harmondsworth: Penguin, 1976); Bernard F. Dukore, *Money and Politics in Ibsen, Shaw, and Brecht* (Columbia and London: University of Missouri Press, 1980), with interesting comparative readings; Christopher Innes, *Modern British Drama: 1890–1990* (Cambridge: Cambridge University Press, 1992), which explores Shaw's central position in the canon and the importance of social institutions such as censorship; T. F. Evans, ed., *Shaw and Politics* (University Park: Pennsylvania State University Press, 1991); Laurence Kitchin, *Mid-Century Drama* (London: Faber, 1960); John Elsom, *Post-War British Theatre* (London: Routledge and Kegan Paul, 1976); John Bull, *New British Political Dramatists: Howard Brenton, David Hare, Trevor Griffiths and David Edgar* (Basingstoke: Macmillan, 1984); and Geraldine Cousin, *Churchill, The Playwright* (London: Methuen, 1989).

Samuel A. Weiss, ed., *Bernard Shaw's Letters to Siegfried Trebitsch* (Stanford, Calif.: Stanford University Press, 1986), includes some letters that are also in the Laurence volumes, though seeing them gathered together like this gives unique insight into the literary management and international dissemination of Shaw's work by his German translator and friend with whom he corresponded through two wars.

Shaw's estate deposited papers in the British Museum, London School of Economics, and National Library of Ireland, where they are accessible for public scrutiny. His house at Ayot St. Lawrence was left to the National Trust in perpetuity. His art collection (largely portraits of himself) was given to public galleries in England, Ireland, and the U.S.A. He also made significant bequests to the Royal Academy of Dramatic Art and National Gallery of Ireland.

NOTE

1. Shaw, *The Intelligent Woman's Guide to Socialism and Capitalism* (New York: Brentano's, 1928), 11–12.

Index

About the Author

TRACY C. DAVIS is Associate Professor in the Departments of Theatre and English at Northwestern University. She has contributed to numerous books and anthologies, and is the author of *Actresses as Working Women: Their Social Identity in Victorian Culture* (1991).